GOD
Knows My Size!

GOD
Knows My Size!

Silvia Tărniceriu

By Harvey Yoder

Cover and Layout Design: Vincent Haley, Design Inspiration,
   Orrville, Ohio

Editorial Committee
Tabitha Beachy, Lois Miller, David Troyer
Proofreaders
Lorna Dueck, Wilma Dueck, Naomi Lapp, Cornel Marza

ISBN # 1-885270-14-3

Printed in the USA

To order additional copies of *God Knows My Size!*, please contact:
TGS International
PO Box 355, Berlin, Ohio 44610 USA
Phone: 330-893-2428
Fax: 330-893-2305

For more information about the work of Christian Aid Ministries, or to sign up for CAM's monthly newsletter, please contact:

Christian Aid Ministries
PO Box 360, Berlin, Ohio 44610 USA
Phone: 330-893-2428   Fax: 330-893-2305

Preface

I thank God for the privilege of writing *God Knows My Size!* My faith has been strengthened and I am continually in awe of a God who so miraculously worked in the life of a girl who was born and raised behind the Iron Curtain.

When Silvia was relating her story in preparation for this book, there were times when the awesome presence of God was so real as she recounted some experience, that we had to stop and pray. It was very emotional for Silvia to relate her prison stories and even though she wanted this book to be written, it was always hard for her to relive her past.

One thing kept surfacing over and over again. "If someone can have their faith strengthened, or if someone will come to God because of this story, I am glad to share it."

Don't look for perfection. Silvia is the first to realize that she made many mistakes in her life. But the recurring theme is that God always knew just where she was and that He cared deeply for her, even as He continues to do until this day.

We tried to be accurate and keep the facts just as they happened. However, we also took some writer's liberties to keep the stories flowing smoothly. Some names have been changed to protect the privacy of the people involved. If there are any errors that crept into the story, I accept them as mine. Silvia did a wonderful job in remembering details that made this book a joy to write.

Special recognition needs to be given to Tabitha Beachy, my long-suffering editor from CAM. Her fine-tuning is just what we needed to keep the story flowing smoothly.

So we present *God Knows My Size!* to you. It is a story born of real issues, real experiences, and yes, a story born with tears and yet indescribable joys. The joys of knowing that God knows the size of every one of us!

- Harvey Yoder

Dedication

I dedicate this book to the glory of Jesus Christ, my Saviour. He gave His life for my salvation and I give my life back to Him.

I also dedicate this book to the memory of my dear parents: my Tata, Pricop Tărniceriu, and my Mama, Elena Tărniceriu. Their influence has had lasting effects on my life and on the lives of all their children.

I also dedicate this book to my brothers and sisters: Mihai, Margareta, Rodica, Costel, Victor, Ştefan, Ana and Dan, and to their families.

– Silvia Tărniceriu

Acknowledgments

I give a special recognition to my pastor, Marcu Nichifor, and his wife, Ada, who had perhaps the greatest influence in my spiritual life. In fact, Marcu was the servant of God who helped me fall in love with my Saviour. He taught me how to reach heaven with my prayers of true personal repentance.

I want to make a special mention of the faithful pastors who encouraged and fed me spiritually during my childhood and then during our trying times as we labored together during the communist times. I know their messages and encouragements have not been in vain.

Then, there were my brothers in Christ—Iosif Tzon, Aurel Popescu, Pavel Niculescu, Liviu Olah, Vasile Brânzei, Vasile Taloş, Geabou Pascu, Simion Cure and others—whom I highly respect for their faithfulness and steadfastness in those very difficult years of persecution. And I want to make special mention of Daniel and Daniela Brânzei and Iosif and Sanda Morcan. Daniel and Iosif were more like my blood brothers, being close in age and in spirit. We were all like strangers in our own land.

Thank-you, Iosif and Sanda, for hiding me and Elena in your house when the police were watching us after we came out of prison.

I would like to mention all my close friends from Iaşi with whom I spent unforgettable days and nights in prayers, fasting, working, crying, laughing and rejoicing in the Lord. Each one of them had their part in helping me grow spiritually and loving the Lord and people. Among many of them are Elena (Boghian) Mârza with whom I shared even the cell in prison; Genovieva, Tudorică and Constantin Sfatcu; Dănuţ and Mihaela Mănăstireanu; Iliuţă (Marabou) Niculiţă; Magdalena Popa and many others.

I want to give special recognition to all the wonderful people at CAM who have been my American family. Thanks to David and Erma Troyer, who opened their house and took me in when I arrived in the US. Thanks to Paul and Orpha Weaver, and Ura Miller and his beloved wife, Clara, who has gone to be with the Lord. Clara was like a real mom to me. To the CAM board of directors, and to all the secretaries who also encouraged me to write this book, thank-you.

Of my many American friends, I will mention a few special ones who have been a wonderful inspiration to me: Larry and Alice Agnew, Cherie and Larry Yoder, Esther and Larry Mast and their daughter, Gina Yoder.

I would also like to mention my American friends who encouraged me to write this book while they were serving the Lord in Romania: Bill and Ellen Mullet and their children, Willis and Esther Bontrager and their children, Nathan and Martha Bange, Ben and Lena Lapp and their children, James and Sarah Nolt, Alvin and Lil Stoltzfus and their children, and Johnny and Ruth Miller and their children. Thanks also to the many others who visited Romania in that time, and to all those who in the first ten years in the States asked me to write this book.

And thanks to everyone else who should be mentioned here, but that would take pages! I praise my dear Lord for all of you dear friends and I hope you will not be offended because I didn't put your names in. Each one of you meant a lot to me in my adjustment to a new country and language. May God bless each one of you, "real good"!

And last of all, I would like to say a big "Thank-you" to my writer Harvey Yoder and his sweet wife Karen who had such patience and love to listen to all these stories and cry with me and laugh with me while writing this book.

And finally, to the many dear friends and acquaintances who have prayed for me and with me through my walk in this life.

I count each one of you special and my life has been enriched because of your love.

–Silvia Tărniceriu

Glossary

Romanian Spellings, Pronunciations, and Definitions in the order they appear in the book.

Chapter One

    Bombonel *(BOHM boh nehl)* — Candy
    Tata *(TAH tah)* — Daddy
    Tataia *(Tah TY ah)* — used for Daddy or Grandfather
    Dănuţ *(Duh NOOTS)* — nickname for Daniel
    Ştefan *(Shteh FAHN)*
    Fănel *(Fuh NEHL)* — a nickname for Ştefan
    Ana *(AH nah)*
    Nuţi *(NOOTS ee)* — a nickname for Ana
    mămăliga *(mah mah LEE gah)* — cooked cornmeal
    Moşu *(MOH shoo)* — a term of endearment and respect for an elderly man or grandfather
    Lolu *(LOH loo)*
    Tărniceriu *(Tuhr nee CHEHR yoo)*

Chapter Two

    Lazăr *(LAH zuhr)*
    Sora *(SOH rah)* — sister
    Măriuţa *(Muh ree OOTS ah)* — a nickname for Maria
    Pace *(PAH cheh)* — peace, used as a greeting among the Romanian evangelical believers
    Sânnicolau Mare *(Seh nee koh LAH oo MAH reh)*
    Iuliu *(YOO lee oo)*
    Estera *(Ehs TEH rah)*
    Incze *(IN tzee)*
    Iaşi *(Yahsh)*
    Tanti *(TAHN tee)* — a term of endearment and respect for a woman or aunt
    Pricop *(PREE kope)*
    Rodica *(Roh DEE kah)*
    Nenea *(NEHN yah)* — a term of endearment and respect for a man

Chapter Three

Angela *(Ahn JEL ah)*
Elena *(Eh LEHN ah)*

Chapter Five

lei *(LAY)* — Romanian currency
Cluj *(Kloozh)*

Chapter Seven

Albu *(AHL boo)*

Chapter Eight

Cruceru *(Kroo CHEH roo)*
Isacov *(Ee sah COHV)*
Ionel *(Yoh NEHL)*
Dacia *(DAH chyah)* — a Romanian-made car

Chapter Nine

Mihai *(Mee HY)*
Radu *(RAH doo)*
Stănicel *(STUH nee chel)*

Chapter Ten

Marian *(Mah ree AHN)*
cireşe amare *(chee REHSH eh ah MAR eh)* — literally,
    bitter cherry, a wild cherry, used mostly for jams
    and jellies
Popovici *(POH poh veech)*

Chapter Eleven

Marcu *(MAHR koo)*
Ada *(AH dah)*
Andrei *(AHN dray)*
Margareta *(Mahr gah REHT ah)*

Chapter Twelve

Mihaela *(Mee ha YEH lah)*

Chapter Nineteen

Anica *(Ah NEE kah)* — derived from Ana
dinar *(DEE nar)* — Serbian monetary unit

Chapter Twenty

Alexandru *(Ah lehk SAHN droo)*

Chapter Twenty-four

Lenuța *(Leh NOOTS ah)* — derived from Elena
Veronica *(Veh roh NEE kah)*

Chapter Twenty-five

Ceaușescu *(Chow SHESS koo)*
Sofica *(Soh FEE kah)*
Stănescu *(Stuh NEHS koo)*
Ileana *(Eel YAH nah)*
Stoicescu *(Stoy CHES koo)*
Tănase *(Tuh NAH seh)*
Tereza *(Teh REHZ ah)*
Daniel *(Dahn YEHL)*
Brânzei *(Brn ZAY)*
Dana *(DAH nah)*
Mica *(MEE kah)* — sometimes derived from "mother"

Chapter Twenty-six

Tudorică *(Too doh REE kuh)*
Lidia *(LEE dee ah)*
Florica *(Floh REE kah)*
Mureșan *(Moo reh SHAHN)*

Chapter Twenty-seven

Larisa *(Lah REE sah)*
Natalia *(Nah TAHL yah)*

1

My Tata's God

The hill behind our house was as much a part of my world as the mud-brick, two-room cottage where I lived with my family. The contours and slopes of the hill were so familiar to us that the hill seemed to be ours. There were special places that were only known to those of us who lived close by. One such place was the spring which provided sparkling water in a little ravine. Wild rose bushes grew there, the roots reaching deeply into the moist soil to draw the water up the thorny stems to nourish the pale pink single rose blossoms.

We also knew where to find the sweetest rose hips in the fall. But I and my siblings knew that we must check early if we were to be the first ones to gather the sweet fruit. For the city spread around the hill, and the slope was often dotted with the children from the houses on the city's outskirts.

Our frequent trips up the hillside always included faithful *Bombonel,** our family dog. Whether we were taking the family goats to graze the sparse grass, hunting for the early spring cress, or just exploring, Bombonel was always with us. His shaggy white coat dotted with black patches is one of my earliest childhood memories.

I knew too, the part of the hill where my father dug out the yellow clay to repair the walls of our house. Of course, everyone knew where the clay pit was because there was a road up the slope where the two-wheeled carts would trundle

* Refer to glossary on pages xi - xiv for pronunciations or definitions of italicized words.

1

back with the clay. But there were other, less known paths on the hill too. Some of these seemed to lead aimlessly about at first, but each had a particular destination. Some led in a roundabout way to the monastery that crowned the very top of the hill. Other paths led to places where a person could sit and gaze out over the city.

But as a child, I hardly ever just sat and looked. I looked as I ran about from one place to another. I looked across the cluster of village houses on the outskirts of the city to the big office buildings and the stores downtown. I especially looked at the railroad foundry's huge twin smokestacks that pointed up into the sky like some giant fingers. For it was there that my father, my *Tata*, worked.

Like the sun, Tata was such a vital part of my life. Even if he was away at his work, just like the warm Romanian sun sometimes hid behind the clouds, I knew an inner delight in merely thinking about dear *Tataia* returning to our home. Mama was always busy caring for the baby, *Dănuț*, or for the other two children who were younger than I. And there were the older children to clothe and feed and try to provide for. Altogether, there had been 12 children; two had died in their infancy, and one had died when he was 3. Truly, Mama was busy. But Tata always had time for me.

Life with Tata was not only secure, it was also fun. When the outside walls of our house needed to be repaired, we had to mix the yellow clay from the hillside and the barnyard straw from the monastery stable. It was Tata who told us girls to hitch up our skirts and the boys to roll up their pant legs and mix the clay, water and straw with our bare feet. And it was Tata who laughed along with us children when the wet, oozing clay squished up between our toes.

My father had the gift of making the ordinary, extraordinary; the mundane, special. I even thought of my father as having the same miracle-working abilities that God has. I was very familiar with the Bible stories of God leading the children of Israel through the Red Sea, of water gushing from a rock, of manna floating down from heaven and of the miracles that Jesus did. And I was sure that Tata could also perform miracles.

Once when Mama had taken her mending to spend the evening with her parents, Tata had turned the preparations for our sparse supper into a special event. Scarcely had the yard gate closed behind Mama when Tata wondered who would find the biggest cooking pot and fill it with water? Who would bring some kindling in to start the fire in the mud brick stove? And would anyone be interested in going to borrow just a little bit of sugar from a generous neighbor?

— · —· —· —· —· —· —· —· —

Victor ran out the door to fetch the water. Five-year-old Ştefan, Fănel, we called him, went to gather the chips, and I brought back the sugar in a cracked cup. With excitement, we crowded into our lean-to kitchen. We watched as the fire crackled into a bright flame and as the oven plate was removed so the cooking pot could be set right over the glowing coals. Then, we eagerly waited for the water to boil. What special food was Tata going to make? I had heard Mama say despairingly that we had only a little bit of flour left and she did not know what to make for supper. The meager wages that the state-run foundry paid Tata were never enough to provide for our needs, and sometimes there simply was not enough money to buy food. That was when Mama's voice quivered and her brow wrinkled up like a freshly furrowed field. But now, Tata was going to make supper for us! What could it be?

We crowded around the stove as Tata took some flour, found a little bit of oil, heated some water in a saucepan and stirred the mixture together to make a batter.

"Is the water boiling yet?" he asked as he leaned over to peer into the pot at the back of the stove. His skinny frame made a sort of arch over the stove. His face was flushed by the heat and his smile was as warm as the stove.

The flour batter was spooned slowly into the hot water, and as the mixture cooked, it formed into small dumplings. The aroma of something cooking filled our simple kitchen and we all realized just how hungry we were. I gave a little giggle as I felt my insides rumble. I patted my middle and waggled my finger at my stomach. "Shh," I admonished.

3

"Let's take one and put a little sugar on it." Tata dished up a plump noodle that was shaped like a fat pillow and carefully I sprinkled a teeny bit of the precious sugar on it. Then Tata broke the small dumpling into tiny pieces and gave each of us a crumb to taste.

With what delight we each took our tiny portions and placed them in our mouths. How we gently munched the slightly sweet dumpling and carefully savored each bit before we reluctantly swallowed. When a crumb clung to a corner of 3-year-old *Ana's* lips, I gently took my forefinger and pushed the crumb into her mouth. I felt my own throat tremble and I swallowed, too, as I watched Ana, or *Nuți* as we called her, swallow the last teeny bite.

So it is no wonder that I thought Tata was like God, because as we sat around the table and ate the delicious warm dumplings that evening, I was vividly reminded of the time when Jesus fed the 5,000 with a small boy's lunch. My father could do miracles, too!

— ·— ·— ·— ·— ·— ·—

I gave another experimental pat to the saucer I was making. The clay had been just right to make a set of play dishes. Victor, even though he was 9 and sometimes thought he was too old to play with clay, had looked with interest at the cups and bowls that Fănel and I were making. Soon we three children were busily making pottery. Even Nuți had her own lump of clay and tried to make a bowl, but spent most of the time watching the wet clay squeeze out from between her fingers.

"I will make a teapot," I announced as I set the saucer on a board to dry. In my mind, I could picture the spout gracefully curving from the squat body, just like the teapot Mama used. I frowned thoughtfully for a moment at my lump of clay. "I need to look at the big one," I decided and with a quick spring to my feet, I was up and running noiselessly across the yard. My bare feet were nimble and I crossed the hard mud floor of the porch and went into the entry.

"Oh, we must have guests," I thought to myself when I saw that the door to one of the rooms was closed. I could hear the murmur of voices, first Mama's voice and then Tata's voice. Even though I knew it was Mama's voice, there was a different tone to it, almost as if she were crying.

I didn't like when Mama cried. Mama had cried, too, when instead of bringing a baby home from the hospital as we all expected she would, only Mama came home. And when Mama cried, it made me feel as if somehow our home had a crack in it. A big, black crack that ran down one of the sturdy white walls and allowed some unknown threat to come in and destroy our happiness. So the sound that came from behind the door stopped me from going into the kitchen to look at the teapot.

Then I heard Tata's voice again. A rush of warmth swept through my being as I heard my beloved Tataia's steady and calm tones. But there was also something different about his voice that was not quite steady. A pleading tone that I was not used to hearing in his everyday voice. I didn't really mean to eavesdrop, but with my usual directness, I wanted to know what was happening. I stepped closer and pressed my ear against the door.

"You know we have no food in the house. You gave us these dear children and we love them all. But You also know we have no food. And supper time is coming and we need to feed our dear children."

Tata's voice came quite clearly through the door. In my mind, I could see him kneeling beside the cot that doubled as our bed at night, work-worn hands folded in prayer, talking with God.

"God, I know that You love us. You have promised us that You will never leave us nor forsake us. You fed Elijah in the wilderness. You helped the widow and her boys. And now we ask You to help our children. We have borrowed from the neighbors and we are ashamed to beg from them again. Please God, help us. Strengthen our faith."

Tata was pleading for food! I suddenly realized how desperate our situation was. We almost always had *mămăliga* (corn mush), the poor man's staple. Even if we got tired of it, there always had been enough mămăliga to take away the emptiness from our stomachs. And now we didn't have

5

mămăliga either?

As I heard the kind, yet pleading voice of my Tata, my whole being longed to comfort him. "I am not hungry," I whispered to myself. "I will not need to eat. I can do without food." I so desperately wanted to do something to fulfill the longing I heard in my father's voice. "I can just wait until . . ." my thoughts went in circles. Until when? I suddenly realized that we would need food sometime. The voices of the children playing outside were real voices. They would need food. Even the older children needed food so they could go to school or go to work. Everyone needed at least some food!

The hinges of the yard gate squeaked. Someone was coming! I suddenly realized that I was eavesdropping and Tata must not find me here. I quickly turned and went back outside.

"Silvia!" It was our neighbor, *Moşu Lolu*, who lived in the house behind ours. Moşu sometimes would stop me on the way home from school and give me a cup of milk or maybe a slice of white bread. That is, if his wife did not see us. She never shared willingly with our noisy, happy family, even though we were neighbors. I had heard her sharp remarks about people who had children in litters like animals. Once I even heard her say that "the *Tărniceriu* family is no different from the uncivilized Chinese who have huge families." They themselves had successfully raised their family, and living next door to such a large family was disturbing to her.

But Moşu Lolu always liked me. And now, his kind face was relaxed and smiling. "Where is your Tata?" his hearty voice boomed out.

"Tata!" I called, running into the house. The closed door opened and I eagerly searched my father's face for any sign of turmoil. But his face shone as bright as the sun that was now dipping toward the western horizon. There was not a trace of worry, just a calm trust.

"Do you have anything for supper?" Moşu Lolu asked in a friendly way. "My wife is visiting her sister, and I have a big bucket of milk from our cow. Do you need it?"

Need it? I could scarcely believe my ears! How could Moşu Lolu know how desperately we needed that milk? How was it possible that tonight his wife was gone and that he had thought about the large family next door?

But Tata's voice was calm and he said, that, yes, we would be glad for the milk. And no, we didn't have any bread in the house. But we would be thankful for the milk.

"Give Silvia a pail and we will go for the milk," Moşu Lolu said as he turned to leave.

I not only returned with the pail of foamy milk, I also clutched a handful of coins with which to buy bread.

Bread! Sometimes for a treat we might have bread on Sunday mornings. But this time, Tata sent Victor to the bakery right away for a delicious loaf.

As our large family gathered around the table for this unexpected feast, Tata led in a prayer of thankfulness and praise to the God Who answered our prayer and loved us in such a wonderful way. I didn't mind that the prayer was long, but every once in a while I opened one eye and peeped at the bread. Yes, it was true. And there was a big pitcher of milk in the center of the table. Bread and milk. Manna from heaven.

"We thank You that You hear our prayers. And we thank You that You moved in Moşu Lolu's heart to share with us in such a wonderful way. We bless Your name and praise You!"

The words flowed from Tata's mouth. It was more than a prayer. It was a hymn of praise.

I wiggled with slight impatience, but the words of Tata's prayer were now also echoed in my heart. Now I realized that when Tata prayed, God answered. Prayers were more than just something that people said. Prayers were talks with God. Talks about needs. And God was Someone Who heard when Tata had needs.

In my heart, I prayed, too. I didn't know where we would get food for the coming days, but I did know that Someone loved and cared for the Tărniceriu family! God did!

2

No Home

Somehow, it seemed we always did have food, even though there was never plenty. I became more keenly aware than ever of my parents' constant struggle to provide for us children. Whenever Tata would pray and ask God to provide for us, I would remember the time I overheard Tata pray for food. But most of the time, we younger children did not even think of ourselves as poor. Oh, yes, there were many times we were sharply reminded that we were different from other families with fewer children, but life was too interesting for us to dwell on such issues. Why, who else had such interesting times as when we spent whole afternoons on the hillside searching for the best places to take the family goat? Victor was responsible for the goat, and often I, Fănel, Nuţi and sometimes even Dănuţ accompanied him. While the white goat grazed contentedly, we found all sorts of things to do. Victor carved remarkable figures out of wood and I taught Fănel how to whistle on blades of grass. The warm sunshine shone on our already brown skin and the fresh breezes cooled our faces when we lay on the grass to rest after our vigorous games. So what if we did not have enough shoes so that we all could go to church at once? Or, for that matter, if we were not able to afford the tram tickets so the whole family could attend church services on the other side of the city? We were used to taking turns to go to church and if we couldn't go every time, it made it all the more special when we could go.

But I knew that our poverty weighed heavily on my parents' minds. The worried expression on Mama's face when she was faced with the task of preparing a meal was a constant reminder that want stalked our home.

One Sunday morning on the way to church with my parents on the tram, I was delighted to see Maria *Lazăr*. *Sora Măriuţa*, we called her. Maria was one of those women who had a heart big enough for everyone. To me, Maria was not only friendly, she was also someone who knew how to share. God had never given her and her husband any children, and it seemed like Maria just opened her big heart and claimed all of her friends' children as her own. So when I saw Sister Măriuţa on the tram, I eagerly pushed my way through the crowd and stood beaming at the friendly lady.

"Silvia! What a nice surprise! Sit here beside me. Are you going to church, too? Oh, there are your parents. *Pace*, Brother and Sister Tărniceriu. Now we can go to church together!"

There was still room for my parents to sit next to Maria. As the grownups talked, I remembered the gift Maria had given to me on my last birthday. Maria's nieces lived in the capital city, Bucharest. They had brought the gift from a special store in the city.

That pencil box was the nicest gift I had ever received. The wooden box was painted a soft blue-gray color on the outside. When the lid was opened, there were little compartments to hold the erasers and pencils, a space for a ruler, and even a place for a small tablet. I had never seen such a pencil box before! And this was something that was all my own. I usually didn't mind sharing with my brothers and sisters, but it was very special to at least have the pencil box all my own!

As the tram rounded a street corner, I swayed slightly to the left and leaned against Maria's comfortable side. Then I became aware of what she was saying.

"I know, Brother Tărniceriu, that you are having a difficult time providing for your family. God has not blessed us with any children and I would like to make a suggestion to you. Would you consider letting Silvia live with us? I would take care of her and buy her the clothes she needs. It would make it easier for you with your big family."

I looked up at Tata. Then I looked at Mama. My parents looked at each other. Mama raised one eyebrow questioningly at Tata.

Tata seemed to be at a loss for words. Was he considering the offer, I wondered?

I thought about Maria's nice house. I thought about the nice clothes Maria could afford to buy for me. And, more than anything else, I remembered the wonderful food Maria always fixed for me whenever I visited there. Just the thought of the delicious bread, the fried potatoes and gravy, the savory salads and the cakes that Maria served, made my mouth water. But, I also thought of how quiet Maria's house always was. Yes, Maria was friendly and talkative, but I still thought of her house as a quiet house, a house without children.

Was Tata considering giving me away? Tata looked at Mama's face again. Then he looked at me. I looked soberly up at him. My eyes were studying his face. What was Tata thinking?

Tata's voice was not quite steady when he finally answered Maria. "No, Maria, I cannot consent to that. You see, I would miss her too much. And when I would see our daughter in church or we would see her when we visit you, I—I just couldn't stand it. I don't think I could live without my Silvia."

My heart had been beating rapidly as I waited for Tata's answer. When I heard his words of love and saw the special look he gave me, I let out a sigh of relief. I had not realized that I had been holding my breath, waiting for his answer.

———————————————

After that, even though life seemed not much different from before, an uneasy thought kept creeping into my mind. Would my parents really consider giving me away? Was it really that hard for them to feed and clothe our family? I realized my parents worked hard and that the older children were working at jobs away from home in order to help provide for our needs, but somehow it was easier not to dwell on such things.

One evening, Tata told the family that he was going to visit our relatives who lived miles away in the village of *Sânnicolau Mare*, in the far western part of Romania. In fact, Uncle *Iuliu* and Aunt *Estera* lived very near the Hungarian border. "And Silvia, I am going to take you along to visit them. This will be your first train trip!"

Victor and Fănel looked at me. I looked at Tata. Me! Go on the train all the way across the country! Oh, what fun! I was delighted! Plus, I would be traveling with Tata!

It was a strange idea that Tata was to take the train trip. Even though as an employee of the railroad he was entitled to free rail passes, Tata hardly ever traveled anywhere, except perhaps when he went on vacation for a day or two. We couldn't afford the other expenses that went along with traveling.

"When are we going, Tata? I'm so glad that I may go with you. Have I ever seen Uncle and Aunt *Incze*?" I was full of questions.

Tata smiled as he pulled me close and hugged me. He did not speak right away. "We are going tomorrow morning, Silvia. No, I don't think you have ever met your uncle and aunt. I—I hope you will like them. I remember them as—well—kind people."

I looked up quickly at Tata. There was something a little strange about his voice. But the same warm smile reassured me that everything was all right. Or was his smile the same? I was not sure.

The train trip across the central mountainous terrain of Romania was interesting to me. After the newness of actually riding in the coach had somewhat worn off, I glued my nose to the window and watched the passing scenery. Most of the cities and towns looked boringly similar to my own hometown of *Iaşi*. But the eaves of some of the houses in the villages we passed through were decorated with all kinds of wooden curlicues and carved patterns. I was fascinated. This was the first time in all my 12 years that I had been this far from my native city of Iaşi. My soul responded to the beauty and the majesty of the mountains and the valleys we passed through.

When I turned to share my delight of the mountains with Tata, I saw that he had fallen asleep. His face looked worn and tired. Dear Tata! He always seemed quite weary, but something more than just the usual tiredness seemed to be reflected on his sleeping face. Something was not normal. I turned to look out the window again.

The next morning, the sun was already shining warmly when our train chugged into the Sânnicolau Mare station. I had slept rather fitfully in the night, but the new day lay ahead of me, bright and unexplored. Just what kind of experiences would I have now?

"That's their house," Tata said, pointing to a big house on the street corner. A high board fence enclosed the whole yard. We opened the gate and were welcomed by the refreshing shade of a large apricot tree. Even though the walk from the train station was not far, the warm sun had wearied us.

I stared in amazement at the beautiful yard. Well-tended garden plots lined the walk. Red geraniums and pink and white phlox bloomed in flower beds in front of the house. Fruit trees shaded the yard from the warm sun. In the backyard was a fenced-in area where a flock of chickens busily scratched in the ground. The chicken house was painted a deep blue and sunflowers grew alongside one wall.

The house was painted a lighter shade of blue and a large verandah stretched across the entire front of the dwelling. The porch posts, window trim, and wide cornices were all painted a glossy white. Well-proportioned windows flanked the front door. Everything looked so rich and well cared for. This was like a dream to me. We walked to the house and when no one came to answer our knock, we sat on a wooden bench on the porch. I chattered excitedly to Tata about the beautiful house and the yard. Tata smiled lovingly at me and stroked my hand. He did not say much.

I heard the latch on the yard gate click. Then I saw my aunt. The minute I saw her, I knew she belonged here in this beautiful setting. *Tanti* Estera had lovely blond hair, braided and fastened in a bun on the back of her head. Her blue eyes matched her blue dress and a sprinkling of freckles spattered across her small nose. Her lips were a glossy red. Everything she wore looked new, and even though she had been working for many hours, she looked cool and fresh.

"*Pricop*! And this must be your daughter! Silvia, you say her name is? That's a lovely name." Tanti Estera looked critically at me. Her eyes skimmed over the tight blouse and oversized skirt I was wearing. In fact, it wasn't my skirt, but my sister *Rodica's*. True, Rodica, at 21, could no longer wear it, but it was still much too large for me. I had to roll the top over the belt many times before the hem finally was short enough for me. Tanti Estera didn't stare at my clothes, but I was conscious of them and tried to pull the blouse down over the bulge that the rolled-up waistline made around my middle.

I felt myself blush slightly as Tanti Estera reached out and lifted my chin. Her blue eyes met my brown eyes. And then Estera turned to Tata with a laugh.

"What a beauty you have there, Pricop. And by the looks of her, she is intelligent as well! But come inside. There is no need for you to sit out here." She led the way inside.

We were ushered into a tiled hall that was as large as our entire kitchen back in Iaşi. When we entered the living room, I felt like we were in a palace. In the middle of the room was a round table covered with a snowy white crocheted tablecloth. A huge dresser of dark polished wood held sparkling vases and patterned china. Overstuffed floral-patterned chairs and a long sofa gathered around the middle table. On the floor was a soft rug with patterns of maroon and navy blue. A large framed mirror reached almost from the floor to the ceiling and several porcelain figurines stared lifelessly into the mirror from a low shelf. The walls were painted a creamy white with a border of blue lilies stenciled along the top. Lacy curtains swayed softly from the breeze that came through the open windows.

I felt at once overawed and yet delighted. The beauty-loving heart of mine thrilled to the tasteful, richly decorated house, but it seemed unreal that people actually lived in such houses. I tucked my scuffed shoes back under my chair. I instinctively felt that I was not dressed well enough to be in such an elegant place.

When my uncle arrived, he seemed to fit in the setting as well as my aunt did. He was dark-skinned—"just like Silvia," Tanti Estera laughed—and he had a strange accent. During the grown-up conversation, I soon understood that *Nenea* Iuliu Incze was a Hungarian by birth. I was fascinated by his black hair and his brown eyes, even darker than mine, and by his courtly manner.

I heard Tata and my aunt and uncle talk about their jobs. When the relatives heard how little the government job paid Tata, they clucked their tongues and shook their heads. Tanti Estera was a doctor and Nenea Iuliu was a businessman, and it was clear that money was no problem for them. They had never had any children and so were used to spending their money freely for whatever they wanted.

After a bountiful supper, Tanti Estera showed me where I would sleep. The room was cosy, decorated with stenciled flowers and blue curtains at the window. The well-ordered room seemed to reach out with inviting arms to my weary body. At first, the soft bed felt so good, but after awhile it seemed too big for me and I missed Nuți's comfortable little body snuggled against me. I would even have welcomed Fănel, although I usually complained if he wanted to sleep on our narrow cot at home.

When Tanti Estera left and joined the men in the living room, I sat up in bed and looked around in the dim twilight. Everything was so perfectly in order. My aunt had helped me hang my few clothes on the hooks behind the door. In spite of the rise and fall of the adults' voices in the living room, I felt almost engulfed in silence. But I was tired and I laid my weary head on the pillow.

On Sunday afternoon, it was Tanti Estera who first approached me. "Dearie, last night while you were sleeping, your Nenea Iuliu and I talked with your Tata. And guess what! We are going to provide a home for you with us! Won't that be wonderful!" Tanti Estera raised both shapely eyebrows and beamed at me.

"We know that your parents love you, but they have so many children and it is very difficult for them to raise you and provide for your needs. Nenea Iuliu and I have never had any children," Tanti Estera paused for a little chuckle, "and we would like to have you live with us. I'm sure you'll like it here."

My mouth was dry. I tried to swallow. I looked at Tanti Estera and then at Nenea Iuliu. Finally, I looked at Tata.

Tata was sitting on the edge of the flowery sofa. He was looking at me with a strange look on his face. I had never seen

15

such a look before. I was struck by how lined and tired his face was. With vivid clarity, I realized what a struggle my Tata was facing. He did not want to leave me here. This was not easy at all for him. But I also realized that Tata was keenly aware of his inadequacy to provide food and clothing for our large family. I realized that he did not want this to happen to our family, but he saw no other option.

Tanti Estera's bright chatter continued. "We'll take you to the store and buy you new clothes tomorrow. You can go to our school here. I know some of the teachers and they are very educated and smart."

Nenea Iuliu also welcomed me. "I have for a long time wanted a daughter. I will be proud to have you live with us." His smile was warm and genuine. I felt a little comforted. But I still could not believe this was happening. Tata had said he could not live without me.

The parting between Tata and me was hard. Terribly hard. The invisible bond that bound us together seemed to squeeze my heart until I could hardly breathe. No one seemed to know what to say. When Tata gave his final farewell hug to me and I laid my head against his coat front, all he could say was a choked, "God bless you. My daughter!" I could not talk. My heart felt like stone.

Nenea Iuliu walked with Tata to the train station. But I did not watch them go. Tanti Estera was already busy. She brushed out my hair, even though I usually did it myself. Mama never had time to do her 12-year-old daughter's hair.

Tanti Estera pulled my dark wavy hair back from my forehead. She puffed up the front and then tied my hair with a ribbon. I watched in the large mirror and turned my head slightly in order to better see the glossy cascade of hair rippling down to my shoulders.

And the next day, true to her promise, Tanti Estera took me to the store to buy new clothing. I was fitted with experienced and practiced hands, and a bewildering amount of clothing was folded into shopping bags. Skirts, blouses, a sweater and a jacket. More clothes for me alone than four of us Tărniceriu children used to own together. A stout pair of shoes to wear to school and a pair of sandals were purchased at the shoe store.

"Wear the sandals to go home," Tanti Estera encouraged. My feet felt light and free as we walked back to the house. I had never had sandals before. In fact, I had never had new shoes in my life. Always I wore someone's hand-me-downs, usually Victor's, and by the time he had outgrown them, they were badly scuffed and worn.

In the days that followed, I tried to get used to my home. But, I never really thought of my aunt and uncle's house as "home." Home was where Tata and Mama, Victor and Fănel and all the others were. But I refused to think about home. I would shake my head and deliberately think about something else. Sometimes I would go and tend to the chickens because that seemed the closest thing like my home in Iaşi. Other times I would stay away from the chicken yard because it reminded me too vividly of our own flock and our own yard and my own dear family.

At times the new experiences were interesting and fun. My aunt and uncle did their best to make me feel like their own daughter. One time at the supper table, when Tanti Estera passed a dish of green beans to me, I refused them.

"Yes, you must try some," Tanti Estera smiled at me. "They are good for you!"

"But I don't like green beans!" I wrinkled my nose and looked at the mound of beans in the dish.

"Just take a spoonful and see if you don't like them," Tanti Estera urged.

I dipped the serving spoon into the dish of green beans and put a few beans on my plate. A white sauce pooled under the beans. I shuddered.

But Tanti Estera was watching me, so I quickly scooped up the beans and put them into my mouth. I gave several rapid chews and swallowed.

They were good! I was so surprised! I looked at the serving dish again. The white sauce gave an entirely different taste to the green beans. I reached out and took a spoonful of beans. In fact, I took a large helping.

Tanti Estera and Nenea Iuliu laughed. "So, you like your aunt's beans? And her cooking?" Nenea Iuliu chuckled. They looked at each other and smiled. They thought I was becoming accustomed to living with them. But my longing for my own family was like a constant sharp pain in my side. Sometimes the pain seemed almost unbearable.

3

Homesick

When school started, I soon learned that lessons here in Sânnicolau Mare were quite different from what I had been used to in Iași. The classes were smaller, and the competitive spirit was much greater. Even though I now had clothes that were as good as, or better than, the other students', I felt shy at first. My strange accent and my foreign looks earned me the nickname of "The Moldovan Girl." I was not from Moldova, but I was from a part of Romania that had once belonged to Moldova.

But it did not take the teachers long to recognize that I had a quick mind. And *Angela* the top brain of the school who used to hold the honors in all the subjects, suddenly found her position seriously challenged. So, in spite of being the poor girl from Moldova, I soon was known as the best student in the class.

The music teacher soon found out that I had a natural talent for music. After hearing the melody of a song once, I could hum the tune with hardly any mistakes. I was given the solo parts and from then on my popularity in school increased dramatically.

"Silvia," the music teacher told me one day, "we are going to attend the area competition for musical choruses and I want you to learn this song. You will be dressed in a national costume and your solo will be the final performance for our group."

I shivered with excitement. I recognized the importance of this competition. And for me to be given such a special part was a great honor. I remembered how shy and out-of-place I had felt when I first attended school. Now, I was given this special attention from the entire school. Girls who at first had turned up their noses and walked on the other side of the street suddenly wanted to be my friends. Of course, Tanti Estera was enormously pleased. She eagerly repeated to Nenea Iuliu what the teachers were saying about me. Sometimes, my aunt and uncle even referred to me as "our daughter."

One evening, I came home from school in a sober mood. At choir rehearsal that day, the teacher had encouraged me to put more life into my solo. "Let yourself go when you reach the chorus. Sing:

'I am the darling of the mountains,
Even though I live in the valley!
I am the sweetest of all the girls,
Sweetest in the whole country!'

Tap your foot as you sing. Your voice is high and sweet, but your body is stiff. You need to dance a little."

Dance! I had stiffened up even more when I heard the teacher ask me to dance. What would Tata say? Indeed, what would he say if he heard the words of my song? After that, the song practice just didn't go very well. I had tried halfheartedly to jiggle my feet when I sang, but the movements were not natural. The music instructor had not been very well pleased with me.

Just the thought of Tata caused me to remember other things with regret. I knew I was pressured to do things and attend places that Tata would not have liked. But the constant praise and encouragement of my teachers and of Tanti Estera dulled the uneasiness of my heart.

Finally the day for the competition came. All day long, the choruses from different schools performed. When it came time for the Sânnicolau Mare chorus to sing, I followed the other group members up onto the stage. We sang one song after another, the girls all dressed in hand-embroidered blouses and colorful skirts, the boys in embroidered shirts and dark pants.

I looked out over the sea of people, and spotted Tanti Estera and Nenea Iuliu in the front row. I smiled at them and when the time came for my solo, I tried to step forward bravely in front of the audience. At first my voice quivered, but the long hours of practice came to my rescue and helped me gain control. I tried to put feeling into my song and because I loved to sing, I put my whole heart into the melody.

When I finished the last note and curtsied before the crowd, I slipped nimbly back into place.

The audience erupted into applause. They clapped and clapped. I could see the wide smiles of my relatives. My teachers from school were clapping and nodding at each other.

After the competition was over, I joined my aunt and uncle. A group of their friends surrounded them.

"Where have you kept her all this time? You mean Estera refused to forgive you until now? I bet if she would have known what kind of daughter you have, she would have long ago forgiven you!" The speaker was a friend of Iuliu's, and he was very vocal in his opinion.

"Come over here, Silvia. Stand there beside your father," a lady with short, curly, red hair chattered. "See the resemblance? Brown skin, dark eyes and black hair. Shame on you, Iuliu, for keeping her hidden so long." The lady laughed loudly.

The protestations of Estera and Iuliu were brushed aside. No, their friends insisted, they would not believe such things. They could see that I resembled Iuliu too much to believe his declared innocence.

—·—·—·—·—·—·—·—·—·—·—·—

One day after school several weeks later, I took my crocheting and sat outside on the verandah. The days were getting shorter but the sun was still warm enough to make it pleasant outside during the middle of the afternoon. I pushed my hook through a loop and began to add another row to the doily. Tanti Estera had been patiently teaching me how to make the intricate patterns of a small table mat.

I sighed and looked up. My gaze went beyond the board fence and I looked at the hills surrounding the town. Suddenly my ear caught a sound. A beautiful sound that somehow I had unconsciously been longing to hear. It was the gay music of children laughing and playing. An indescribable feeling came over me. A door in my memory was slowly opening. Time and time again, when memories of my home tried to penetrate into my mind, I pushed them resolutely away. But now the childish voice lifted in glee was opening that door.

An invisible cord seemed to draw me from my seat on the bench and lead me around the corner of the house. From there, I could see straight into the neighboring yard.

Two small children were running around in the back yard. A boy perhaps 3 years old and a girl of about 5 were playing. Someone, probably their father, had balanced a board on a section of a log, and the two children were happily seesawing up and down. When the end where the boy was sitting on hit the ground with a thud, he would throw back his head and laugh gleefully.

I stood and watched the lively scene. My chest rose and fell under my heavy sweater. My hair was neatly combed and my skirt was clean and spotless. My sturdy shoes were only slightly scuffed. I just stood there in my nice clean clothes in the well-groomed yard, and stared hungrily at the children playing next door.

It was unusual for me to stand still for so long, but something was happening to me. I could no longer keep the door to my memory closed. The memories were too many.

Suddenly the door burst wide open and into my mind tumbled all the memories of my home. Memories of my brothers and sisters and I on the hillside behind our house. Memories of waiting at the gate with the other children to see who could first see Tata coming home from work. Memories of sharing the bottle of chicory coffee that he often brought home for us children instead of drinking it himself. And yes, memories of the family gathered around the table, eating our humble yet delicious meal. Memories. Of Mama and baby Dănuț. Of Tata. My dear Tataia. It had been so long since I had heard his loving voice or felt his tender, work-hardened hand smoothing my hair. I felt like a statue. A well-dressed, clean, cared-for statue. Successful in school, liked by my teachers, approved of by my aunt and uncle, and yet something was missing. It seemed I had no heart.

Slowly, I began walking toward the chicken yard. Several of the hens were in the yard and as I walked toward them, they came over to the fence to see if I had some tidbits for them. But I had nothing.

I stooped and put my fingers through the wire that separated me from the chickens. The hens cocked their heads sideways and made strange little noises. Then, seeing there was nothing for them to eat, they wandered off.

I pressed my face against the wire. A tear formed into a drop in the corner of my eye. The rough wire pressed against my face and suddenly I sat on the ground. I didn't care that my skirt would get dirty. I didn't care that my shoes would need to be polished again before I could go back to school. In fact, I didn't care anything about my looks or my clothes right now.

I cried quietly. A steady stream of tears coursed down my cheeks and dripped from the wire fence. My crying was not a wild sobbing, but a crying of deep heartache, of loneliness.

The chill of the evening finally forced me back into reality. I knew that soon my aunt and my uncle would come home. They must never find me out here, crying.

That evening, Tanti Estera was barely inside the house when she called to me. I was sitting on my bed, just looking out the window.

"I'm going over to see *Elena*. She has a pattern for a crocheted bedspread that I want to see. I don't know when I'll be back." Tanti Estera breezed out the door.

When Nenea Iuliu came home after dark, I was in the kitchen. "Where's your aunt?" Iuliu questioned.

"She went to see *Elena*," I replied.

"Why?" Nenea Iuliu breathed heavily.

"Oh, she wanted to borrow a pattern for crocheting," I answered.

Iuliu prowled restlessly around the house. He went into the darkened living room and pulled the lace curtains aside. He shoved both hands into his pockets. Then he removed his hands. He stood at the window, his back turned. He leaned close to the glass and peered into the street. Even after he sat down and began to page through a magazine, he would get up and peer out the window again.

Over an hour later, Tanti Estera's quick steps came up the

walk. When she entered the hall and slipped off her coat, Nenea Iuliu was standing in the living room doorway.

"Where were you?" he asked coolly. His voice was clear and distinct, and I could easily hear it from my room.

There was a little silence, and then Tanti Estera's voice rippled out in laughter. "Why do you want to know? Didn't I tell you where I was?"

"I want to know where you really were. Not where you said you were." Nenea Iuliu's voice was cutting.

Tanti Estera's voice rose. "Now you are accusing me of lying! You don't trust me! Why do you think you have the right to know where I am all the time? Ask Elena if you want to know if I was there or not." She flung the words out at her husband.

When the three of us gathered around the table for our evening meal, Tanti Estera chattered to me.

"How was school today? You know, I am so glad you are doing so well in your studies. I'm sure that coming here to our school has been a real help in your education."

I tried to answer Tanti Estera's questions, but it was difficult to carry on a conversation while Nenea Iuliu sat eating quietly, hardly saying a word. He kept glancing at his attractive wife, and several times he scowled at her when she tried to draw him into the conversation.

That night, even with my bedroom door closed, I frequently heard the voices of my relatives shouting in their room. Then abruptly, all would be quiet, but later the shouts would begin again. I fell into a troubled sleep.

The next evening, Tanti Estera and I were in the living room when Nenea Iuliu came home. He strode purposefully into the room, fire shooting out of his eyes as he glared at his wife. He completely ignored me.

"I found out where you were last night. You liar!" he shouted. He flung his heavy briefcase straight toward Tanti Estera. The black case flew across the room, missed Tanti Estera, and crashed into the heavy framed mirror. The mirror shattered into pieces and the glass showered down upon the shelf below. Shards of glass flew out from the impact and landed on the soft carpet and the flowered chairs. Some pieces even flew onto the table in the middle of the room.

There was a deathly silence, broken only by the sound of Iuliu's heavy breathing. A piece of glass fell from the corner of the mirror, tinkling among the other broken pieces. Again there was silence.

I was terrified. I got up slowly and sidled out the door. My aunt and uncle didn't notice me. They stood very still, staring at each other. Nenea Iuliu's cheek twitched. I fled to my room, closed the door and, without undressing, slipped under the covers.

I drew the floral-patterned comforter up over my head and lay shivering in a heap.

"Where can I go?" I wondered. "I don't know anyone here well enough to run to their house. What shall I do? I can't stay here. I need to—I want to go home." My thoughts were confused.

When the shouting began again, I could not bear to hear any more. I opened my window, and without getting my shoes, I fled into the night. I hardly knew where I was going. I only knew I must get away.

I raced across the yard and opened the door to the chicken house. I slipped inside and shut the door behind me. There, in the little room where the chicken feed was stored, I groped my way in the darkness and sat on a pile of straw.

I was shivering all over, but not from cold. I drew my legs up and wrapped my arms around my knees. I lay my head on my arms and sobbed.

My world was shattered. Shattered just like the big mirror in the living room that Nenea Iuliu had broken.

I drew more straw around me and huddled deep into the pile. For some reason, the prickly straw gave me a sense of comfort. It brought a feeling of reality to my situation.

"Why am I here?" My mind rebelled. "Why me? Why did Tata ever leave me here in this awful place? I don't want to live here and be their child. I don't need these people's money to buy me things. I don't need sandals. I don't need the dresses they buy for me. I don't need to eat their meat every week. I don't need their things!"

It was much later when I realized I could not stay in the

25

hen house all night. My rational mind told me the best thing to do was to go to bed and try to forget all about it. Pretend nothing happened. That's what my aunt and uncle did. That's what they would do in the morning. In the morning all the glass would be cleared away.

So I went on cat-soft feet back across the yard and easily climbed back into my room through the window. The house was deathly still and dark. I undressed in the dark and once again huddled under the covers. It was a long time before I dropped off to sleep.

4

Conflict!

The empty space where the mirror used to be was an ugly reminder of what had happened. Every time I went into the living room, I tried to avoid looking at that corner where a lace curtain covered the hole. Now the arguments were no longer overheard only at night. If there were no arguments, there was often a sullen silence. I spent much time in my bedroom, studying. I threw myself into my lessons and tried to become absorbed in my books. But the air in the house was electric, the atmosphere tense.

It was obvious that when Tanti Estera went visiting at her friends' houses, she drank too much of the homemade wine that was served. After such parties, her voice was slurred and she giggled incessantly. And far too often, Nenea Iuliu himself stayed out late into the night. When he came home, he was the typical drunken male, belligerent and jealous.

On some evenings, they pretended nothing was wrong. Tanti Estera would make delicious meals, Nenea Iuliu would be pleasant, and they would ply me with good food and try to make me feel welcome. But I knew it was all a cover-up and in my nightly prayers, I would ask God to help me endure my stay there. I did not dare think about how long I would be in that house. That thought was too dreadful. But I had a vague idea that perhaps after school dismissed in the spring, I would be allowed to go home.

One evening after I was in bed, the wind seemed to howl around the house with unusual vigor. The bitter cold reached even into the house. When I heard the front door slam shut with a bang, at first I thought it was a result of the wind.

But then I heard the voices of my aunt and uncle raised in an argument. Suddenly, Tanti Estera cried out in pain. I sat upright in bed. My scalp prickled. What was happening?

Again came the cry. Then the sound of running footsteps. They were having a fight! I could hear the loud curses of Nenea Iuliu and hear the whack of his hands striking his wife.

I was horrified. This was the first time I had known Nenea Iuliu to hit his wife. He must be horribly drunk to be in such a rage!

The bedcovers were not thick enough to cut off the sounds. Kitchen utensils rattled, there were more cries, and harsh, violent words were spewed out of the warring partners' mouths.

At first, I stifled the sobs rising in my throat. But suddenly, it was as if something broke inside and I started crying. I couldn't stop. My horror was so intense, my fear so huge, that there was nothing I could do to stop crying. I stuffed my bed sheets into my mouth to muffle the noise of my crying.

Then suddenly, all was quiet. I heard only the mournful sound of the winter wind and the wild thudding of my heart. But in just a short time, I heard voices outside. Loud voices. Angry voices! The voices of my uncle and aunt. Again the cries of Tanti Estera. Again the blows of Nenea Iuliu as the fight continued.

I didn't know how long I lay under the covers, shivering and heaving long, shuddering sobs. I was aware of the front door opening and closing. Then all was silent.

The next day was Saturday, and Nenea Iuliu did not go to work. After Tanti Estera left for her work at the hospital, Nenea Iuliu came and sat on a chair beside me.

"I'm sorry that our home is not a happy home. But your Tanti Estera is a bad woman and I will not stand for it. I thought maybe after you came to live with us, she would change. But she hasn't changed, and I think maybe it was a mistake to have you come and live with us. You'd better just go back to your family. Even though your family is poor, I can see that you are better off there than here." Nenea Iuliu was not drunk now. His face was haggard, his eyes were swollen and puffy, and his voice was a dull monotone. Gone were his handsome looks and courtly manners.

I studied the pattern on the carpet. "Maybe I can call your Tata at work," said Nenea Iuliu. "Maybe he could come and get you."

A wild surge of hope sprang up in my breast. Tata! Home! Oh, what joy! I looked at Nenea Iuliu with tears in my eyes.

But in the following days, nothing more was said about me going home. And I was afraid to ask. Afraid the answer would be no. I became pale and had to force myself to eat. I had wild dreams and would often wake to find my pillow wet with tears.

Tanti Estera tried to cheer me up. We went to restaurants and ate fancy dinners. Tanti Estera bought more clothes for me and encouraged me to invite my friends from school to their house.

The long winter wore on, and finally spring came. Warmer weather meant more time outside after school, and I spent a lot of time with the chickens. And sometimes I watched the neighbor children playing on the other side of the board fence. Or on the other side of the prison walls. For now, this beautiful house and this beautiful yard seemed more like a castle than a home, and the fence was like a fortress. I was the prisoner. When could I escape?

For a long time now, there had been no more arguments, no more fights. Any casual observer would have been impressed by the good relationship between beautiful Tanti Estera and handsome Nenea Iuliu.

But I knew. I knew it could only be a matter of time before war broke out again.

"Silvia, school will be dismissed for the summer in only two more weeks," Tanti Estera crossed her elegant legs as she sat on the sofa beside me. "You could go home and visit your family for the summer. I know that two of your uncles and their wives are planning to travel in three weeks, and you could go with them on the train."

"Oh!" was all that I could manage to say. "Oh, yes!"

Estera continued, "In the fall, your Tata can bring you back to live with us again. We want to help educate you. You have such good marks in school that I am sure you could be a doctor like I am. We will help pay for any expenses."

I did not hear any more of the conversation. Come back again? Back here? Would I have to come back? Did my parents not want me? Must I come back?

But all of my questions vanished when I thought about going home in three weeks' time. Home! I was going home!

Suddenly I was jerked back into reality.

What was Tanti Estera saying? "You see, we are thinking of adopting you. We would change your last name to Incze. Silvia Incze. Doesn't that sound nice?"

Silvia Incze. There was nothing musical to such a name. It had no nice sound like Silvia Tărniceriu. I liked my family name. I didn't want to change it for something like Incze.

"Tell your parents you want to come back and make sure you bring your documents along with you. Then we can do all the legal work here." Tanti Estera prattled on as if everything were all arranged.

5

Going Home

The day had finally come! I was actually on the train, going to meet my relatives in the next town. Then we were going to travel to Iaşi together. I hugged my traveling bag to my chest. I did not have many clothes to take along. "Just your summer clothes, Silvia," Tanti Estera had told me when we were packing my clothes. "You won't need your winter clothes there, because you'll soon be back." She didn't ask me how I felt about it all, just made the statement and thought I would agree. After all, I was only 13, and she must have thought that I did not know what was best for me.

I had thanked my aunt and uncle for everything they had done for me and with eager steps I had boarded the train. Home still seemed far away, but at least I was on the way!

Now, I was nearing the station where I would meet my uncles and their families. Yes, the train was already slowing down. There was to be only a short stop here, but we had to board a different car to go to Iaşi.

The departing passengers got their bags together and I followed them off the train. When I got on the platform, I quickly looked around for my relatives. I expected a group of people, but I saw only one of my Tata's brothers.

"There you are," my uncle said. "You know, there has been a change of plans. Your relatives already left on the morning train. But that's all right. You may stay with us. We'll take care of you until—"

"Already left?" My voice lifted in fear. "Why did they leave? No! I don't want to stay with you! I'm going home!"

"I—well—you see they—" my uncle began.

"Why did they leave without me?" I repeated. "I want to go home. I am going home! I know the way. I can go by myself. This train goes right to Iași. I know I'll be all right!"

"But," my uncle began to protest, "you are only a young girl and I don't think it is wise for you to travel all by yourself. Why don't you wait and we'll—"

Again I interrupted him. "No! I will not stay! I know I can go by myself! I'm going home!" It seemed every time I said the word "home," my resolve grew stronger. Home!

I became very upset! My voice trembled and I started babbling loudly. "Just help me buy my ticket. Then I'll be fine. Where is the ticket booth? Help me, please! I'm going home!"

My uncle was almost helpless. He didn't know that I could be this determined. "One might as well try to stop the wind from blowing," my uncle said in amazement.

Reluctantly, he helped me buy the ticket and I boarded the train. I barely turned to wave to my uncle, but scurried to my seat in the compartment assigned to me. I was still worried that somehow, something might yet interfere with my plans of going home. My breath came and went in short gasps.

When the train finally started moving, I relaxed a little. I was sitting on the very edge of the seat, leaning forward. I had only my bag of clothes and personal belongings with me.

Though I was very tired, I could not relax. I was exhausted from the strain of finally being able to leave Sânnicolau Mare and start my journey home, the disappointment of having my relatives leave without me, and the consequent struggle of minds to be allowed to go by myself. I had not eaten at all that day, for it had been early in the morning when Tanti Estera had put me on the train.

"Where is your inter-city ticket, young lady?" The conductor was at the door of the compartment, punching the tickets.

I looked at him blankly. "I—I just have this permit. I don't have anything else," I stammered.

"Who are you traveling with?" He glanced at the other occupants of the compartment, a middle-aged man and two young men in their 20's.

"No one. I am traveling by myself." I answered politely.

"And you have no ticket? How did you get on the train?" He was puzzled.

"My uncle bought my ticket. He gave me ten *lei* and the ticket cost eight and one-half lei. See, here is the change. But I have no other ticket."

The conductor lifted his cap and ran his hand through his hair. "What shall I do? Make you get off at the next town? You can't travel on the train without the extra ticket!"

"I want to go home," I said in a small voice. "I have been away from home since last summer and I want to go home to Tata and Mama and my family." The last words almost came out in a wail. Was I going to be forced to go back? The very thought struck a cold fear in my heart.

The train rocked on its way toward the east. The rhythmic "clack clack" of the wheels was the only sound in the quiet compartment. But to me, the quietness was loud. My heart pounded and my breath came quick and fast.

"Let her stay." It was the middle-aged gentleman who spoke. "Probably the ticket agent took her money and kept the ticket to sell again. Allow the poor little girl to go home to her parents."

The conductor swore softly under his breath. He shuffled his feet a few times and then made a sudden decision.

"O.K. I'll let you stay. Now listen. When we get to *Cluj*, I get off because my shift is finished then. But I will tell the next conductor about your situation. I know him and he will help you get to Iaşi. But just don't speak to anyone about this." The conductor left the compartment.

It was already the middle of the day and when the businessman dug into his bag and got out some bread and a slice of cheese, I was reminded how long it had been since I had eaten last. I knew that I did not have enough money to buy anything to eat. So I just hugged my bag tightly and looked out the window. I had been hungry before. At least I was going home!

"Here, take some bread." It was the businessman again. He was offering me a big piece of bread. How good and wholesome it looked.

"Thank-you. You are kind," I said softly as I took the

bread. I laid it on my bag and bowed my head. I thanked God for providing this food for me. Then I ate. It was delicious.

"Why don't you lie down and sleep? There is room for you here on the seat." The man indicated the soft seat between us. At first, I shook my head, but finally my weariness overcame me and I lay next to the friendly man. All the while, the train moved onward—eastward—homeward.

When I woke up, it was dark outside. The train had already passed through Cluj, and now we were traveling through the lovely, mountainous countryside. As we whizzed past lighted homes, I could see families gathered around the supper tables. Sometimes I caught a glimpse of children playing games. Each scene left a vivid impression on my mind. It heightened my eagerness to reach my own city.

I began to have doubts. How would I be able to find my way all across the city from the train station to our home? It would be after midnight when the train arrived, and I knew the trolley buses did not run after twelve o'clock.

"God, help me," I prayed. "Maybe someone I know will be there and I can follow them. I—I know how to get there, but it is dark and—and—will I be able to find my home in the dark?"

The train was slowing. I smoothed my hair, clasped my bag tightly against my chest, and waited. That morning, I had felt so sure that I could go home by myself, but now that the time had come, I suddenly realized how big a task lay ahead of me.

I stepped off the train. The station was well lit, and even at that hour, many people were walking about. Everyone else seemed to know just where to go or what to do.

I stood under a street lamp at the edge of the platform. Beyond the circle of light, the darkness loomed large and black. The next street lamp with its pool of light looked far away. Did I dare leave and brave my way toward home?

A lady came walking past, her clicking heels a staccato beat on the concrete sidewalk. Something about her made me look at her closely. As the light shone fully on the lady's face, my eyes opened wide in amazement. I recognized her! I didn't know her name, but I knew this lady lived only several streets away from my house. I had often seen her going toward the

34

bus stop along our street.

When the lady walked into the blackness, I followed. I trailed the woman down the sidewalk and no longer was the darkness of the night looming over me like a giant. Now I could find my way home!

Through the poorly-lit city we went. When a service tram stopped to pick up some workers, the lady seized the opportunity to get a ride since it was going in our direction. But I was not going to be left behind. I, too, hopped on the tram.

I watched the lady closely throughout the trip across the city. When the woman got to her feet in preparation to leave, I knew we were close to our destination.

Again, I shadowed the woman closely. No longer did I need the woman to show me the way, but I felt better going with someone I knew rather than going through the dark city by myself. The lady was like an angel leading the way. Leading the way home!

First, a left off the main street into a side street. Then, a right onto another street that bisected the first street. By then, I did not need anyone to guide me at all. When the woman's heels "click clicked" on down the street, I made a right and made my way rapidly toward home. My feet seemed to have wings. Past my school, past the kindergarten, and past the Orthodox church building I went.

I turned down a little alley and went swiftly into the darkness between the tall board fences that separated the yards from the street.

The sound of dogs barking didn't usually bother me, because almost everyone in my neighborhood had a dog to protect the yard. And dear Bombonel accompanied us children almost everywhere we went. But Bombonel was not here, and there was a pack of dogs snarling and fighting somewhere in front of me. I was scared!

My footsteps were no longer quick and fast. In fact, I stopped when the pack of howling, yelping dogs came down the road toward me. There was enough light that I could see them. Three dogs. And now they were no longer fighting among themselves. They were barking at me.

With my heart thumping loudly in my chest, I edged past. When I got past them, I did not dare turn my back. The dogs barked and barked. I backed slowly down the street, and the dogs seemed to get braver as they came snarling and barking, closer and closer.

Suddenly I remembered how Tata used to chase dogs away. I quickly bent down as if to pick up stones and with a swift movement of my arm, I flung an imaginary stone at the snarling dogs.

It worked! The three yelped and ran several feet away. But now they only barked louder. Their shrill yelping and yapping echoed between the fences and they began to edge closer.

Again I bent over as if to pick up stones. This time, as soon as I flung my arm in their direction, I turned and ran.

The dogs cringed back in fear and retreated. But it did not take them long to see that I was running. So, with excited yelps, they followed my fleeing figure.

By this time, I was almost sobbing in fear and exhaustion. Once more, I sent them back with a wave of my arm and with the next dash, I turned the corner. Now I was on the street where my home was. Safety at last!

Miraculously, the dogs did not follow. My steps slowed and I tried to go softly down the dirt road so I would not disturb any more dogs.

One more house, and there, right there, was home! I almost wept in joy to see my home once more.

I quickly felt for the latch of the gate. I pushed against the rough wooden fence boards. Not here. Not down here either. Not here either!

I stood stock still. Was I dreaming?

This was our house! I knew it was. But where was the gate? I couldn't find it!

I fumbled in the dark. My fingers made desperate efforts to find a break somewhere in the monotonous sameness of the fence boards and find the gate, but their search was fruitless.

A sudden barking behind me startled me so much that I yelled. Not another dog!

I desperately felt along the fence. The dog barked and barked at me. He yapped and yelped and snapped at me and all the while, I frantically searched for the missing gate.

"I can't find the gate! I must jump the fence!" I cried to myself. I grasped the top of the boards that were higher than my head and, with a scrabbling and a scrambling with my feet, I clambered up the side. The dog's frantic barking and snarling at my heels lent strength to my wildly flailing limbs. When I reached the top of the boards, I flung myself into the yard. I was safe!

After only a few seconds on the ground to regain my breath, I ran to the door. In vain I turned the latch and pushed. The door was locked.

"Tata! Mama!" My voice rang out into the night. "It's Silvia!" I pounded on the door. "Tata! Mama! Open the door!"

"The house was quiet. There was no light inside.

"Where is everyone?" I asked.

I beat frantically on the door. Again and again I called. I felt so excited, yet everything was so strange. No gate in the fence! No one to open the door!

I went to the window, stood on my tiptoes, and knocked against the glass. Surely someone would hear me!

To my great relief, my older sister, Rodica, pushed aside the curtains and looked down at me.

"Rodica! Open the door! It's me, Silvia!"

But Rodica—or Rhoda, true to her Biblical name—left me outside and ran into the next room. "Tata! Mama! Someone is outside, and I think it's Silvia!"

"Open the door! I want in!" Again my voice rang out into the night.

Suddenly the door opened and somehow I was in Tata's astonished arms. All the frustration and stress of my trip home, and the long parting from my family, were too much for me. Exhausted, I sobbed upon the secure shoulders of my father, my Tata. I felt so safe.

"But where is the gate?" was my first question when I could think clearly again. "I couldn't find the gate and the neighbor's dog kept barking and no one came to help. I had to climb the fence to get in. Where is the gate?"

"I moved the gate to the other corner of the fence so Mama

can see when someone comes while she is working in the kitchen. We didn't like that people could come into the yard before we knew they were here," Tata stroked my hair. "And we had been up until after two o'clock this morning visiting with the relatives. That is why we didn't hear you knock. Oh, Silvia, how did you get here? Who brought you?"

As the awakened household sat listening in astonishment about my trip home, they shook their heads in disbelief. But to me, how I had come home didn't matter. I was home! That's all that mattered right now.

I lay down next to Nuţi and cuddled up against my little sister. But, as tired and sleepy as I was, a worrisome thought kept coming back to me. Would I have to go back to Tanti Estera's house? Finally I fell into a fitful sleep.

6

Safe Haven

The summer months were all that I had longed for, and even more. The first day at home, I wandered around the house and the yard. I did find the new gate, and saw where I had flown over the fence in the night. I was amazed that I had been able to get over the barricade. But I also remembered how terrified I had been.

When I met Bombonel, I hugged his shaggy body. "Where were you last night?" I scolded him. "I don't remember anything of you! You should have been there to scare that other dog away!"

There just wasn't enough time at first to get used to the changes in my family. Nuṭi barely seemed to recognize me, and at first Dănuṭ had refused to have anything to do with me. When I saw how Fănel just sat and looked and looked at me during breakfast, I realized that I must have changed some, too.

In the bustle of that morning, the grown-ups busily visiting and the cousins getting acquainted, more than once I sighed a deep sigh of contentment. To be with my family once more, to see Tata and Mama and all my brothers and sisters, was all my lonely heart had longed for. And the mămăliga was delicious! Each mouthful was savored and then swallowed. Nothing at Tanti Estera and Nenea Iuliu's house had ever tasted half as good!

All of this was the security for which my heart had longed: to be at home with my beloved Tata, to be with Mama and the children, to go to church when it was my turn, and to hear my father read the Bible and to listen to him pray. My world that had been turned upside-down was now right-side-up again. I was home once more.

But all during the following weeks, I would be reminded of what Tanti Estera had said. "You'll be coming back in the fall."

Most of the time I was quite successful in pushing such thoughts into the back of my mind. But more than once, in the middle of the night, I would suddenly wake up and the thought of going back would loom above me like a living nightmare. I would shiver and huddle under the blankets, no matter how warm it was.

As usual, we youngest ones of the family went to spend three weeks with relatives who lived in a distant village. The joy of being able to run with the other children through the meadows made my stay in Sânnicolau Mare seem even more distant. To feel the dust puff up between my toes as we walked down to the river, to gather wild flowers along the roadside and make posy crowns for our heads, to splash and wade in the cool water: all of these happy times were a healing balm to the tempests that I had experienced during my stay in the west.

The leaves began to change from green to yellow, the days began to shorten, and the winds no longer blew warm and balmy. I was reminded that autumn was rapidly approaching. That meant school would soon begin.

I had not seen Tata and Mama for three weeks now. Before long, we would need to leave the village and go back home. And then what?

I wasn't really prepared to see Tata when he did arrive. Or actually, to hear Tata. That afternoon, I was in the back yard that bordered the fields. Suddenly I heard Tata's voice in the house. What was he doing here? He hadn't planned to take us all home this soon.

With a quick realization, I knew. He was coming to take me back to Tanti Estera and Nenea Iuliu's house!

I panicked! Back to Tanti Estera and Nenea Iuliu's arguments and fights! Back to huddling under the covers, scared and shivering! Back to being pressured to do things that bothered my conscience! Away from Tata and Mama and the family!

No! I was not going back!

I darted away from the house and fled into the cornfield. The shocks, waiting to be harvested, stood tall and comforting in the rows of corn stubble. I streaked away from the house and then flung myself behind a shock. My heart was beating wildly and I tried hard not to breathe too loudly, lest someone should hear me. I pressed my hot face against the rustling corn and tried to squeeze among the stalks.

"Silvia!" a clear call came from the house. "Where are you?"

It was Tata! Tata was calling for me!

All of us children had been taught from infancy that when Tata or Mama called, we must respond. Now when Tata's voice came calling across the meadows, I had to steel myself against answering. It seemed as if my feet were going to carry me away from the corn shock and take me to Tata.

But there was something stronger than my childhood training that kept me from going to my father.

"Silvia! Come on, it's time to go!" Again and again Tata called. My cousins and my brothers called. But I just pressed more tightly against the corn stalks and kept saying, "I won't go back! I don't need their things! I won't go back!"

I could hear the voices of my family moving from place to place as they searched and called for me. Then suddenly, everything was silent.

I do not know how long I stayed there. Darkness was already stealing across the land when I cautiously peeked out to see if anyone was around. But all was quiet. I slowly went back to the house.

Tata had already left on the train. The others kept questioning me, asking me where I had been. They told me that Tata had come to take me back to Sânnicolau Mare and that they had called and called me and looked for me but they just couldn't find me. I refused to answer their questions.

It was only several days later that Victor, Fănel, Nuţi, Dănuţ, and I went back home. When Tata came home from work and saw us children come running out through the garden gate, he looked tenderly at me. He hugged each by turn, and when it was my turn, he tilted my chin up and looked deeply into my eyes. I looked back at him. We gazed long at each other.

Tata's arms tightened around me. And suddenly, I knew that Tata understood. He knew why I had not come when he had called. I suddenly wondered if Tata had really wanted me to come.

So it was settled that I did not need to leave home. Tata must have talked to Mama about it, but it seemed Mama just didn't understand like Tata did.

"Don't come asking for shoes or dresses. You will just have to wear what we can provide for you. You could have been well provided for at Tanti Estera's house," Mama said wearily. "I know that God has always provided for us, but there sure are times when it is difficult to know how to care for everyone!"

"I won't ask for anything, Mama! I would much rather be at home with my family than wear nice clothes and have good food all the time! Home is so much nicer than anywhere else!" I threw my arms around my mother's waist. There were no more dark or heavy thoughts to push away from my mind. I was not going back!

7

My Size

I shifted uneasily beside my mother on the church bench. The church house was well filled with people this Sunday evening. But I allowed the words of the song we were singing to drift by unnoticed. I was reliving an embarrassing and troubling time I had had in school just this past week.

I was 13 years old now, and in the seventh grade. At first, it had been so good to be back in my familiar school with the neighbor children and the classmates I knew. I was especially glad to be in the same school with my brothers, even though we were in different rooms. Just knowing Victor and Ştefan were in the same building was somehow comforting.

In Sânnicolau Mare, nobody had found out that I was from a Christian family, and I didn't tell anyone about my beliefs. Everyone who knew my aunt and uncle had no reason to think that I might come from a believing family.

But here, in Iaşi, most of the children knew we were believers. And since I had new subjects and new teachers this year, I was being taught things in school that were very troubling to me.

In spite of the group of worshipers singing in church, my mind was very far away. I shuddered slightly as I thought again of what had happened.

I had been in Teacher Maria *Albu's* class, studying anatomy. The teacher was giving a lengthy explanation of the origin of man and how, through millions of years, man evolved from some common ape-like ancestor. My mind rebelled against what she was saying, because I did not believe in the theory of evolution at all. As the teacher gave more and more explanations of our "kinship" with monkeys, I became very ill-at-ease. And then Mrs. Albu had made the statement that there were some idiots who think that man was created by One named God.

A ripple of laughter and excitement swept across the room. A babble of voices rose as my classmates excitedly told the teacher that "Silvia Tărniceriu believes in God!"

Mrs. Albu's eyebrows rose in astonishment. "So, we have a repentant—a believer in God—in our class! How interesting!"

"Who is God? Did you ever see Him?" the questions came in short bursts from Mrs. Albu's red lips. Her tone of voice mocked as she asked, "Did your mother ever see God?"

A small wave of laughter rippled across the room. Several of the boys snorted in derision.

"And what does God give you? Does he give your father a new car? Where does God live?"

It seemed as if Mrs. Albu was using the opportunity of having the entire class' attention to drive home a point "Our country doesn't need God. We don't need weak people who put their hands together and close their eyes and pray to someone who doesn't exist. We need people who open their eyes and get an education and help our country to become rich and prosperous. God doesn't do anything for us. We have to do it ourselves!"

Even now, years later, I still feel the shame and scorn that Mrs. Albu had put into her voice. And that had not been the first time. It seemed as if she hunted for opportunities to make sarcastic remarks about "people who believed in God."

The voice of the pastor suddenly reached through the fog of my thoughts. "You need to know for yourself that God is real! Believing in God because your parents believe in God is not enough. Or just because the pastor says God is real will not give you your personal faith in Him. You need to know Him personally!"

I listened attentively. The pastor was speaking directly to my need!

"You children, and young people especially, are being continually told in school that God doesn't exist. But everyone can have a personal knowledge that God exists. It doesn't

44

matter how young you are, you can have a deep heart knowledge that there is a God, and that He cares for you."

I allowed the words to sink deeply into my soul. I knew that my parents believed in God and that they took their cares to Him. But the many things I heard in school about it being foolish to pray and to believe in someone whom nobody can see caused doubts to niggle in my mind. Was God real?

The pastor was continuing to speak. "Just talk to God and ask Him to reveal Himself to you personally. Young people, just talk to God like you talk to your parents. Tell Him everything. All your doubts, your struggles, anything! God loves you and He wants to reveal Himself to you!"

After the services were over, I did not chat with my friends like I usually did. I mulled the pastor's words over and over. He had said that God wanted to reveal Himself to me? Wanted to? That was what the pastor had said.

Without really knowing just when I had made up my mind to put to test what the pastor had said, I knew that I must do this all by myself. And, I wanted to be alone when I asked God to make Himself known to me.

Alone? I knew that in a two-room house crowded with our entire family, it was not easy to be alone. I would not go outside, for by the time we got home, it was already dark.

The Tărniceriu family tradition for as long as I could remember was to sing while everyone prepared for bed. The small children were tucked under the covers on their cots, and while the older ones and Tata and Mama settled down on their beds, everyone sang. Mama's clear soprano voice led the songs and Tata sang bass. Since the older children sang in the church choir, they all knew the hymns of the church. Each of us younger ones had heard the same songs many times and everyone sang one part or another. Our whole family's voices blended in songs of praise night after night. Usually, the younger ones fell asleep first. After singing for awhile longer, the adults would fall asleep, too.

Tonight, I joined in with the singing as usual. When finally I heard the little children's treble voices dropping out, I was still wide awake. I held myself tense, waiting until the last notes of the last song died away.

When I heard no more restless moving from anyone in the room where I slept, I slipped out of bed. I knelt down on the floor and laid my head on the bed. "I don't know if this is a prayer or not. The pastor said I could talk to you as if you were Tata. I have a problem. In school, my teacher says there is no God. She says no one ever saw You. She mocks me and the other children laugh at me. The pastor says that You exist. And I know my parents pray to You and they believe that You answer their prayers. But, God, You have never answered my prayers. And I need to know. Is there a God? Can You do miracles? Do You know everything like the pastor said? Do You? I need to know!

"How can You know everything? Do You know about me? The pastor said You know each one of us personally. There are 12 people in our family. Do You know about each one of us? There are many families in Iași, and even many more in all of Romania. How could you know everyone in the whole world? And how can you know everything about me if there are so many other people in the world?"

I paused in my talk with God. The room lay in darkness. The even breathing of the sleeping children was interrupted now and then by someone turning restlessly. But for me, sleep was far away. I was wrestling with conflicting thoughts and my heart was pouring out my confusion.

"The pastor said You answer prayers. Tata says You answer his prayers. But, God, You have never answered my prayers personally. And the pastor said we can ask You to reveal Yourself to us, even though we are young. I am only 13 years old but I want to know. I want to know if You really are and if You can do miracles and if You do know everything.

"If this is true, You know I don't have my own shoes. I have to wear Victor's shoes even if they are too big and even if I have to stuff newspapers into the toes to keep them from flopping when I run. I have to hurry home from morning school so that Victor can wear the shoes when he goes to afternoon school. Can You make a miracle? The pastor said You could. And he said I can talk to You as if I were talking to Tata. When I need something, I can ask Tata. So, now I am asking You. Send me a pair of shoes. And I need a sweater.

And send me a coat. I want this to be mine. Then I will believe that You are real. I don't want to be selfish, but I do need clothes and the pastor said You can do miracles.

"You see, I am having such a difficult time believing that You really are. In school we are taught there is no God. The teachers are atheists. I am given unfair grades because I go to church. I am given school tasks to do on Sundays so I can't go to church. Our family is very poor and we are constantly mocked because people say God does us no good.

"So, You see, I want to know. I must know! I must know for myself! My teachers say one thing, the pastor and my parents say something else. Now, I must know!

"I really don't know if this is a prayer or not, but I am just talking to You." I hesitated for a moment, then whispered, "Amen."

As I crept into bed, I lay awake, staring into the dark. I could hardly wait for the morning. For miracles happened immediately, didn't they? Would there be shoes under my bed, a coat on the hook behind the door, and a sweater folded on the small table beside my bed? How would they get there?

When the first faint rays of daylight began to steal through the curtains, I was awake. In a flash, I was out from underneath the covers and peered under the bed. It was still too dark to see properly, so I stuck my arm under the couch and carefully felt all along the front. Nothing. I got up and looked behind the door. Nothing. I looked all around the room for something unusual, some unfamiliar package. Nothing.

All that day, I was in a state of expectancy. I wasn't too sure just what I expected, and yet I kept looking into the corners of the room, and I kept listening to my parents' conversation. No mention was made of the need for clothes for me. Nothing was mentioned about the need for miracles to happen.

But, somehow, I had a different feeling about God. I kept my nightly "talks" with God on an informal level. I kept pleading with Him to reveal Himself to me in a miracle.

"Help me know You are real," I kept praying. And every morning, I kept on checking under the bed and behind the door, and I kept looking around the room. Maybe God would at least give me one of my needs. Perhaps just a pair of shoes. Or the sweater. Maybe I could do without the coat because it was not terribly cold yet. But I wanted the miracle to happen. I wanted to know if God really did answer prayer.

A week passed by, and still there was no answer. I continued to be torn by doubts and when Tata prayed in the mornings, I wondered whether his prayers did any good. But at other times, when our whole family sang together, I rested securely in my parents' faith. However, there was still that deep longing within my heart to know for myself that God really did exist and that He knew me personally. I still kept my nightly trysts with God in prayer talks. I still asked God to make Himself known to me and I asked to be able to believe in Him.

One evening, we children were out at the gate, waiting for Tata to come home from work. This was always an exciting part of the day for us. School was over, supper preparations were under way, the older children were home from work, and now the best time of the day was approaching. Tata was coming home!

Swinging on the yard gate, playing games, tussling with Bombonel; we whiled away the moments.

"I see Tata!" Fănel yelled, and the race was on. As I tried to outrun my younger brother, I noticed that Tata was carrying a brown cardboard box. Perhaps he was bringing a box of wood shavings home as he sometimes did. But usually he brought the shavings home in a bag.

Dear Tata! As soon as the running children reached him, he set the box down on the road and took turns greeting each one. He tossed Nuți up in the air and she laughed with delight.

"What's in the box?" we pelted Tata with questions.

"I don't know!" Tata told the children.

"Where did you get the box?"

"Where is it from?"

"I got a notice from the post office that a package was sent to us. So when I got there, they gave me this box. I have no idea where it is from."

Fănel and I looked inquisitively at the box. There was strange handwriting on it. We could make out our family name, Tărniceriu, and the city name of Iaşi, although it was spelled "Jash."

"It's a foreign language! What do you think is in it?" I shook the box slightly. It wasn't very heavy, yet it felt solid.

"I don't know what is inside," Tata said patiently. "We will take it home and see. We will see what God has sent to us."

As was customary whenever a gift was given to us, we all knelt on the hard-packed dirt floor and Tata prayed. He thanked God for whatever was in the box. He thanked God for Christian brothers and sisters in other parts of the world. He thanked God that Christians were bound together by the love of Jesus, though they were often separated by distances and many times spoke a different language. He thanked God that they all spoke the same language of the heart. He thanked God for caring for them.

I could not keep my eyes closed. Was this in some way connected to *my* prayer? Why didn't Tata hurry up? It seemed Tata just couldn't find the amen! I fidgeted nervously on my knees.

When the amen had finally been said, Fănel carried the box to the table. Mama and all the children watched while Tata cut the twine that was tied around the package. Then he carefully cut the brown tape that sealed the package.

"I wonder what God has sent to us," Tata said as he opened the cover flaps.

For some reason, I could feel my heart beat in my ears. I tried hard not to push my way closer. Could this box in ANY way be connected to my prayer?

On the very top of the box was a pair of shoes. Girls' shoes! A pair of beautiful brown girls' shoes with small heels! The shoes had a delicate design punched in the leather. And they were new!

"They are mine!" My voice sounded strange even to me. "Those shoes are mine!" My breath came in short gasps. The other children looked at me in amazement. Mama frowned and shook her head slightly at me. Things were never "mine" in our household. Everyone knew that we all needed to share, and whoever needed an article of clothing would wear it until someone else needed it more than they did.

"Mama!" I tried to bring my voice under control. "Could I see if it fits my—if it fits our—my foot?" The question came out in barely a whisper.

I can't remember if I took the shoe or if someone else gave it to me to try on.

"It fits!" I breathed in awe. Everyone could see that it fit. It was not too big, but it was not too small either. I slipped the other shoe on and stood up.

New shoes my size! Girls' shoes! Girls' shoes with a feminine heel. Shoes I would not need to share with Victor because no boy was going to wear such a pair of shoes. Girls' shoes with a delicate punched design on the toes. These were *my* shoes!

Suddenly, I remembered something! I had told God that I would like for Him to provide something extra—some surprise that would really convince me that God is real.

"God knows my size!" I thought in amazement. "I forgot to tell Him what size I am! God knows everything! And I forgot to tell Him I am a girl! But He knows! He really does know everything!"

Tata looked into the box again. He pulled out a sweater. It was a new, soft, gray sweater with a vee neck and a row of pearly-gray buttons down the front. It was not a pullover that could be worn by boys and girls alike. It was a cardigan—a girl's sweater.

I did not say, "That's mine, too!" Just a little noise escaped from my mouth and my arm began to reach toward that soft, new sweater.

It was far too big for Nuți and far too small for Rodica. But—but—it looked like just the right size for me.

Finally the words came out, unbidden. "That's mine, too!" I reached for the sweater.

"Silvia!" Tata looked at me. Hardly ever did I show such a streak of selfishness.

"Could I just try it on to see if it fits?" I asked in a small voice.

Mama gave the sweater to me. It fit perfectly. The sleeves were just the right length. And it had pockets! Two patch pockets. I twitched my shoulders and looked to one side. The sweater fit perfectly across the shoulders, too. Slowly, I took the sweater off.

"What else is in the box?" Victor wanted to know.

As Tata lifted a burgundy-colored garment from the box, I already knew what it was. A coat! A long warm coat with a silky, black fur collar and fur cuffs. A girl's coat. And it looked like it would fit . . .

I could not say "That's mine" this time. I already knew. My entire prayer was being answered right before my eyes. Yet I asked, "Mama, could—could you just hold it up on my back and see if maybe— it fits?" The last two words were almost more of a statement than a question.

Mama held the coat with the rosy color and the warm fur collar against my back. I could feel the soft fur brush softly against my neck. I peeked around the side and saw that the coat was slightly longer than my skirt. It fit! I knew it did.

"It's strange," Mama mused out loud. "It's almost as if someone took your measurements, Silvia. Who would know us and know what size clothes you need?"

Tata and Mama looked lovingly at me. They saw the flush of red that shone through the brown skin on my cheeks. They saw the rise and fall of my blouse as my heart pounded in my excitement.

Suddenly I felt myself weeping. I wanted to be alone. I wanted to talk to God and tell Him that I knew He was real. I wanted to thank Him for the miracle He sent to me.

Tata saw that something unusual was happening to me. "Yes, Silvia, God knows everything. He knows your size. Did you think He didn't?" Tata's voice was so loving, so tender.

So I told him everything. How I had struggled with ill feelings and discouragement with the treatment I got at school. How I had doubted and wondered if God really did exist. And then how the words of the pastor had gripped me and how I had begun to talk with God.

"But I forgot to tell Him my size. When I saw that the things I prayed for were in that box I knew that God could do miracles. And when I felt how everything fit me just right, and I remembered that I had forgotten to tell Him my size, then I knew that God knows everything!"

I noticed that Mama's eyes were also wet with tears as she folded the coat and laid it on the table. But Tata took the sweater, placed it on top of the folded coat, and placed both garments in my arms. Tata took the shoes that I had placed carefully on a chair, and placed them on top of the sweater. Then he folded me in his arms and kissed me.

As we prayed together, I could almost see God. There was no longer any doubt in my mind that God existed and that He could perform miracles. And I really was no longer that interested in finding out who had sent the package or from where it had come. Tata had said that the Christians in the other parts of the world must have heard about the massive flooding that had occurred here in Romania during the heavy rains. Somehow, someone must have received our address and packed the box for us. But I knew that whoever had sent that box had been moved by God to do so. And I knew that God had answered my prayer. God seemed so close to me. I thought I could almost see Him. In my mind, it seemed like God looked a little like Tata.

As Tata prayed, I prayed also. My heart was overflowing in thankfulness and my whole being was rejoicing in my newfound faith. This time, I was not waiting impatiently for Tata's amen. But over and over again I kept saying, "God knows my size! He knows my size!"

8

Orange Shoes

I hurried through the swirling snow, going past the bleak apartment buildings and trying to keep the rapidly accumulating drifts from burying my feet. This was hard to do because I was wearing my only pair of shoes. Handed down from Rodica, they had long ago faded into a hopelessly washed-out shade of orange. And the low-cut sides were almost no protection at all for my numb feet. I had thought perhaps there would be enough money for another pair of shoes, but then Dănuţ, had needed medicine for his persistent cough. So the new shoes had disappeared down his throat, so to speak. Not that I minded that much, for I was used to such emergencies cropping up. But my feet minded, and so I hurried even faster.

It was good to be outside after having been in school all day. I had just started high school and, since the school was between my home and the church, I had been given the task of starting the fire for the evening services. The bitter, winter cold would have seeped into our church house and I knew I must hurry. The sooner I could start a fire in the metal stove, the sooner there would be an oasis of warmth for the worshipers who gathered for the usual Friday night service.

I pushed the snow away from the gate leading to the church yard. No one had even made a path to the front door. As soon as I unlocked the door, I shook the snow off my coat in the entry. Then I looked for some kindling in the room with which to start the fire.

Only a few pieces of shriveled bark lay scattered on the floor, and I used this to start a small blaze. When the flames started curling around the kindling, I added several small sticks of wood. I closed the stove door, adjusted the damper, and then realized I needed to get more firewood.

I slipped on my coat and ran outside. The wood shed held a fair amount of wood, but to my dismay, most of the pieces were too large. So, I grasped the ax firmly and set to work, splitting kindling from a dry chunk of pine. This exercise warmed me up and I soon had my basket filled with the size wood I needed.

I put the ax in the corner, stepped backwards, and immediately yelped in pain! I knew right away that I had stepped on something sharp. I looked down, and saw that a board with the sharp point of a nail sticking up was stuck to the bottom of my shoe. By the pain that shot through my foot, I knew that the nail had gone deeply into my arch.

I picked up my foot with my hand, and balancing myself on my other foot, jerked hard at the piece of wood. I grimaced in pain as the nail pulled on my throbbing foot, and it took another wrenching jerk before it came free. Immediately I slid my foot out of my orange shoe, and looked at the wound in my foot. Only a little blood showed where the nail had gone in, and I was surprised that it didn't hurt more. But as I held my foot in my hands, I realized that it was too cold to have much feeling.

That gave me an idea. I limped outside with one shoe on, tiptoeing on my injured foot. Then I rubbed my bare foot on the snow, numbing it even more. I hardly felt any pain at all.

But I knew I had no time to waste taking care of my foot. So I limped back inside, slid my cold foot into my even colder shoe, lifted the load of wood in my arms, and went back into the church house. I turned the doorknob with one hand and opened the door.

A cloud of gray, acrid smoke came billowing out of the room! I dropped my armload of firewood on the step and the pieces of wood spilled out into the snow. As I looked in through the door, I saw that the room was filled with the smoke!

Without thinking, I dashed in to find out was happening. I could barely see, and the smoke burned my throat and made my eyes water. Holding my hand over my mouth, I peered through the haze. I could see no flames and at first could not figure out how the smoke had filled the room.

But with a sinking heart, I saw that the stovepipe, running horizontally from the stove all the way to the end wall, had somehow come apart at the first section. The smoke was seeping out of the crack. I immediately realized that the stovepipe was much too hot to push back together, so I dashed outside and scooped up snow in the water bucket. Then I opened the stove door and flung the snow onto the fire.

The snow sizzled and hissed as it melted on the hot firewood and sent out an additional cloud of smoke and ashes. But to my relief, the large amount of snow extinguished the flame.

However, the room was still filled with smoke, so I quickly opened several windows and the front door. Using my coat, I tried to waft the smoke away. The bitterly cold wind swept through the room and created a strong draft that helped my frantic efforts.

The smoke soon cleared, and after I closed the windows and the door, I stared in dismay at the room. A quick glance at the clock told me that I only had a little over an hour before the first worshipers would come. And there I was—no fire, the room even colder than before, and the ceiling black above the stove where the smoke had been the most dense. To make matters even worse, my foot began to ache in pain again.

I didn't know what to do. I was not one to cry easily, but this situation looked hopeless. Then suddenly, the words of Pastor *Cruceru* seemed to echo in my mind: "When the situation seems hopeless, lift your eyes in prayer to God. That is what He wants: our dependence upon Him." So I began to pray, even as I looked for something with which to push the hot stovepipe together again so I could start a fire once more.

When my eyes lit upon the mat by the door, I knew that I could use it to protect my hands from the hot stovepipe. It didn't take long to push the loose pipe back into the other end. Thankfully, the fire had not been burning long enough to make the stovepipe extremely hot. But it did take awhile to retrieve the scattered wood pieces from the snow, crumple newspaper and get the fire going again. When a slight bit of warmth began radiating from the stove, I stared ruefully at the ceiling. Everybody would see there had been some kind of disaster that day. How could I ever clean it? Even if I stood on the backs of the benches I knew I still could not reach the high ceiling.

My foot began to throb again, but I was determined somehow to get the smoke washed from the ceiling. Glancing around the room, I was seized with an inspiration.

I jerked the tablecloth off the small table that Pastor Cruceru used as a pulpit and pulled the table close to the stove. Then I pushed two of the pews together and heaved the table on top so that the legs were resting on the benches. Next I put a wooden chair on top of the table. Unsure of how stable this improvised ladder was, I carefully stepped onto the table top and then very carefully on the chair. I stretched my arm up, and to my delight, I could wash the blackened area.

After going down to get a bucket of water, I climbed back up the pyramid. I carefully wrung out the cleaning rag and gingerly began to scrub. I tried not to move my feet at all because I was not sure if the chair or the table would slip off the benches.

In very little time my water was black, and it seemed at first all I did was streak the ceiling even more. I had to change water repeatedly. When I had finally washed as much as I could reach without moving the benches and the table, it was easy to see just how far I had been able to reach.

"I wonder if anyone will look up and see that clean spot and notice that the rest of the ceiling is still smoky," I said to myself. A quick glance at the clock showed me that I did not have time for any more cleaning.

I had slipped my shoes off to stand on the table, but when I remembered that I still needed to clear the snow from the path so people wouldn't track snow into the church house, I hurriedly slid my feet into my low shoes again. Ignoring the pain that was still making my foot throb, I went outside.

The snow swirled around the fence that separated the street from the church yard. I took a shovel and began. At times it almost seemed useless because the wind continued to blow snow into my newly-shoveled path.

But finally the job was done, and besides, the first arrival had come.

I gave the Romanian Christian greeting of "Pace" to the elderly spinster who came through the gate. Together we entered the church house, and I gave a quick glance at the ceiling to see how distinct the light circle above the stove was. But Sora *Isacov* wasn't interested in the state of the ceiling. She wanted to get to the warm stove. I, too, went to the stove to warm my hands. And my feet. In all the excitement of trying to get the church house ready for services, I had not had time to warm my feet one time. But now, I could finally warm my feet on the fender of the stove.

Other people were coming in and gathering around the stove. I pushed my worn orange shoes under the stove and warmth began to creep back into my chilled feet. My injured foot began to throb again.

"These young people," Sora Isacov's voice broke through the chatter of voices. "Silvia! Why are you wearing such shoes in the wintertime? I don't understand such things. Here it is winter and you have to wear your fashionable shoes instead of wearing some sensible winter shoes or boots! Young people are more interested in fashion than they are in being sensible!"

Just then the song leader announced the opening of the services and everyone went to their seats. But my mind was not on the song. I was indignant!

I felt sorry for myself. I had worked so hard to get the church house ready for services, and I had hurt my foot. For all my hard work, this was the thanks I got! By now I not only had an injured foot, but also an injured spirit because of Sora Isacov's remarks about being fashionable.

True, there were times when I was tempted to wish for fashionable clothing. But—I almost laughed—there was hardly enough money to clothe all the children in our family, much less to be fashionable!

Even more funny, how could anyone think I was trying to be fashionable in those horrid orange shoes! I don't know where Rodica had gotten those shoes, but by the time they were passed down to me, there was surely nothing fashionable about them anymore. That this old woman thought I would wear such shoes on a cold winter night by choice was ridiculous.

However, the calming influence of Pastor Cruceru's sound Biblical preaching soon healed most of the hurt the critical remarks toward me had caused. By the time the service was over, I had all but dismissed the incident from my mind. But, as I plowed through the snow in the dark to catch a tram ride home, I was reminded again how woefully inadequate my orange shoes were.

The next morning, I was still sleeping when I heard a rather familiar voice out in the kitchen with Mama. Why on earth was Sora Isacov here at our house so early on Saturday morning? Had she discovered the black streaks on the church house ceiling after all and come to complain to my parents about it?

"You know, that daughter of yours, what is her name? I could not sleep because of her! What did you say her name is, the one who makes the fire in the church house? Silvia, yes, that is the one. Well, I could not sleep last night because of her!"

I could hardly believe my ears. What in the world had I done? Surely the smoke was not that bad! Sora Isacov said she couldn't sleep?

"I lay in bed and suddenly it was the Lord Who was talking to me. 'You did wrong tonight. You said the girl was trying to be fashionable by wearing those low slippers. That was the best pair of shoes she had.' That is what the Lord told me."

She went on. "And I couldn't sleep. Because the Lord told me, 'Give half of your pension to buy a pair of shoes!' And I said, 'But how will I live?' But all the time I could not sleep and the Lord continued to tell me to give half of my pension for her shoes."

What a marvelous thing! Sora Isacov was here at our house, having come all the way across the city by tram to tell us this!

"Sora Isacov, you don't need to give any money," Mama protested. "We will make out somehow."

"Yes, I must give the money. I told the Lord that if He would let me sleep at least several hours, I will bring the money to you this morning. Here. I hope I can sleep tonight!"

Mama called me into the kitchen and briefly told me what I had already heard. I thanked Sora Isacov. Even after the old woman left for home, I marveled at how the Lord had spoken to this elderly sister in the night.

So it should not have been much of a surprise to me what happened next. That afternoon, Nenea *Ionel* stopped in to see if Tata could help him in his shredding business. This man often needed help to turn used clothing and rags into kapok for comforter batting. His business had prospered and if work was slow at the foundry, Tata earned extra money by helping him.

When Nenea Ionel's cheerful figure came into the room, I glanced out the window to see if he had come in his car. Sure enough, there it was. A blue *Dacia*. To me, anyone who had a car was rich. None of my friends' parents owned a car, and very few of the students in school had ever even ridden in a car.

"Are you going to go back home?" Mama asked after Tata had agreed to come and work for Nenea Ionel.

"Yes," Nenea Ionel answered as he buttoned up his heavy coat.

"Silvia needs to buy boots. Could she go along with you to the store and buy them? It would save her from walking or going with the tram."

"Sure! Silvia, get ready and come with me. I will take you."

I sat in the Dacia, feeling like a princess. As we motored down the street away from our house, I wished the neighbors would look out their windows and see me. I was riding in a car! In all of my 14 years of life, I had never had a ride in a car before. I secretly wished some of my schoolmates might be on the sidewalks so I could wave to them.

How swiftly we traveled. But when we came to the store where Mama had instructed me to buy the boots, Nenea Ionel kept right on driving.

"Where are you taking me? Mama said to buy the boots at

this store." I was perplexed.

Nenea Ionel calmly kept on driving. "I know where I want to take you. I want to get good boots for you."

"I don't have enough money for expensive boots!"

My protesting made no difference. Nenea Ionel stopped in front of a shoe store that I had never even dreamed of entering. As we went into the store where rows of shoes lined the shelves, I stared in amazement.

The clerk politely asked us what we needed. I didn't say anything. I knew I did not have enough money to buy anything in that store.

Again my protesting made no difference to Nenea Ionel. He calmly asked the clerk to "fit the young girl with a pair of fur-lined leather boots." And when I slid my red feet out of the hideous orange shoes, Nenea Ionel promptly instructed the clerk to find a pair of warm socks. Then he took my shoes, those orange shoes that Sora Isacov thought I had been wearing for style, twisted them with his strong hands, and threw them into the wastebasket. I had to hold back a giggle to see with what force he threw those worn-out shoes away.

The new boots almost seemed too nice to use for walking, and it was like a dream to have warm feet. Almost before I knew it, we were outside and I was wearing the new boots. When I told Nenea Ionel that Mama would think I asked him for more money to buy the expensive boots, he told me that if Mama fussed, he would explain everything to her.

I did have enough money for the bus fare home, but I was so happy to have a pair of warm boots that I wanted to have the experience of having warm feet while walking through the cold snow. So, I walked from one bus stop to the next in order to try out those wonderful boots. Again, God had provided for my needs. Indeed, He did know my size.

9

God Wants Me

The winter wind that moaned between the new apartment buildings snatched at my coat and tugged insistently at my scarf. Little twinkles of stars were barely visible between the high-rise buildings, and the electric street lamps made harsh stabs of light on the concrete sidewalks. No one chose to linger outside longer than necessary on such a night, and yet I was not striding briskly as usual. In my mental anguish, I was all but oblivious to the night outside. Because I knew the way home so well, I did not have to concentrate on when to turn the corner or climb the slight grade that led to my home.

My thoughts went back to the past spring. I remembered clearly how, after I had finished the eighth grade, I had approached my mother and asked if I could take the examinations to enter high school. At first my mother had scoffed at me for even wanting more schooling. "You know we cannot afford to let you even try to enter high school. We don't have money to bribe the teachers to let you enter, nor do we have connections with anyone there. No, just get the thought of further schooling out of your head. Besides, you need to get a job at a factory and help with the household expenses. Your father's job is not enough for our needs."

It was then that Rodica had spoken. "Mama, I think you should let Silvia try to enter by taking the examinations. You know she has been a good student and she has excellent marks in all her subjects. I have been sorry that I had to leave school after only completing six grades and now I think you should let her try. I know you needed my help when there were so many little children, but now I think we could manage."

Mama had stopped scrubbing the table top to look at us. "And where would we get the money to buy Silvia's uniforms? And her books? I hardly know where we get enough money to keep the younger children in school, much less let Silvia enter high school. None of the rest of you children went. Why should she?"

Mama had turned to her work again as if the subject had been closed.

"I will help her," Rodica said firmly. "I will use my salary and help Silvia buy her things. I know it is too late for me to get a better education, but I want to help Silvia."

"We can't afford—" Mama's voice trailed off. Perhaps she suddenly remembered that Rodica could have kept all of her wages from the sewing factory for herself instead of generously sharing her salary with our parents, for she was already 23 years old.

Suddenly, Mama had capitulated. "O.K. Let her try. She might not pass the exams anyway." Mama abruptly had left the room.

I remembered how disappointed I had been when, after successfully completing the spring examinations, I was rejected from entering the high school. The educators said, "There is no room for more students in school." It had been a double disappointment when I found out that others who had scored lower on the tests than I had were accepted.

When the fall examinations were held, however, I had tried again and scored even higher. This time the educators seemed rather impressed by my ambitions, and I had been accepted.

High school was difficult. Like all the communist schools in Romania, the teachers were strict disciplinarians and we students were expected to study hard. The lessons were all graded on a scale of one to ten, and anything under an average of a five meant that the grade had to be repeated. And because of the struggle with my mother about even entering the school, I had tried hard to keep my marks up.

I had been doing well the first quarter. But as the lessons became harder during the second quarter, my grades had slipped. So, I had determined that I was going to be a model student and study diligently.

And now this. I had made the mistake of staying up late the night before an examination. True, the teacher didn't always call on all the students the same day, but no one knew just when the teacher would call out one of our names to check what we knew about the lesson. And, the grades were given after the teacher decided whether the pupil knew the lesson. That was what worried me, because I knew I was not ready for the exam.

I kicked at a frozen clump of snow. Why had I ever gone to visit my brother *Mihai* and his family in their new flat? I was honest enough with myself that I knew why I had gone. I had heard that a new TV program would be aired that evening, and so I had asked Mama if I could go visit Mihai's family. Mama didn't ask me if I had homework. I knew I must keep my marks up in order to graduate from high school, and usually no one had to remind me to do my homework. So it had been with guilty feelings that I had sneaked away from my homework and gone to see the show on Mihai's new television.

The winter wind seemed to numb my soul. I felt so condemned. My conscience had pricked me several times during the show, for the characters had been silly and the whole episode was unrealistic and not at all edifying. But the action and the drama had captured my heart, and the images dancing on the screen had been so fascinating, that I had tried to shrug off any uneasy feelings.

It hadn't been until I was outside by myself, going home after ten o'clock at night, that I had really begun to think about what I had done that evening.

It wasn't only that I had watched the show, even though my conscience smote me for getting so involved in worthless patter. My heart was also heavily weighed down with the time I had wasted. Time that I needed to prepare for the examination tomorrow.

I tried to pray as I neared the railroad tracks. But it just didn't seem as if God was listening. It seemed that the knife-sharp wind just whipped my thoughts away and that God never even heard the cry of my heart.

Usually, I enjoyed walks at night through the city. Often

when Victor and I walked home from church, we would discuss the evening services and then pray. Victor and I shared many thoughts with each other. I knew I could share anything with Victor and he would understand. Victor's love for God was a definite encouragement to my own faith. Together, we usually prayed until we reached our home. Often, it was almost with regret that we reached our front yard gate.

But tonight, I was alone. Alone and miserable.

When I finally reached my home, I quietly went inside and sat on my bed. Rodica was already sleeping, but when I switched on the light, she turned and gazed blearily at me. I drew my schoolbooks toward me and opened a textbook. Rodica let her head fall back on her pillow and closed her eyes. She was used to seeing me study in the night.

I tried to concentrate on my math book. The numbers all wanted to swim in front of my eyes. All I could see was the people of the show. I squeezed my eyes shut and shook my head. I had to concentrate.

It was no use. Every time I began to analyze a problem, I could not find the solution. The daring men, the laughing ladies, the movement and excitement of the show began to dance through my thoughts.

In desperation, I knelt beside the bed. "Help me, God," I prayed. "I want to study. I need to study! I am sorry I wasted my time on such a stupid show. I am sorry I didn't do my homework first. Oh, God, I am sorry that I even went at all. Forgive me!"

But it all seemed to be in vain. Even in my prayers, the dancing images just would not go away. I couldn't even concentrate on my prayers.

In exasperation, I attacked my books again. But now, I had more problems. Not only the memories of the show wanted to intrude and destroy my studies. I was also getting drowsy because of the lateness of the hour and the warmth of the house after my cold walk home.

When my head nodded and I felt myself falling asleep, I tried to rouse myself by making a cup of coffee. I took my book along out to the kitchen and tried to study while I warmed the water. Then, I sat at the kitchen table and sipped the coffee.

That only revived me for a while. When I suddenly woke up with my head on the surface of the table, I almost panicked. I had to study!

I did not want to get a bad grade. I *had* to do well. The thought of receiving shamefully poor grades spurred my desires to do well. I remembered vividly how terrible I had felt when I had received a three in elementary school. It was such a great shame that when Tata had asked me if I had gotten a grade, I had lied and said I was not graded that day. That night, I had wrestled with my conscience and had not been able to sleep until I had written a note and confessed my lie. I finally found peace after quietly getting up and putting the paper into Tata's pocket where he was sure to find it the next day. And receiving Tata's forgiveness was a blessed experience. But this time, I realized there was nothing my Tata could do for me. I would have to fight this battle myself.

Finally, at five o'clock in the morning, I turned the light off and crept to bed. And then it was not to sleep the peaceful sleep of the weary. I tossed and turned. I dreamed my teacher gave me a two after finding out that I did not know my lessons, and throughout the dream there were always moving figures, mocking laughter and gay, dancing music.

I dreaded going to school in the morning. When I met my seat mate, Elena, and told her that I was in no way ready for the examinations, her horrified reaction increased the fear already in my heart.

The class was in session. I scooted down in my seat and propped the book up in front of me. The neckline of my green jumper rubbed against my chin as I lowered my head in an unconscious effort to hide from my teacher. Nervously, I chewed the corduroy jumper and when the teacher picked up the grade book, my heart raced.

"She is paging back toward the T's," Elena whispered.

"Be quiet!" I mouthed back at her.

After the teacher had quizzed several students, I began breathing more easily. The teacher was past the T's now.

"She is paging backwards now," Elena whispered.

I did not dare to look up. I could almost hear the teacher call my name, "Tărniceriu, Silvia," and ask me to close my book and begin to recite. A cold sweat broke out on my forehead. How could I bear the shame of failing? If the teacher would ask me why I was not ready, what could I say? That I had wasted my evening watching a worthless show on television?

"She stopped on your page now!" Elena's whispered voice broke into my thoughts. "Her finger is pointing to the top of the page."

I knew that my name was the last of the three names on the grading book. *Radu, Stănicel*, Tărniceriu.

I began to pray desperately. My whole life seemed to be wrapped up in this awful moment.

"God, I need You. I want to give myself totally to You so that these things don't happen. I believe in miracles but this time I can't ask You for a miracle because this is my fault. I just pray that You forgive me and help me. You know all about me. You know my size and You know that I need You."

"Oh," the teacher said just as her finger reached Tărniceriu, Silvia. "Look at the time! We must move on into the next lesson." Then she put the grade book back into the drawer.

Elena looked at me. My jumper neckline was wet from being stuffed into my mouth. My look of relief was so evident that Elena looked at me with pity.

"Was it really that bad?" she sympathized. "Weren't you ready for anything at all?"

I could only shake my head. I felt weak and my head wanted to swim.

At home that afternoon, I was subdued and chastened as I attacked my homework persistently. As I studied and memorized and read and reread my lessons, I felt that something more was needed. I had promised God something that morning in school.

When the house was quiet, I slipped out of bed to have my nightly talk with God.

In the quietness of the hour, God spoke to me. I realized with crystal clarity that even though God had sent me a miracle in the box of clothes just my size, and even though I prayed to Him continually, I had never really seen my need of a Savior. Yes, God had become real to me and yes, I had often been comforted by God's presence. But I had never before clearly seen my need to repent and give my heart to God.

The many sermons I had heard throughout my youth came into focus. I saw that I was a sinner. I saw that too often I had succumbed to the temptations of the flesh, like yesterday when I had gone to see that show. And I understood that I needed the cleansing power of the blood of Christ to save me from my sins.

In the comfortable darkness of the room, I brought my need of a Savior to God. "God, I am sorry for my past life. I repent of my sins and I will be all Yours. I believed in You before and You revealed Yourself to me in a wonderful way when You showed me You know all about me and sent clothes my size. But now, I give You my everything. Not just my heart, but my eyes, my ears, my hands, and even my feet, so I will not go places I shouldn't go, or listen to things I should not listen to. Thank-you for loving me and being my Savior."

For a long time I knelt and prayed. Such a sweet communion with God as I completely surrendered my spirit and my entire life! Peace filled me and a great joy of heart and mind flooded my entire being. When, finally, I got up and crept under the covers, I was so thrilled with my experience that I continued my talk with God until I fell into a contented sleep.

10

Growing Pains

The light of dawn was just beginning to creep across the eastern sky as I closed the yard gate and started up the street toward the hill. Summer days had fully arrived, and there was no need for even a light jacket. When I reached the point where the road turned left for a more lengthy route to the monastery, I hesitated just a moment. Then I plunged into the woods at the base of the hill and followed the well-worn path that went straight up the side.

The wood thrushes were already calling their first notes to each other in the high reaches of the trees, and a faint light sifted through the green canopy overhead. I felt as if I were in a large cathedral. The song of the birds, the hush of the morning, and the silent trees stretching their limbs upward touched my soul. My prayers winged their way upward as I steadily climbed. My heart was filled with song and my soul was in tune with the world around me.

Did it matter that my errand was one that most teen-aged girls would despise? Gathering horse manure to repair the walls of our house was not any more glamorous to me than to any other normal young girl.

But gather horse manure I had decided to do. The financial situation at home was not any better than it had ever been, and I was keenly conscious of my parents' constant struggle to provide clothes and food for the growing family. I remembered my Mama's comment when I had begged to be allowed to go to high school.

"If you would have stayed with Tanti Estera and Nenea Iuliu you could have gone to high school without any question. Or, you could have gone on to the university or any other school you would have wanted to attend."

"But, Mama, I want to be at home. You don't know how it was to live with them and have them constantly arguing and fighting. I like my home much better!" I had tried to explain how I felt.

Mama had shrugged her shoulders and said she hoped there was something I could do in order to help care for the needs of the family.

It wasn't that I didn't help at home. But I needed to spend so much time on my homework so that my grades would not suffer. And then, after the last examination was finished and school was dismissed for the summer, I wanted to find some way of helping with school expenses. Uniforms and shoes did not grow on trees and I did not want to ask my parents for clothes for the next school year. I tried not to mind too much when I had to wear clothes that were too small, but if I could not close the buttons, something had to be done. So, I quickly wanted to gather the horse manure that Tata needed to repair the walls of our house where moisture had softened the mud and the plaster was beginning to crumble.

I knew, as did all the villagers who constructed their homes with mud bricks, how valuable the horse manure was both in repairing existing mud walls and in forming new bricks. The horse dumplings were mixed with the red clay, and the organic material and bits of straw in the manure made a perfect binding material to make bricks or plaster. Plaster made without horse manure had a tendency to crumble and disintegrate quickly. So, the prized horse manure was in great demand for the many village houses huddled around the city.

No, it was not a pleasant-smelling job, and to many finicky girls, the idea of gathering horse manure by hand would have been quite distasteful. But to me, this was a way I could help my parents.

I reached the edge of the woods on the brow of the hill. Meadows surrounded the high stone walls of the monastery. In the early morning, there was no sign of the goats or cows that were allowed to graze there. It was only later that the village children would bring the animals up and either tether them with ropes or stay with them all day.

The wooden gate that opened into the monastery stable yard was slightly ajar. That meant that one of the monks was already at work, feeding the horses or perhaps milking the cows.

I entered the yard. The horse stalls were empty, so that meant the horses were already harnessed and at work in the fields or out in the pasture. Quickly and deftly, I began to fill my pails.

There was not enough manure in the stable to fill the pails, so I climbed through the wooden bars and went into the pasture. The first rays of the sun gilded the top of the bell tower that guarded the entrance to the monastery.

I walked toward the lower end of the pasture. Were the horses here or were they in the fields working? I rounded the hedge and there they were, grazing. Now it would not take long to fill both pails.

Instead of taking the shortcut through the woods, I decided to take the winding road back to the city.

"Silvia!" a voice called out as soon as I reached the base of the hill. "Do you have enough horse manure for us, too? There is a small place right beside our front door that needs repairing. I was going to try to patch it with just clay, but you know that doesn't usually last long."

"Why sure, I already have two pails full," I laughed and turned toward my neighbor *Marian*. "If you need only a little, I am sure Tata won't mind."

"Thank-you. What luck that I met you."

Marian was several years older than I, and the two of us had been childhood playmates. But Marian had left school because he could not afford the added expenses, and like many others, did whatever work he could find. "Tata said he saw you yesterday morning with your pails and he told me to watch for you today," he said.

I was conscious of how I looked after my early morning excursion. Even though I had stopped and washed my hands at the spring on my way down the hill, wisps of hair had escaped from my braids, and the hem of my skirt was wet where it had dragged on the grass.

71

But Marian didn't seem to mind. He chatted with me and soon I was no longer conscious of my clothes. After he took his portion, we lingered and talked as the noises of the village reached us from outside the wooden yard fence. When my stomach suddenly growled from hunger, Marian laughingly said, "It is time for my breakfast too, and I imagine you have not had anything to eat either since you got two pails filled so early in the morning. Were you up at the monastery?"

"Yes. That is the best place to go even if the hill is steep. I am going to go back to pick *cireşe amare* after I have eaten breakfast. I saw they are ripe and you know there will be many others after them." I picked up my pails to leave.

"I wish I could go with you!" Marian said as he watched me go through the gate. "But Tata wants me to repair that wall before the whole house comes tumbling down on us!"

We both laughed and I shut the gate behind me.

—·—·—·—·—·—·—·—·—·—

"See, Silvia," Dănuţ called as he held out his small pail. "I already covered the bottom!"

"Good for you!" I encouraged him. "Let's see how much Fănel and Nuţi have. Maybe we have enough to fill the pail."

We four Tărniceriu children had been steadily picking the small cherries since breakfast. The sun was high overhead and our progress was hindered because others were picking the ripening cherries also. It seemed the ravines where the cireşe amare bushes grew were alive with people. Mothers set their babies on blankets and attacked the bushes with nimble fingers. Children rattled their buckets as they picked and picked. When I saw the many people already on the hillside, I steered my younger siblings around to the other side of the hill. Here, the bushes did not grow as luxuriantly as they did closer to the village houses, but fewer people knew about this place.

"My bucket is full." Fănel sat on a stone to rest. "I got my arms all scratched, though." He ruefully looked at the red marks that crisscrossed his brown, tanned arms. "It always seems like the best cherries grow among the hardest-to-reach places."

72

"I know," I said as I poured the cherries into the large pail we hoped to fill. "But I am thankful there are so many cherries this year. I guess the heavy rains we had this spring gave the right amount of moisture to make the cherries grow big and plentiful."

"Do we have enough?" was Nuți's question. She was tired and hungry. The forenoon seemed like an entire day to her.

"Not quite," I surveyed the pail. "I'll pick some more while you all rest. Here is some bread that I brought along."

"I'm thirsty," Dănuț complained. He took a hunk of bread that I offered and crammed it into his mouth.

"You'll get even thirstier if you eat all that bread," Fănel chuckled. "We can get some water from the spring when we go back to the village."

But I shook my head. "We are not going back past the spring. I don't want to risk having the groundsman take all our cherries again. Remember how he did last year?"

Of course the children remembered. We had all labored long and hard to fill our buckets. When we had almost reached home, we had met the groundsman who claimed the cherries "for the monks and the friars at the monastery." Everyone knew that the religious order did not mind that we villagers harvested the cherries and other edibles that grew on the hill. So we had watched in dismay as our day's work was carried away.

It took another 30 minutes before I was finished picking enough cherries to fill the bucket. But Fănel had gone to the spring and come back with water for us warm and thirsty pickers.

"Do you want us to come with you?" Nuți asked me. "Shall we all go to the market?"

I looked at my little sister's tired face. Dănuț was still sitting on the ground pushing a stick into an ant hill and watching the little creatures scurry around in alarm.

"I'll go by myself," I decided. "Fănel, I want you to meet me at the market with the soup bowl so I can measure out the cherries for the customers. And," I looked at my skirt, "ask Mama to send an apron along."

I set off for the market. The bucket of cherries was heavy

73

and I changed it from one hand to the other quite a number of times before I reached the busy market.

It was already midday when I arrived. I set my bucket at the end of the row of vendors and waited for Fănel. I had looked to see if many others were selling the bitter cherries and had only seen one other vendor with a small pailful. It was still early in the season so I should have no problem selling the cherries.

All along the sidewalk, were tables of vegetables. Lettuce, radishes, tomatoes and other garden produce made a colorful display. Housewives bustled along the front, asking questions, testing the freshness of the vegetables and bargaining with the sellers. The air was noisy with the shouts of vendors extolling the virtues of their produce and the haggling of buyers.

"Here you are," Fănel said, slightly out of breath. "I brought a stool for you to sit on."

"Did you remember my apron?" I wondered. I peered into the bag and removed the bowl. Then I saw the apron at the bottom of the bag and I tied it around my waist.

"I need to go back home," Fănel explained. "Mama said I must weed the potato patch."

Fănel had barely left before my first customer came. "How much for your cherries?"

"One and a half lei for a bowl," I answered. "I picked them just this morning."

The lady picked up a cherry and put it into her mouth. "I want two bowls full. I was just thinking this morning how ready I am for good cireşe amare jam again."

The afternoon wore on and the pail became emptier. I was glad for the stool and rested whenever there was no one looking at my cherries.

". . . have been looking for some kind of berry," a familiar voice broke in upon my thoughts. "My mother is coming and we will make the jam together while she is visiting me."

I tried to shrink back from view. It was Mrs. *Popovici*, my history teacher from high school. And Mrs. Popovici was the one who was always ridiculing me for being a Christian. What would I say to her in the market? Perhaps she wouldn't recognize me or would pass on by.

"Look!" Mrs. Popovici's lady companion said. "Here are some cireșe amare. They make good jam."

The two fashionable ladies stopped in front of my table. The bowl was heaped high with the dark red cherries.

"Just the right thing! How much—Oh, why it's Silvia. Silvia Tărniceriu. Are these your cherries?" Mrs. Popovici looked at me in surprise.

"Yes, Mrs. Popovici. My—my brothers and my little sister and I—I picked the cherries this morning."

"Well, I never expected to see you selling cherries in the market. But, I can see that you probably need the money." And Mrs. Popovici looked at my faded and worn blouse.

Her companion looked at me.

"Silvia goes to your class?" she asked Mrs. Popovici. "Silvia goes to high school?"

I felt my cheeks flush in embarrassment. I lowered my eyes and then looked at my history teacher again.

"Yes," Mrs. Popovici answered shortly. Then to me, "I will take three bowls of cherries. Put them into this bag."

I carefully filled the bowl three times and emptied the cherries into the bag. Then I put the four and one half lei into my apron pocket.

The two ladies watched silently. Then Mrs. Popovici and her companion turned to leave. Before they disappeared, I heard Mrs. Popovici say loudly, "Silvia is one of the children from one of those Christian families. They pray to God . . ."

I had been embarrassed when I first saw my history teacher come and find me selling cherries in the marketplace. I had felt the scorn from my teacher while she was purchasing the cherries. I knew no one else from our school who would need to sell cherries in order to have money to buy school uniforms or books.

But all at once none of those things mattered. "—children from Christian family—pray to God—." Even though Mrs. Popovici had said the words in scorn to her companion, I felt a surge of joy flow through me. Yes! I did pray to God! And not only was I from a Christian family, I myself was a Christian!

The 15 lei I might get for my cherries would be enough to

buy three meters of fabric and Rodica could help me make a dress for school. It would not be any special expensive fabric, but that did not matter. I had the special love of Jesus in my heart and that was worth more than anything wealth could give me.

11

Turmoil

When the tenor and alto voices sang the final phrase, it seemed to me as if the last notes quivered in the air before they died out altogether. The church house had good acoustics and since most of the people had already left for their homes, the almost empty auditorium amplified our voices.

It was a special time for the youth group. Pastor *Marcu* and his wife, Sora *Ada*, encouraged the young people of the church to practice music, and often Brother Marcu led the group in a time of prayer after the services. And then, the church house would ring as we gathered around the organ and lifted our joyful voices in praise to God.

Tonight the singing had gone especially well. Ionel had brought his uncle *Andrei* along. Actually, the boys were more like cousins, because Andrei was only slightly the older of the two. Andrei was a strong tenor, so he sang along with Victor.

"Let's sing one more song," Victor suggested. "Joyful, joyful we adore Thee . . ." our voices blended once more. But even after the song was finished, everyone was reluctant to leave.

Ionel and Andrei walked with Victor and me for the first part of the journey home. I visited easily with the boys for I was used to having Victor's friends come and visit at our house. In fact, Mama often talked about all the friends who came and "cluttered up" our tiny house. She said they hindered the children from their work, such as washing the windows or helping with the cooking. But the rest of the Tărniceriu family was so friendly that the young people came often.

Andrei soon became a part of the group who came often to visit with Victor and the others in our home. He had moved in with Ionel's family and was attending the high school in Iași. He was talkative and friendly with everyone, and he participated heartily in the church choir.

I began to notice that Andrei seemed to enjoy visiting with me. It became commonplace for him to find his place at my side as we were singing or walking home after church.

"God," I prayed one evening in my nightly talks on my knees beside the bed, "I'm not sure what is happening. You know I don't want to have any special feelings toward boys, but it seems like there is one boy coming more and more into my thoughts. I don't want him to come between You and me, for my love for You must always be first. Give me the grace to keep my feelings in the right place."

One evening when Andrei arrived at my house, he handed me a note. "Would you give this to Victor?" he asked. As he passed the note, he looked deeply into my eyes. For a long moment, I gazed back. Then I lowered my eyes and felt a warm blush spread across my face. I could feel my heart beat faster.

"Well, I'd better go," Andrei said. "I have a lot of studying to do. I guess I will see you on Sunday in church." He brushed his blond hair away from his forehead.

"Yes," I replied, looking up at him again. I noticed the small flecks of brown in his green eyes. "I really enjoy our evenings when we sing. We need to have these songs to keep us true in these troubled times. I am often encouraged by the words of songs that remind us to be steadfast in times of trials and troubles."

"Yes, yes," Andrei said hastily. "That certainly is true. Well, good-bye then, until Sunday."

I remembered the note after he had clicked the gate latch shut and I could no longer see him. I looked at the small folded piece of paper. I would lay it on the shelf and give it to Victor when he came home in the morning from his night job. It was rather strange that Andrei gave the note to me, because I knew he often stopped in and visited with Victor at work.

On Saturday afternoon, Victor joined me on the porch

where I was shaking the rugs. "Did he say anything to you?" was his blunt question.

"Who say what?" I asked, even though I immediately knew who Victor was talking about.

"Well, you know, we often talk together and I figured after the note you got, that maybe he said something," Victor said uncertainly.

"I didn't read the note. It was for you," I reminded him.

"You didn't even look at it?" Victor questioned.

I looked at my brother for a moment. "Victor, did you think I would look at a note that was not for me?"

"I guess not," Victor agreed. "But—but—he never told you what was in the note?"

"Silvia, are you coming with the rugs?" Mama opened the door and called to me. "We are not nearly finished with the cleaning. Hurry!"

The next day I was very aware that Andrei was watching me. Once when I was looking at him, he smiled. I felt a warm feeling steal across my heart. I smiled back.

"You know, I thought you would read the note I gave you," Andrei said as we walked home after church. I inhaled the fragrance of the autumn leaves we scuffled through. Even though the air was cool, I felt no need of a sweater. Walking was such an invigorating exercise, especially if Andrei was walking with me.

"I never thought about reading your note," I laughed. "You said it was for Victor. What did it say?"

"You mean Victor didn't tell you? I thought you knew!"

"You tell me. I didn't read it and Victor didn't tell me. I want you to tell me yourself."

Andrei hesitated. "It was a Bible verse. Mark 10:7-8. Do you know what that says?"

We walked together in silence through the city. I was deep in thought. Andrei's question seemed to hang in the air.

Jesus taught about marriage in Mark 10. I was almost sure of that.

"I think I know," I almost whispered. My thoughts were whirling wildly.

"Well, I did want you to know that I am thinking about

79

that. And I do like you very much. I want you to be my special friend. My girlfriend!" He turned his head toward me. In the semi-darkness, I could feel his smile.

"I feel honored to be your friend," I said shyly. "I never wanted many boyfriends because I have been firmly convinced for a long time that I don't want to give my heart to someone and then later have to withdraw my feelings for him. I believe God wants me to only have a serious relationship with one person."

"Yes, yes, that's so," Andrei said quickly. "You know, you are special to me and I want you to be serious about me."

All the rest of the way home, my feet were light and gay. As we neared home, we walked more slowly to prolong our conversation. There was so much to talk about.

"I have to leave right away," Andrei said softly as we reached the front gate. "I am already behind in my homework. I'll try to come and see you again soon."

I hugged my friendship with Andrei to myself. Of course, Victor knew about it because he was with us most of the time. And because I knew that Andrei and Victor had prayed about our courtship, I felt very sure that it was from God. I had a lot of confidence if Victor felt good about the whole matter.

I had a certain longing within me to share my special experience with Rodica. But it seemed the age difference between us at that time made it difficult for me to talk about my affairs of the heart. And Mama was always so busy that she never seemed to have time to just sit down and talk. I was sure Tata would understand, but somehow, I never did find the right time to talk to him.

The days sped by on wings. I felt like singing all the time. Often I burst into song on my walk to and from school. My heart felt as light and free as the swirling, dancing autumn leaves.

At night, I poured out my thoughts to God. I thanked Him for bringing Andrei into my life and I prayed earnestly to be led by the wisdom of the Holy Spirit. I felt convinced that the Lord would guide us now and in the future.

It was on a Thursday evening that I heard Andrei's voice calling my name out by the front gate. With winged feet I met him.

"Good evening," he greeted me with a wide smile. "It sure is cold. Winter must soon be here."

"I don't even feel the cold," I laughed. "I guess I am warm-blooded."

"I would say you are warmhearted," Andrei teased me.

"Come inside," I invited. "It is too cold to visit outside, I know."

Andrei entered easily into the noisy family chatter. Tata was there, Ştefan was trying to fix a pair of shoes, and Nuţi and Dănuţ were playing with some toys Tata had made for them.

I went into the kitchen to get a drink for Andrei. Mama was scrubbing a kettle with vigor. "So you think you need boys? Silvia, you know you are only 17 and you are not nearly finished with school yet. I need you to help me in the house and often you are gone. Now you bring a boy home and expect to entertain him. Who will do the work?" Mama's voice went on and on.

I stood still in shock. What was Mama saying? Didn't she want me to be friends with Andrei?

"Mama," I whispered frantically. "He will hear you!"

"Maybe he will," Mama said without lowering her voice. "You have no time to spend with boys. You wanted to go to school and now you bring boys to the house!"

I went back into the room with the rest of the family. From the uninterrupted chatter I knew that none of Mama's words had penetrated through the wall.

But I was worried. What if Mama came into the room and Andrei sensed how she felt? He must not know that Mama did not like him.

"Andrei, I—I think it would be best if you would leave. You know, I have to study tonight—and I really think I should. Is that all right?"

Andrei looked at me with a slight frown. Then he shrugged his shoulders and grinned. "Oh, that's all right. I really should study, too."

I walked with him to the gate. The wind already had an icy chill and dark clouds scudded across the starry sky. I suddenly shivered.

"I'll see you on Sunday, then, O.K.?" Andrei said with one hand on the latch. "Then we can spend lots of time together. No need to study then."

"All right, Andrei." I did not feel like talking anymore. Knowing that Mama did not like Andrei's presence was unsettling.

The next time Andrei and I met, I poured out my heart. I told Andrei that Mama thought I was too young to get serious with a boy and that Mama thought I had no time for boys at 17. In fact, it seemed like Mama thought I did not need any time for myself at all.

Andrei listened and sympathized with me. And so it was that Andrei hardly ever came to our house anymore, but we met at my school and talked. And we still saw each other at church and enjoyed our time of singing together.

I felt somewhat guilty, because I knew Mama did not approve of my spending time with Andrei. However, I justified the time I spent with my boyfriend by reasoning that I was old enough to make some of my own decisions. After all, my oldest sister *Margareta* had married when she was 18.

With Mother, I was distant and cool. I did my required chores and helped with the housework, but I was not my usual self.

As the winter set in, it was too cold to meet for long periods outdoors, so Andrei and I spent even less time with each other. Most of our time together was with the church youth, singing or praying.

Andrei was at his best in these public settings. He was friendly with all the youth and at times it seemed to me that he was as friendly to the other girls as he was to me.

"I don't mind that you are friendly with the other girls," I told him on one of our walks home. "I just want to know how you really feel about me. I want to be special to you."

"You are special to me," Andrei protested. "But you know, we really can't get that serious about each other since your mom doesn't like it. And maybe it is best nobody else really knows how we feel about each other."

"Andrei! I want everyone to know that we are special friends. Haven't we prayed about it? Isn't this what God wants for us?" I stopped walking and faced Andrei.

"Come, Silvia, let's not argue about it. You know I like you and that you are special to me. We are the only two who need to know how we feel about each other."

We started walking again. Filled with new thoughts, I was quiet. My mind was in turmoil.

Once more, I poured out my heart to God in my nighttime prayer. "God, my thoughts are getting confused. I do love Andrei very much and I think he loves me. But now, it seems like his heart is not only for me. And You know I have no feelings for sale. I want only one true friend. I don't want many boyfriends, I want only one. I want only Andrei. Didn't he pray about it? You know I have prayed about it, too. I don't know, something doesn't seem quite right. Help me, please, Lord!"

Something else bothered me, too. Since I did not have my mother's support for our friendship, I sensed all the more a need to depend on God for guidance and wisdom. I wanted my friendship with Andrei to flourish with God's blessings. Whenever Andrei and I were together, I felt we should spend time in prayer together.

But I was always the one to suggest to Andrei that we should pray. I was the one who would steer our conversation into spiritual channels. That bothered me. I felt that Andrei should be the spiritual leader.

"God, does Andrei love You like he should? Why doesn't he ever suggest we pray together? I know he prays when I say something, but I want him to lead out. One of the things that first attracted me to him was that he seemed such a sincere Christian. But lately, his mind seems to be filled with other things."

The next afternoon, I slipped on my coat and started for the door.

"Where are you going?" Mama questioned me. "I want you to finish the ironing while I get supper ready."

"I was just going to go out on the street and see one of my friends," I said simply. "I can do the ironing when I get back."

Mama's flying fingers never stopped busily darning Ştefan's stocking heel. "I don't know why you need to go out so much. There is so much work to do here. The windows haven't been washed at all this week and the floor needs sweeping. And I need you to help with the ironing."

The latch on the gate clicked and as we looked out the window, we saw Andrei coming toward the house.

"Him again!" Mama said and her mouth tightened into a hard line. She thrust her knitting away from her and rose swiftly to her feet. In a few steps, she was at the front door.

"Andrei! I want to talk with you. Come into the kitchen," Mama said in a voice that showed she expected to be obeyed.

Andrei looked at me in surprise. Mama was already leading the way into the kitchen. At first Andrei just stood rooted to the spot, then he slowly followed her. After he was in the kitchen, Mama firmly shut the door.

I felt trapped. What was Mama going to tell Andrei? Would Andrei be too scared to say anything? I went close to the wall and listened. I could hear Mama's voice rise and fall in a continual, steady stream. There was hardly any break in the flow of words. And I knew how Mama could talk. Sometimes it seemed Mama was talking all the time—telling us children what to do; wondering how they were going to clothe the children; complaining about the low wages that Tata received at work.

And now Mama was talking to Andrei. But what was she telling him? My active imagination darted to all kinds of things. Was she saying that I had no time for boys? That I did not help enough at home? And what was Andrei thinking? Did he see how unfair Mama was? Did he understand how Mama tried to run my life?

I lost track of time. The rest of the family was silent. Everyone understood that some kind of crisis was in the making, so no one talked directly to me. And I continued to agonize. What could Mama be finding to talk about so long? Whatever could Andrei be thinking? When would this ever end? I ceased to think of the woman in the kitchen as my mother. I felt a cold hardness creep into my mind as I imagined what all was being said.

All at once, Andrei was in the room. His face was red. He looked at me as I went over to him. I did not know this Andrei.

Finally he said, "I guess you need to live your life like your mother wants you to." Then he turned abruptly and went for the door.

"Wait! Andrei! I need to talk to you. I need to discuss this with you!" I couldn't believe this was happening to me. Didn't Andrei understand? Why was he leaving?

"I must leave," was all Andrei said. He did not wait. The door closed behind him with a dull thud.

I went into the kitchen.

"What did you tell him? Why did he leave without speaking to me? Tell me what you said!" My voice was trembling, yet firm.

Mama looked quickly at my face. "I told him what I needed to tell him," she said. "I told him you need to finish school and not be with boys. I told him you wanted to go on with your education and that I was not going to let you run around and neglect your schoolwork. That's what I told him."

I felt dizzy. I needed air. I needed to think. "You ruined my life!" I finally said. My words sounded toneless, flat. I turned and left the room.

Bundled up in my coat, I walked to church. I talked to God and argued with Him. I complained about Andrei. I was very upset at him. Why didn't Andrei tell Mama that our friendship was the will of God?

I felt like my life was over. Andrei had left me—left me because Mama had chased him away.

I tried to sort out my thoughts. All the children in our family knew that Mama voiced her opinions freely. We all knew that Mama scolded and complained about our situation in life. At times, she would fuss at Tata and try to goad him into doing something that would improve our situation. And she would fuss at the children. She would try to get us to care more about our appearance, or to help more in the house, or to get good jobs in order to bring more money home.

That was just the way Mama was. I had known that all my life and I was used to having our home dominated by Mama. But now I began to see my home in a new light. Tata was always such a peace-loving husband and father that he did not withstand his wife's talk. He tried to maintain peace and quiet by loving us children more and taking time to be with us and give us the needed attention. But he never talked back to his wife. He never caused a ruckus or a fuss. He was always the one to try to keep our home calm.

Now, I saw what had happened. Mama was the boss. She was the one who ruled how things should be done. And Tata allowed her to do it. This realization came to me with clarity. My respect for Tata also withered. Tata should not have allowed Mama to rule our home. He should have asked Mama to give him the leadership role and should not let her be the dominant parent.

Tata was too good. He did not even stand up for what was right. I did not want to be like that. I knew that when something was right and the Bible taught it that way, I should defend the Bible teaching. Tata, in my mind, lacked strength. Yes, I was convinced he was a man of God and that God heard his prayers, but for the first time, I recognized a weakness in my dearly beloved Tata. I wept because of that realization.

But I felt it was all Mama's fault. It was Mama's strong mind and ceaseless tongue that made our home this way. I knew I should honor and respect my parents, but I felt a hardness creep into my heart when I thought again what Mama had done. She ruled our family's lives and now she wanted to rule my personal life also. Did rule my life. And ruined it, too.

In the next weeks, I lived in a vacuum. I went to school, tried to study, tried to function. But my heart seemed cold, and I detached myself from my family.

When I saw Andrei, I tried to detach myself from him. Even when he did try to talk with me again, I was too unsure of my emotions to respond. He seemed to regret what he had told me and tried to win my friendship again.

My realization of the situation with my parents caused a deep chasm to separate me from my mother. I no longer called her Mama and only answered when I was directly spoken to. I intentionally avoided my mother and often just shrugged rather than giving any verbal answer when questioned.

Everyone in our home felt the tension. Victor pled with me to talk with our mother and to forgive her. Rodica said she thinks "someone needs to take Silvia in hand." Tata tried to talk to me. But to all their pleas, I turned a deaf ear. I continued my silent existence. I was too deeply disturbed to really care about anything.

My spiritual life suffered. My talks with God seemed mostly like surface talks. I had made a public testimony of my faith in Jesus earlier and it was scarcely six months ago that I had sealed my faith with water baptism. I had rejoiced to be able to join the band of believers. As the church prayed together and encouraged each other to remain faithful in the repressive times under communist rule, my spiritual life had blossomed.

But now, my life was like a deflated balloon. The joy, the spark, was gone. When I prayed, it seemed I only went through the motions. There were times when I wondered if God even heard me.

One evening, Mama began to complain that life was really giving her a hard time. She said that when I was little, she cared for me, clothed me, fed me and trained me. And now, this was the reward she received: a daughter who did not even talk to her. And, Mama went on, Tata did nothing about it.

Everyone sat silently.

Mama's voice went on and on, listing how life had been so unfair to her. I sat still and silent on my chair. I moved my face slightly away from my family and looked out the window.

Again Rodica spoke up and urged Tata to do something. "This can't go on all the time! Our family is being destroyed. Tata, make Silvia talk with Mama and stop being so uncommunicative!"

Tata looked at me. He stood up from his chair. "Come with me, Silvia," he said and we went out together onto the porch.

"Silvia, you must get over this. It is not right that you don't speak to your mother." When I refused to look at him, he reached out and gave me several spanks.

It was so unexpected that I gasped and lifted my eyes to my father's face. A slight quavering sound came from my lips.

Tata's face was a picture of misery. Urged by his wife and Rodica, he had tried to restore happiness to our home. But his heart was not in the discipline he had used and his anguished face betrayed his torment.

That evening, after the house was silent, I knelt by my bed to pray. This time, my prayer was not just words, but a cry from my heart.

"Why does no one understand? Where are You, God? When I need You, You seem so far away. Ever since You showed me that You know my size, I have felt Your presence. But now, nothing seems to make sense. Mama ruined my life and yet she doesn't understand why I can't speak to her. Tata is taking Mama's side against me. And Andrei doesn't understand me, either. You know I love him. But why? Why do I love him? Why did You make me with feelings? I do want Andrei's love back again. Even if I know he doesn't feel for me like I feel for him, my heart keeps wanting him back. And I don't know why. I already gave my feelings to him and I can't take them back. Oh, God, what shall I do?

"If my mother wants to talk with me, I will talk. But she will have to come to me, because she is the one who ruined my life. I do not want to hate my mother. But I do not understand her. Help me, God."

Once I began crying out my heart to God, I again found a relief for my deep ache. My questions were not answered and I found no solution to my problems, but a certain sense of being loved by God began to penetrate my broken heart.

Early in the morning, I was still not sleeping. When I heard a soft knock on the door, I did not want to answer. The door opened slightly and I heard Tata's voice whisper, "Silvia!"

"I—I need to talk with you." Tata was crying. "I couldn't sleep all night because I kept thinking of what I did to you. Can you forgive me? When you needed me, I turned against you. Oh, I—I'm sorry."

I sat up in bed. "Yes, Tata, I can forgive you. I know you love me." Then I stopped talking. I wanted to say, "You should not let your wife rule you. You should stand up for what is right." But I could not say that to Tata. It would make him feel even worse.

Even though some things had changed in my heart, nothing changed outwardly. I waited for my mother to approach me and ask to discuss the problem. But nothing happened. I yearned to have peace restored, but I felt nothing could be solved unless my mother wanted to talk things out.

Another evening came. Tata sat on one cot with his eyes closed. I was studying my homework on the other cot where Ştefan was already sleeping. It was hard to concentrate, but I had to study. My grades were slipping, and I knew that if I did not do better, I would have to repeat the eleventh grade.

Suddenly, it was as if Tata was a changed person. He stood and kindly, yet firmly, said, "Silvia, if you love me, go talk to Mama. She is alone in the other room and now is the time to talk!"

I looked up from my books. There was something different about Tata's voice. Something commanding.

Yet I hesitated. "She should come to me first. She is the one who ruined my life."

Although Mama was in the other room, she had heard what Tata had said. She was quick on the defensive. "The daughter should come to the mother. That is the way it should be."

Everyone waited to see what the outcome would be. Tata still stood, looking at me. "If you love me," he had said.

Five minutes passed. Ten minutes. Time stood still.

"It is Satan who is trying to keep us apart," I said. "He will not win!" And I walked into the room where Mama was waiting. Tata and the others left for the kitchen, leaving us alone.

Mama nervously smoothed the cover on the bed. "What do you have to say? Why is all this trouble come to us?"

"I am willing to have these troubles put away but I think first we must talk," I began. "I must tell you how I feel. Why is it that you are always the one who tells the whole family how to do things? Why don't you let Tata be the head of the family? It seems like you push and shove with your words until everyone does just what you say. Then when Andrei wanted to be a special friend to me, you began to try to push him away. Don't you want your daughters to get married? What do you think he will tell the other boys about my mom? And I want to know why the house is always so important that you never have time to visit with guests or with us. Why are you always so busy with earthly things and why do you continually complain about not having enough food and clothes? Tata always prays about his problems, but when have we ever seen you on your knees or when do we hear you praying about your problems? Do you love God? Are you a Christian?" I myself did not know where all my questions were coming from. It seemed that a dam had broken and the words came pouring out.

Mama sat in complete silence. Several times she opened her mouth slightly, but I kept on talking.

"When Andrei came to see me, I wanted to talk with you about it and share with you. But you didn't like him from the start. I could not tell you how I felt because you were not interested. You said you took care of me when I was small and when I needed you. I need you now. I need someone who likes me and is interested in how I feel. I need someone to share things with.

"Sometimes it seems like you resent everything I do, and that you are always finding fault with me. When I was younger, you wanted to give me away. I often wonder if you really love me. What is wrong with me? Do you wish I would not be active in the church and want to serve God? I want to go to heaven. Why don't you like what I am doing? Would it be better if I would drink and dance and smoke? What do you want from me?

"You turned everyone against me and you got Tata to spank me. You ruined my life with Andrei. You don't know how much you hurt me!" I was crying by now. All my self-control was gone and I could not stop talking.

Mama was crying too. She covered her face with her apron and she sobbed.

But I was not finished. "I know that you cannot bring Andrei back again. I lost him and I lost you. But I am willing to try again. I am willing to call you Mama again. And I ask that you forgive me for not talking to you. I know now that I hated you. I'm sorry!"

It was a long time since I had started talking. There was complete silence in the kitchen where the rest of the family was

90

gathered.

"Mama, it's up to you. I want to try again," I said.

But Mama was crying too hard to reply.

"Do you want to say anything, Mama? Tell me your part. I've told you now what I told you many times in my mind and at night when I could not sleep."

But there was no reply. Mama seemed to be in a state of shock. I knew that no one had ever spoken to her like this. Not from our family.

I looked at the clock. It was three in the morning. I wondered if the rest of the family were still in the kitchen. I left the room and found them huddled around the door listening. I knew they had heard everything I said, but I didn't care. Everything was out now. Everyone knew just how I felt about this situation.

Since it seemed that Mama did not want to talk, I went out to the kitchen to get something to eat. I got a dish of mămăliga and some soup. I decided I would just eat it cold and study while I ate.

I heard soft footsteps come into the kitchen. It was Mama. "Here, let me warm that for you," Mama said in a low voice.

"That's all right. I'll just eat it cold," I protested.

But Mama insisted that she would warm it up. She bustled around and then set the dish of warm mămăliga in front of me.

"Do you want me to sit with you while you eat, like in old times?"

I looked at her. There was something different about her voice. Something softer. While I ate, she sat quietly on the edge of the bed on the other side of the table. We didn't talk. Each scrape of my spoon against the bowl seemed loud and harsh. When the bowl was finally empty, Mama broke the silence.

"I'll wash your plate," she said and then she made a request that I had never heard before. "Would you like to pray with me? I kept thinking about the things you said. And I know that too many of those things are true."

So we, mother and daughter, knelt on the humble kitchen floor, and I heard the anguish and pleading of my mother's heart. Mama prayed for forgiveness for being such a thoughtless mother and for neglecting her duties as a mother and wife. She pleaded with God to forgive her hardheartedness. Mama's voice broke and she wept bitter tears. Even as Mama was praying, I too prayed for forgiveness. I asked God to forgive me for not being more willing to follow my parents' wishes, and for hardening my heart against my Mama. As we prayed, the healing love of God bridged the chasm that had been between us.

For a long time we prayed. At times, we would talk to each other, both confessing our failures, and then we would pray again. We hugged each other and wept on each other's shoulders.

The kitchen had become a holy place. A temple where peace and love were restored. And the place where I found a true mother.

—·—·—·—·—·—·—·—·—·—·—·—·—

It took me a long time to get over my feelings for Andrei. But as time went on, I saw that he was losing out in his spiritual life. He still came to church, but I realized that he was not anchored strongly in God. I could see now that he was not at all what I would want in a true spiritual leader for a Christian home. I realized the foolish mistakes I had made. In my heartache, I turned to God.

"Lord, forgive this foolish young heart of mine. Now I can see that You were all-wise in not letting me continue my friendship with Andrei. He was not grounded on You. I sensed this when I would talk about spiritual things and I always had to ask him to pray, but my heart was saying other things. I gave him my special feelings, and I'm sorry. I wanted someone to love me and I reached out to him. But now, Lord, I will love You. You are my first love. And I can even thank You for letting me go through this experience because You gave me a true mother. Thank-you, Lord. I know again that You know everything. You know what I need just like You knew my size."

12

In the Mountains

I rested my hand on the sagging wooden yard gate and took a deep breath. I gazed beyond the two-story school building across the road and my eyes rested on the forest-covered mountains that climbed abruptly from the village nestled around the base of wooded slopes. The brisk autumn air was laced with wood smoke spiraling up from the humble cottages. I took a deep breath and filled my lungs with the fresh mountain air.

It was over a year now that I had been teaching school in the Carpathian Mountains. As I reflected how I had been hired to teach, I marveled once more at the direction God had given me.

"We must have looked like the city people we were," I chuckled to myself. I could still see our group of seven young people headed up the mountain side with our "city" shoes and carrying clumsy cardboard suitcases.

There were seven young people who had decided to take a vacation in the mountains. In this group was my brother Victor and his new bride, *Mihaela*. Actually, it was Victor and Mihaela's honeymoon! But the couple had invited the rest of the group to accompany them on their trek through the countryside.

And it was in this very village that we young people had stayed with our Christian friends. During the day we hiked up the steep slopes, and in the evening we visited or attended the Christian church in the village.

I felt a sudden homesickness as I remembered the evenings when we used to gather in the small church. Victor was at the organ and I had my guitar as our group sang hymns until late in the evenings. That was what actually had landed me the job of teaching in the first place. When the church leader heard that I had finished high school and was looking for a job, he met with the elders of the church and then surprised me with a job offer of teaching the children's choir in the church!

When I first mentioned it to my parents after our return from the mountains, they hesitated about having me leave home when I was only 18. But Tata reflected that I had tried in vain to get a job in Iaşi. Now there was a need for a music teacher in a village with fellow believers, so they gave their consent.

"Try it for several weeks," Tata had said.

I smiled to myself in memory of how those several weeks had stretched into more than a half year. And how I had enjoyed it.

I was glad for every bit of training I had taken in school when I began forming the village children into a children's choir and orchestra. Thankfully, the children had natural musical abilities and the musical instruments that were carefully brought out of their storage places were tuned and practiced on.

It wasn't only the children who took an interest in the music lessons. The older people and the youth of the village began to gather for musical evenings. The news about the singing village spread to a neighboring village. When a vacancy for a teacher at the grade school suddenly opened, the director had offered me a job of teaching the fifth through eighth grade classes.

Since summer with its busy times had arrived, our music classes ended and I had gone home to Iaşi. But now I was back, teaching school for a lively group of mountain children. I stirred from my memories and hurried across the road to the school. The students would soon be arriving.

— · — · — · — · — · — · — · — · — · — · —

"*Adrian*, since it is getting colder and you seem to have a constant cold, could you please remember to bring a handkerchief along with you when you come to school?" I asked gently. I was trying to be patient with the constant stream of sniffs coming from his corner of the room.

Adrian looked at me with a glint of mischief in his eyes but he answered meekly, "Yes, Teacher Tărniceriu."

"Where is *Ionică*?" I asked as I scanned the room and saw the empty desk that belonged to the biggest boy in the class.

Empty looks and shrugging shoulders indicated that no one in the class had any idea.

"Well, I guess—" but I had no time to finish my sentence, for suddenly a tousled head peered around the doorway leading into the classroom.

"Here I am!" Ionică said loudly. He rolled his eyes and smirked at the children.

"Ionică! Come here!" My voice was unusually stern.

But Ionică withdrew his head and slammed the door!

Even as I took several swift strides from my desk to the door, I heard Ionică scurry down the hall.

I jerked open the door and called, "Ionică! You come back!"

The only answer I received was a mocking laugh as Ionică clattered down the flight of steps to the first floor.

"This time you have gone too far!" I said under my breath and I started off in pursuit. Ionică's constant escapades had been a source of frustration many times, and I had tried being patient with him. But with a sudden resolve, I decided that it was time to deal with him.

My feet pounded on the wooden steps. When Ionică heard his teacher coming after him, he looked upward in surprise. The startled look he gave me through the banisters of the stairs spurred me to even greater speed.

Ionică darted out the front entry, taking time to slam the door just as I reached the last step. But in a second, I too was out the door. The chase was on.

Ionică was a big boy of 13 who was used to climbing mountain slopes taking care of sheep who were only slightly more nimble than he. So, when he ran down the village street to get as far away from Teacher Tărniceriu as possible, he thought he could easily leave me behind.

But what Ionică did not know was that I had trained as a track runner in high school, and even had the offer of competing in other countries. But I knew, and I was determined to catch the runaway.

As the boy fled down the dirt street between the board fences, he glanced backwards and saw that his teacher was not far behind! And what was more, I seemed to be gaining!

Ionică put forth more effort and ran faster. But I ran faster too.

An old woman was driving her gaggle of geese along the roadside and as Ionică came racing toward them, the geese scattered across the road. He stumbled as he tried to avoid the honking fowl, and the old woman yelled angrily at him. But she stood rooted to the spot with her mouth hanging open wordlessly as I dashed after the running boy.

A horse tethered beside the fence jumped skittishly as we ran past. I was now only a few steps behind Ionică.

Ionică's breath was coming in big gasps. No one had trained him how to breathe and how to save his energy in long distance running. He knew how to sprint, but this race was much further than he had imagined.

He no longer threw quick glances backwards to see where I was. On and on he drove his tired legs, trying in vain to outrun the footsteps that drew ever closer. He ran with his mouth wide open and his chest heaving.

When we reached the end of the street where the board fences no longer hedged us in, Ionică dashed wildly down a little footpath between two gardens. He clambered over a pile of logs and scrabbled to jump over the high wooden fence.

But it was here that I grasped Ionică firmly by his collar. With one last effort, he tried desperately to wrench free. But his energy had all been used up in running and his strength was no match for the vise-like grip that held him firmly.

With great gasping breaths, Ionică began to sob. Huge tears rolled down his cheeks. His panting breathing made rasping noises as he sobbed and panted in turns.

I, too, was panting. My face was hot and my hair clung damply to my forehead.

"Sit, down, here—and we'll get our breath," I panted as I steered Ionică to a log.

The two of us sat side by side, each drawing deep breaths. I was still holding onto Ionică's shirt collar. I knew we made quite a spectacle: teacher and student sitting side by side on a log, both panting for breath and Ionică's tears streaming down his cheeks.

"Why are you crying?" I finally asked when I could speak.

"I lost my money for bread," Ionică sniffed in distress.

I smiled to myself. That wouldn't account for the fearful trembling and the scared look on his face. Ionică was afraid.

"I'll give you money for bread." And I drew out of my pocket enough money for three loaves of bread and gave it to Ionică. He looked at the money in amazement and then he dared to sneak a look at me.

"Ionică, I am not going to spank you. Nor am I going to call the principal or the police. You don't need to be scared of me. I want to talk to you."

I addressed him in a soft voice. "Ionică, you know we have been having problems in school. You are continually doing things that disrupt the class. When I ask you to do things, you either don't obey or you mock my authority. And that makes it difficult for all of us."

Ionică stopped sobbing so he could listen. His eyes seemed fastened to the ground and he sniffed several times, then was silent.

"You have repeated this grade three times and I know you can learn your lessons. You do have a good mind and I can see that you are very intelligent in numbers and doing figures. But because you don't stick with your lessons, even your math grades suffer. Ionică, what do you do with your sheep if they continually break away and run away from the flock?"

Ionică lifted his dark eyes and looked at me. He swallowed and then said in a low tone, "Tie their legs together."

"Do you think they enjoy that?"

A sideways shake of his head gave me encouragement to continue. "Of course, they don't. And if the sheep don't learn, you continue to keep close watch over them and restrict their freedom. But if they learn to listen to you, they can be free to go with the other sheep and don't have to be tied up.

"Ionică, you are like a sheep that needs to be tied up. Because you constantly make trouble, I constantly have to 'tie you up.' Do you understand what I mean?" I looked deeply into Ionică's eyes.

At his nod, I continued. "Running away this morning did not solve anything. You would still have had to come back to school someday. And that is how you try to handle your problems. You ignore them or try to run away from them. But the problems still exist."

I was confident my message of reproof was getting through to my student.

"Are you willing to try again? I will not punish you if you promise that you will try hard to learn your lessons and try to be obedient. And remember, if you run away again, I can catch you again!"

Ionică gave a little chuckle. "I didn't know you could run that fast!"

When we returned to the classroom, there was a silence that was filled with questions. All the pupils wondered what had happened. Why was Ionică walking alongside Teacher Tărniceriu? How had I caught him? They had seen the beginning of the chase from the second story windows and they had assured each other that Ionică could easily get away. Now here he was, meekly sitting at his desk and diligently attacking his lessons. And Teacher was going ahead with class as if nothing out of the ordinary had happened.

Questioning Ionică after school didn't give the other children much satisfaction either. But one thing he did say and everyone believed him. "Don't ever try to run away from your teacher!"

And Ionică did try to do better. Both his attitude and his grades improved, and when he saw that I treated him with respect as he tried his best, he put forth even greater efforts. It was soon evident that this would be his last year in this room, for he had progressed enough to move to the next grade.

But I soon found, as many teachers do, that mischief can arise in unexpected places. One chilly evening, when I tried to start a fire in the little stove that warmed the one room I lived in, smoke began to pour out of the stove. In a matter of minutes, the small room was filled with choking fumes.

I fled gasping out the door and stayed outside until the fire had gone out. My landlady lived in the same yard and I went to her for help.

As we entered the smoky room, the landlady opened the stove top and peered in. A few wisps of smoke still rose from the kindling that had been burning when I started the fire.

"It is obvious that something is blocking the flue," she murmured. The stovepipes were not hot, so she pulled the pipe out of the chimney. "I should be able to see daylight, but there is something up there. And it is not the time when birds build their nests. Did you have a fire yesterday in the stove?"

"Yes," I answered. "I had a fire in the morning but by the time I came home in the afternoon, I didn't add any more wood because I was gone all evening."

Just then, one of the landlady's children came in. "I saw *Manole* on your roof this morning. He probably stuffed something in your chimney."

I knew where Manole lived so I went up the slope and knocked on the yard gate. I lifted the latch and stepped onto the wooden porch and knocked at the door.

When Manole's mother answered the door, I saw the white curtain at the window move slightly. Someone was peering out the window.

"Is Manole here?" I asked pleasantly.

Out of the corner of my eye, I saw the curtain fall into place again.

"Yes, what do you want?" Manole's mother asked as if it were nothing new to have teachers come and ask for Manole.

"I'd like to talk with him."

The middle-aged woman turned. "Manole!" she called out. She whirled and darted into the room. "No! You are not going to run out the back door! The teacher wants to talk with you. What did you do this time?"

When his mother pushed Manole forward, I spoke to him in a normal tone. "Manole, I need your help. Something seems to be blocking the chimney at my house, and I need someone spry to climb up on the roof and see what might be blocking the chimney. Could you help me, please?"

Manole shifted his eyes from the floor to me. Then he looked at his mother briefly. His eyes darted back to my face again.

"Why do you need Manole?" his mother wondered curiously. "Can't any of your landlady's children help you?"

"I prefer to have Manole do it. I like to have my students help me sometimes. Could he come, please?"

"Well, I guess. Manole, you go with the teacher and help her. Then you go on to the store for bread. You will have to hurry because we are not finished cleaning out the barn and we want to finish before Sunday."

We walked in silence to my house. When we entered the yard, my front door was still standing open. "I tried to start a fire this evening, because I was chilly and I needed to check some papers, and then smoke started pouring into the room. I had to leave the door open to get rid of the smoke and now I am sure it will take a long time to warm up my room. Well, can you climb up on the roof and see what is in the chimney?"

I could plainly see that Manole knew the easiest way to scramble up onto the roof. But he didn't seem to know what to do with the old rags and shoes that he pulled reluctantly from the chimney.

"Just toss them down here in the yard. I'll take care of the stuff," I told him. Again his eyes had difficulty meeting mine.

After he got down off the roof, I smiled at him. "Thank-you, Manole. Now I think I can start a fire. I'll see you at school on Monday."

Not a word did I say about how the stuff got into the chimney. But I could tell that Manole was uneasy because he shifted from one foot to the other instead of leaving right away. "I—I can take care of the rags," he finally managed to say. He gathered up the pile and turned to leave. "I'm sorry," he murmured. "I shouldn't have done that to you."

"I forgive you," I replied, placing my hand on his shoulder and smiling at him. I could tell I didn't need to worry that he would play any more tricks on his teacher.

—··—··—··—··—··—··—

I wished all my problems were as easily solved as the ones that came up in the classroom.

We teachers had a room where we often gathered after school to talk and relax. As we got to know each other, we began to talk about spiritual things. I shared my childhood experiences with them and I told them what an impression it had made on my life when God sent the clothes, just the right size, in answer to my prayers. I told them of the joy that came into my life the night I asked Jesus to forgive my sins and cleanse me with His blood. Although I could tell that several of the teachers weren't interested, two of the women asked many questions about God. One day, I brought in my guitar and started singing songs of faith in God. After that, we often spent much time in singing and talking about the things of God.

In the evenings, several of us began meeting regularly in my rented room to listen to preaching tapes. Their questions showed a definite interest in the Bible and I could sense a hunger for spiritual fulfillment. I was blessed by this opportunity, for wherever I could, even in school, I wanted to be a witness for Christ.

— · — · — · — · — · — · — · — · — · — · —

One day, the chief director sent a message that he wanted to talk with me. As I entered his room, I was at ease, for he had often visited with me and told me that he appreciated the work I was doing in school. It had not gone unnoticed that I attempted to win the confidence of my students and that they did not just obey me because they had to, but rather because they wanted to.

"Silvia," the director said, "I am getting complaints that the children don't like you. Reports are out that you are spanking the children and disciplining the children harshly."

If he had hit me, I couldn't have been more astonished. After all the encouragement he had given me about my methods of teaching, and now this? I could hardly believe he was saying this.

"What do you mean?" I asked. The hurt in my voice must have been evident, for he flinched slightly and turned to look out the window. That he had chosen me for this rebuke was ridiculous. I had often been appalled to see my co-teachers carry sticks with them into the classrooms to keep order, and many times I heard them yelling at the students to be quiet. This didn't make sense! I had never spanked a single student!

The director continued to stare out the window. I was silent, trying to understand this sudden turn of events.

"You talk a lot to the other teachers." The words came out in a monotone, seemingly trying to convey some other message.

Suddenly I understood. He was not upset with me. This was just his way of telling me that I needed to be careful about the religious activities I was engaged in. The long arm of the anti-Christian communist government had somehow learned that I was teaching the Bible to my co-teachers and teaching the children Biblical principles and Christian songs. So, the director had to use this method of warning me. I looked at him with pity.

He finally turned and looked briefly at me. "That's all," he said and nodded toward the door.

After I had left the office, I prayed for guidance. I knew that the situation must be grave if the director spoke to me. On the other hand, I knew that my conscience would not allow me to end my religious activities.

So, I continued my discussions, my Bible teaching and my musical evenings. I was especially close to two of my co-teachers, and when they stopped going to the dances and movies, some of the male teachers were quick to accuse me of influencing them.

Once again, the director spoke with me. He made it plain that he was very pleased with the work I was doing in school, but he also made it plain that he was being pressured to do something about the situation.

I felt sorry for him. There was something pathetic about this man who was being forced into doing something he had no desire to do. I was grateful that he understood that what I was doing was good, not subversive. In fact, as I left, he looked at me with weary eyes and said, "Please pray for me." After that, I had even more of a compassion for him. Perhaps he had been a Christian at one time or had been raised in a Christian home. Somehow, he knew about the power of prayer, and knew that he needed help.

But again, I decided to carry on as I had done before. School would soon be dismissed for the summer and perhaps the opposition to Christianity would diminish during that time. I did not know whether I would be asked to teach another term or not.

One morning when I came to school, I was met with terrible news. The director was dead!

Someone had found him hanging by a cord in his own home. We were all devastated, because none of us had realized that he was having such extreme difficulties. Before my eyes his haunted face seemed to arise. "Pray for me!" he had said at our last meeting. And now he was dead! Some hopeless situation had led him to the deception that he could escape his troubles by choosing to end his life. I shuddered to think of his waking up to eternity without God.

This happening gave me a greater burden to share the hope that I had in Christ. Many hearts were open to the Gospel as the shock of the director's death jolted the small village.

Then what I had expected, happened. A new director was put in charge, and with the information he had about me, there was no chance that I would be hired again. So, I said good-bye to my students and the many friends I had made and prepared to move back to Iaşi.

I have never regretted the experience I had in the mountains. God deepened my love for children and I learned that if I can win their confidence, they are ready to lay down their naughty pranks and put their energy into their lessons. My faith in God deepened and my resolve to share my faith grew stronger. I would not forget the haunted face of that director.

13

Night Work

G*enovieva Sfatcu* and I walked up the hill toward her house. The linden trees were in full bloom and we breathed in the fragrance of the tiny flowers.

"Thank-you for waiting for me," I told her. "I had just gotten a shipment of transistors, and I wanted to put them in their bins and finish my inventory tally."

"So do you enjoy your job at the factory?" Genovieva wondered. "I remember how hard you studied to prepare for the exam before you were hired."

"Yes, I remember, too. Doing a two-year course in ten months was very wearying. Sometimes I was so tired I could hardly find my way home afterwards. But, yes, I do enjoy the work. At first, I was rather overwhelmed by all the responsibilities, but now that I've been working there for a while, I enjoy keeping my department running smoothly. Being responsible for keeping the workers in our department supplied keeps me busy."

Our footsteps were evenly matched. Throughout high school Genovieva and I had been friends. Now, after I had returned from the mountains and started a job at the electronics factory, our friendship continued.

"I am so glad you now have time to work with the children's choir. Wasn't the Sunday evening program good? That little *Edica* can really sing. Do you think we could get her to memorize all the words of "Over the Jordan River" before next month's program?" Genovieva wondered.

I knew why she asked. Little Edica and her sister Carmen, 9 and 11 years old, had been coming to the children's choir for several months now. They both enjoyed it, but they had been having difficulties at home. Their father was a strong communist party member, and when he found out that his daughters were attending church and singing in the children's choir, he became very upset. Their mother, too, was strongly opposed to any religious activities the girls wanted to participate in.

"I think she could," I answered. "But I don't know if we should depend on it. After seeing how their father jerked them around and pulled their hair last Sunday when he came to get them, I just don't know." I dashed at the tears that threatened to cloud my vision. "To see those little girls being abused because they come to church really touched my heart."

Genovieva agreed. "And how my heart bled for them when they came wearing their Young Pioneers' uniforms that one morning. Remember how Edica's face was flushed with shame when she told us how her father had cut slits into their good dresses so they wouldn't come to church? I was so upset."

"Yes," I said. "I know what you mean. But I will not forget how the girls appreciated it when we told them we will not worry about what they are wearing. And when they stood in the choir that morning, to see how they enjoyed singing was worth it."

"Seventy children. And we started with less than 20—" Genovieva broke off suddenly and looked across the street. She nudged me and motioned with her head.

I had seen it, too. A car with foreign license plates was parked parallel to the street. I glanced down the street. Two boys were coming up the walk, swinging their school bags. An elderly lady was limping along, carrying a shopping bag.

Genovieva had checked up the street and she said in a low tone, "I can't see anyone suspicious."

By now, we were alongside the gray car. The woman on the passenger's side glanced up, saw us, then rolled down the window.

"Can you tell us where the cultural hall is?" she asked pleasantly in English.

I could understand what she asked because I had taken

English courses, but it was Genovieva who answered. Her English was quite good.

"You must to go forward, and then you turn to right side of the street. Cultural hall is situated next," Genovieva stated simply. However, we did not continue our walk.

"Are you Genovieva?" the man in the driver's seat asked. His clear blue eyes were friendly.

"Yes," Genovieva acknowledged. "This is my friend, Silvia."

They both nodded at me and smiled.

"We must not keep you. We will meet you at the botanical gardens at seven o'clock." The man unfolded his map and looked intently at it.

Without further words we continued our walk. After we passed the car, I turned around and walked backwards. Genovieva pretended to chase me as I backed up the sidewalk. But all the while, we were both searching the street. When I didn't see anyone who seemed to be paying us undue attention, I fell into step beside Genovieva again.

"Was that the couple who was here before?" I wondered.

"No," Genovieva answered. "I have never seen these people before. The last time there were two men."

Ever since I had come back from the mountains, I had helped Genovieva and several others unload and hide Bibles that were smuggled into Romania. I well remember the time I found out that Tata was involved with Bible distribution. I had gone out with Genovieva to unload Bibles one night, and there was Tata! We both stopped in surprise for a moment, then went back to work. He told me later that for years, an old wooden barrel in our backyard was where he hid many Bibles until it was safe to deliver them. Even Mama was not aware how much her husband was involved in Bible smuggling. It just was not safe to speak about our activities or to let many people know what we were doing. Yes, Mama knew that sometimes Tata was summoned to the police station for interrogations, but then, merely being a "repentant" (a Christian), was enough to provoke questioning.

Because of the frequent times that I had helped with the work of meeting foreigners and stashing Bibles in different places, I knew I was placing myself in a dangerous situation. There were always people willing to work for the government by spying on Christians. Some of these informers seemed to know us quite well, because recently we were increasingly aware of being watched. So every time we received another shipment, we tried hard to observe whether we were being followed.

"Can you stay and help?" Genovieva wondered as we approached her parents' little white house. The typical Romanian high board fence around her house encircled the back yard, the root cellar, and the garden.

"Yes," I answered and followed her through the gate. We went across the little porch and into the front room.

"Good evening," Genovieva's mother greeted us.

"We need to wash the sheets again this evening," Genovieva told her mother. "Silvia will stay and help."

"Since you live by yourself, do you have more time to do other things?" Mama Maria asked pleasantly.

"Yes and no," I laughed. "Sometimes I save time by not doing my housework, but then I can't stand how it gets behind and have to stay up late and do it. I need to wash out another skirt for tomorrow, but I can do it when I get home."

Genovieva was already getting a pile of sheets and taking them outside. We filled the tub with water and swished the sheets up and down.

"You really do go through a lot of sheets in a week," I muttered in an undertone to Genovieva.

She responded with a merry laugh. "I guess we do!"

I took one wet sheet from the tub and flicked the corner of it against her bare arm.

We laughed and carried the load of sheets to the front yard. The clothesline stretched from beside the gate the entire width of the yard. Another line went alongside the house toward the back gate. When we were finished, there was a white line of sheets almost surrounding the house.

"Two more sheets left," I told Mama Maria. I strung them up inside the house, effectively blocking the front door.

After supper that evening, Genovieva and I left for the botanical gardens. Sure enough, the foreign couple was there, and I didn't even see them look at us. They walked past the cultivated rose garden and wandered down the path. Genovieva and I sauntered along behind them, stopping to breathe deeply the fragrance of the roses and admire the flowering bushes. As the couple came to the end of the walk, they turned and started back.

We followed a well-known path down the hillside. Steps led us away from the entrance and the busier flower gardens. Down here, the bushes and trees grew densely and hardly anyone was around. When we came to a huge evergreen tree that made a canopy over a large bare spot, we stopped.

When we saw the man and the woman who were following us come around the bend, we ducked under the low hanging branches. As soon as they were in front of the tree they checked the path both ways, and then they came in, too.

"Praise God!" the man exclaimed. "I am so glad you came along the street this evening. I had used up about three hours parking up and down the street, and I was sure someone was going to become suspicious of us. I kept getting the map out over and over again so people would just think we were lost."

His wife smiled at him and then at us. "And we were praying all the time. Isn't it wonderful how God answers our prayers?"

"Are things going better for you Christians?" the man wondered.

We shook our heads. "No," Genovieva tried to explain. "We must to be watch all times. Brother from church was hit by police for talking about communist evils. He lost job, and wife and six childrens have no food. We share what we can."

The woman's eyes filled with tears. "Oh, Lord," she breathed. "See the sufferings of Your children."

"Yet, I am sure God sees and He will give comfort. We want to encourage you that many Christians are praying for the persecuted churches," the man added with feeling.

"Thank-you," we responded. "It is very good to know that people in the West know about our situation."

"We have brought you supplies," the man said after a silent pause.

"Wait!" I said and walked out from under the tree. I had

caught a glimpse of someone coming down the path. Two people, in fact.

"Genovieva!" I called loudly. "You must come and see the hibiscus superlatim."

Genovieva appeared from the bushes beside the tree. How she had gotten out from under the tree and into the surrounding bushes so quickly, I didn't know.

"Where is it?" she asked as she came up from behind.

We both bent over the tiny pink flower as the two men walked behind us on the path. They looked intently at us. When I gently shoved Genovieva's head close and said, "There!" they walked on down the path.

"Let's make sure they are gone," I said after several moments of studying the flower.

"How did you know what kind of flower that was?" Genovieva asked as we returned to the path.

I looked at her and winked. "Well, some hibiscus flowers *are* pink," I said with a giggle.

She frowned in mock indignation.

I went quickly up the path the two men had taken. I rounded the curve just in time to see them go up the hill and leave. From where I stood, I motioned to Genovieva and she disappeared under the tree again.

"We will be right here," she finished, pointing to a map she had sketched in the dirt.

The man held up nine fingers and raised his eyebrows in question.

We both shook our heads. I quickly held up ten fingers and then pointed to the summer sun shining brightly.

The couple nodded in understanding, and we parted. Genovieva and I followed the path the two men had taken and the foreigners went back the way they had come.

When we approached the entrance to the gardens, I nudged Genovieva. She did not look right away, but she stiffened slightly when she saw the two men sitting on a park bench. They had taken their coats off, but there was no mistaking them. They watched as we came up the path, but we completely ignored them. We chattered about the beautiful day and the wonderful display of flowers in the gardens.

But as soon as were out of sight, we stopped a minute and looked at each other. Were they really following us? Had they been paying special attention to us? Or was it our overworked imagination?

Anyway, we breathed a silent prayer and quickly went to Genovieva's house. I thought again of how good it was to have Genovieva for a friend. Her quick mind made it easy for her to learn English. Actually it was through her mastery of the English language that she had become converted. When she translated sermons for Christians who came into Romania to encourage us in our difficult time of persecution, the truth of the Gospel had spoken to her heart, and she surrendered her life to the Lord Jesus.

But now, we needed to make arrangements to get a car in order to transport the Bibles from the agreed meeting place to Genovieva's house. We tried telephoning a man from church, but no one answered the phone. So we went to a house across from our church house and asked a man we knew there if we could borrow his car. This man was not a Christian, but he seemed to understand that every once in a while we had a desperate need for a car, and would kindly allow us to use his. He never asked what we needed it for.

Driving down the city streets, going about in circles, watching to see if we were followed; in a sense this was routine, and yet in another sense it was not. We could not do our thing in a routine manner, for that would be too suspicious. We must vary our course of action and meeting place every time.

It was dark and the street lights shone bravely among the dense linden trees as we approached our meeting place. We turned down the side street where shadows lay between the glow of the street lamps, and then we saw the car.

Silently, we opened the trunk of the car, and even as we went toward the other car, the woman was already in the back of the car, pushing packages toward the door.

One, two, three; the packages kept coming. Every time, I was amazed at how many packages could be hidden inside the body panels of the car. But there was no time to stare. We moved in extreme haste and yet with utmost caution.

In less than ten minutes the packages were removed, and the car was gone. This was the most crucial time, for if we would have been caught at this time, both the foreigners and we would have been accused of plotting against the government. The sooner the car could be unloaded and we could leave the meeting place, the safer it was for everyone. We knew that somehow, the couple would fill the empty places with something else. That way all the hollow places would sound the same at the border when the guards carefully tapped on all the side panels to check for hiding places. One could not afford to be careless. On the other hand, we were all firmly convinced that God many times heard our prayers and blinded the eyes of the searchers to some small telltale evidence that something unusual was going on.

We went back to Genovieva's house. Since there was a slight slope leading down to Genovieva's house, we shut the car motor off and coasted the last several meters of the way.

The drying sheets made a perfect screen for us as we entered the back gate, crossed the lawn and quickly carried the boxes into the underground root cellar. Anyone seeing us could have easily thought we were unloading garden produce and putting it away for winter use. Mama Maria had turned the radio to the classical station, and the symphony swelled into crescendos and diminuendos. I still think of our night work whenever I hear the classics of Mozart or Beethoven.

When at last we had taken all the Bibles underground, I went with Genovieva's brother *Costică* to take the car back. It was late and we were very tired, so neither of us talked very much.

As we drove along, I thought back to when I had told God that I was going to give Him everything—my hands, my feet, my entire life. When Genovieva had asked me to help with the work, the Spirit had reminded me of the promise I had made. So I had told Genovieva that I would help. Even though I knew the risks, I had never regretted my choice. It was very dangerous. No one in the free countries can know what we went through in knowing we were constantly in danger of arrest. The government was violently opposed to any foreigners bringing Bibles or other religious books into the country for distribution. All such books were considered contraband, and everyone who was involved in any type of this work faced fines and imprisonment if arrested.

But bringing Bibles into Romania was God's work. Of that I was sure. One incident when God worked a miracle and saved us from being discovered was very vivid in my memory. I closed my eyes and let the present slip away as I recalled that particular time.

We had just unloaded a shipment of Bibles into Genovieva's house. Suddenly the front door was thrown open and two secret police stormed in.

My heart leaped as I realized the predicament we were in. Most of the packages had already been stored in secret places, but there was still a suitcase of Bibles in the room we were in, right in front of the tile stove! That suitcase seemed extremely conspicuous and I had thought we were all caught red-handed!

Yet to look normal in any situation was so ingrained in us that we did not once glance at the suitcase with Bibles.

"Stay right where you are!" the harsh command was barked from the police officers. "Don't move!"

Since we were all in the same room, one officer sent Genovieva's niece, *Corina*, to summon two people as witnesses of what was happening. I know it seems ironic to ask for witnesses, but the police always wanted everything to appear legal. Two neighbor women came into the house; one stayed in the room with us, while the other one watched the secret policemen searching the rooms.

"Sir, what are you looking for?" Genovieva started to speak.

"Quiet!" roared the shorter of the two, who seemed to be the leader. "Don't speak!" he shrieked at us. "You will find out what we are looking for! Don't speak and don't move!"

The radio had played on. Beethoven's Ninth Symphony swelled into a crescendo. But our ears were next to oblivious to the music. I sensed rather than saw that the others were praying right along with me. "Please, God!" I begged, "You can close the eyes of these officers. I know You do miracles. You have proved Yourself so faithful in so many ways. You can do it again!"

———·—·—·—·—·—·—·—·—·—·—

While we were under guard, the officers ransacked the
house. They opened drawers and looked behind furniture.
We could hear them dragging furniture away from the walls.
They searched under the cots, looked into closets and
methodically checked every imaginable place.

When they had come back into the room where we were,
they continued their search. To me, that suitcase in the middle
of the room seemed to be so obvious. Why hadn't someone
pushed it under the bed? Oh, one of the officers kicked against
the corner of the suitcase! Surely he could feel that there was
something heavy in there. Something like books. Something
like Bibles!

We did not know for sure that they were searching for
Bibles. How did they even know we were doing anything they
said was illegal? What right did they have to come and search
the house? Had some neighbor been suspicious of unusual
activity and reported us?

But one thing I did know: I thought my heart would beat
so loudly that surely everyone in the room could hear it when
the short commander stood on the suitcase to look on top of
the stove. He strained and stood on his toes as he disturbed
the dust on top of the stove. Then he stepped off the suitcase
onto the floor and peered carefully behind the stove. Back on
the suitcase to make sure he had not missed anything. Oh,
when would he suddenly realize what he was standing on and
open the suitcase and find the Bibles? The suspense had been
horrible.

But all at once, a sweet peace had come over me. In my
prayer to God, I had asked Him to keep the police from finding
the Bibles. And suddenly I was at peace. I did not know if the
officers would find the Bibles or not, but because I had placed
this nerve-wracking episode into the hands of the almighty
God, I was at rest. I looked at the others. It was as if the sweet
peace from heaven itself was in that room. Genovieva was
looking idly at the floor, while Mama Maria and the others
were calmly standing in a line, looking as if this were an

ordinary happening.

I don't know how long those officers searched. But they did not find any Bibles. Not once did they even as much as glance at the suitcase that they continually walked around.

After they had left, without a word to each other, we sank to our knees in prayer. How we praised God! How we blessed His name! Our hearts were overflowing with His wonderful love to us for giving us His presence and for closing the eyes of those men. We trembled at the power and majesty of our God. How worthy His name is to be praised!

—·—·—·—·—·—·—·—·—·—·—·—

I came out of my reverie with a start. We had arrived at my apartment, and Costică walked with me to my door. After I was inside my apartment, I suddenly realized how tired I was. I had been up since four o'clock that morning, and now it was ten minutes before one. I still needed to wash out my skirt so I would have something clean to wear to work tomorrow.

But I still had time. Time to pray and to talk with God. Time to thank Him that another shipment of Bibles was safely in hiding. "How good God is," I thought, and went to get my skirt.

1961 - Silvia at age 10, as a fourth grader in elementary school.

Silvia (standing) was baptized at her home church in Iaşi, on December 22, 1968.

1975 - It is a common practice in Romania for young people to present programs in church services. Here some of the youth are singing at the church in Iași. Silvia is standing in the front row on the far right.

1976 - Silvia at age 25

1976-1977 - The children's choir, directed by Genovieva and Silvia, at a church that invited them to sing. Elena Boghian is in the back row on the far right. Silvia in the third row, the second from the right.

1978 - Co-workers of the factory where Silvia was a department manager. Silvia is in the front row, third from left.

Prison in Timişoara where Silvia and Elena were held for two and a half months.

1982 - Silvia, with her Tata and Mama in pastor Iosif Morcan's house. Silvia and Elena hid for a few months in a back room of this house after they came out of prison. Because they didn't have any jobs, the police had been watching them. Silvia's father brought them fresh bread every so often.

Front row, L to R - Dănuț, Margareta, Nuți, and Silvia.
Back row, L to R - Fănel, Mihai, Rodica, Costel, and Victor.
In July 1989, six years after she left Romania, Silvia is reunited with her brothers and sisters in Constanța, Romania. Because the country was still communist and Silvia's family was scattered, she was afraid the secret police would push her out of the country before she could see all of them on this trip.

14

Questioned

The next morning it was hard to get out of bed and go to work. It seemed every muscle in my body was tired. But I had to be at work by four-thirty and I knew better than reporting late for work.

The sky was beginning to show a tinge of light in the east as I hurried to the factory. This factory was the second largest of its kind in all of Romania. Since we now assembled transistor radios, tape recorders, and ship radios, our country was no longer dependent on wares shipped in from other countries. We were to be a model of socialist efficiency. All of us workers knew that. We were constantly upbraided by the company officials and urged to do our very best.

Another shipment of parts had arrived after I had left for Genovieva's house last evening. Since our factory worked two shifts, there was no way of telling exactly when a shipment of parts would come. But I was the only one of the workers who had a key for my department, so the boxes were waiting for me to open and add to the inventory.

I was soon busy. I enjoyed making orderly lists of all the parts that were there, and could at any time give an exact inventory of everything in my department. I knew it would be easy for the workers on the assembly line to "take" some of these small parts home and build or repair some electronic machine they had. I had appealed to everyone, telling them I kept an accurate inventory at all times of what I had. Whenever parts were taken out, I not only crossed them off my list, but I also wrote down who took them and when. It seemed to work, because I was never accused of coming up short on some part.

Stocking the parts took most of the morning. I was looking forward to the brief lunch break when the door to my department opened.

"The supervisor wants to see you," the supervisor's secretary announced importantly, then left.

This was not too uncommon, although I did wonder what plan Mr. *Nedelcu* wanted to discuss with me. Usually, the department head of this section of the factory summoned me to the office if there were any questions or suggestions that needed to be discussed.

As I walked down the green-tiled hall, I marveled again at how well my job had been going. All through school I had been labeled as a "repentant." I still had many memories of being mocked, and of the teachers telling me I would never be able to hold a responsible position because I believed in some imaginary thing called God. I was told I would end up in some construction job or sweeping the streets. But now, I had landed a job in this prestigious factory. I straightened my shoulders and knocked on the supervisor's office door.

Mr. Nedelcu was sitting behind his desk, looking at some papers that were stacked on his desk. But I could see that he was not reading the papers.

"Come in," he looked up briefly as I came in. "Um—shut the door, and—and take a seat."

Something about the way he talked alerted me. This was not his usual way of greeting me whenever he wanted to talk to me. His brisk, businesslike tone of voice was gone.

He picked up a pen from the array of pens on his desktop and slowly slid it through his fingers.

I sat on the wooden chair facing him and waited. The faint hum of the fluorescent light overhead was the only sound in the room.

Suddenly, he placed the pen on his desk. He looked at me and in a quiet, yet worried tone he asked, "Silvia, what did you do? What have you done?"

"Why?" I asked in surprise. "Why do you ask?"

He did not answer right away, but dropped his eyes and picked up his pen again. "I had a visitor," he stated simply.

"From the secret police!"

I was instantly alert. What did they know? Were those two men yesterday at the botanical gardens spying on us? Had we been watched as we unloaded the precious cargo from the foreign car to ours? Had they shadowed us as we went back to Genovieva's house and hid the Bibles? My thoughts went tumbling over each other, yet I forced myself to remain calm.

I tried to ask in a normal tone, "What did they want?" In spite of my efforts at control, it didn't sound like my voice.

"They asked all kinds of questions about you." His eyes were kind, yet there was a distinct look of anxiety in them. "They asked about your work here, your character, your habits, what you say and do with the other workers, and all kinds of things."

"What did you say?" I wondered.

"Silvia," he began. "You know how much I appreciate the work you do. We all know that you keep your department in such order that you can give us an immediate inventory of whatever is in your charge. There was nothing that I could tell them about any problems with your coworkers. So, I told them you are a good worker.

"Of course, I told them, when they asked, that you are not a member of the communist party. But I knew I did not need to tell them that. They already knew most of the things I told them about you. Silvia, they are watching you! And I want to warn you!"

Mr. Nedelcu looked nervously around the walls. He lowered his voice. "Whatever you do, be careful! The secret police are watching you!" He said it again. "They know a lot about your activities! Be careful!"

I stood up to leave. There was nothing I could say. Even though I was glad for the warning, I could not thank the supervisor for warning me. That could be used against me, because it would mean I all but admitted to illegal activities. It was better to say nothing.

Again the supervisor looked straight at me. "You know, Silvia, that we appreciate the work you do here, and your part in making our factory one of the best in Romania. I can always depend on you to do your work, even if you have to stay late.

You know, you would make a wonderful member of the party. People like you are just what we need to make this country great. Devotion to your work, willingness to get along with other people, and being interested in the production of our factory for the good of the country. There is nothing against you, except your faith in—in your God."

Not once since I had started working here had I tried to hide the fact that I was a Christian. God was too real for me to be silent about Him. Sure, I was mocked and scorned by those who were considered modern and progressive, ridiculed by being asked loudly at mealtimes if I had "prayed yet," and openly scorned when I spoke of what was right and wrong. But I was still determined, whatever the cost, to speak in defense of my Savior, Jesus Christ.

"Sir, the very things you mentioned—being dedicated to the job, friendly, and interested in production—all these things come because I do serve God. That is what makes me do these things. The party cannot make new people. Some idea of man will never change people into productive, useful workers. You have seen that right here in our own factory. Those who preach the idealism of communism are sometimes the most dishonest and deceptive of all. They are not changed inside. The reason I do what I do is because of Christ in me. He makes the difference in my life. I am what I am because I love Him. Don't you understand?"

I knew the words I had just said were dangerous words. To speak against the party was considered treason. But I dared witness to the supervisor. I felt we knew each other well enough that I dared be honest. Besides, I wanted to show him why I was what I was. It was Christ in me.

"All I can say, Silvia, is, please be careful. The secret police are out to get you."

I went back to my job. Yes, my mind went to all kinds of dire possibilities for my future. And I remembered how fortunate I had felt, on my way to the supervisor's office, to not have had any problems on this job. It was a short-lived feeling.

I wondered if perhaps my involvement in the children's choir was the reason the police had come to question the supervisor at my place of work. We all knew how much the government officials hated when young people and children began attending church. Our church people rejoiced to see an ever-growing number of children coming to sing in the choir. But the very fact that there was a constant harassment and persecution of our people, was enough evidence that the police and high officials were upset. Our constitution granted us freedom of religion, but there were other ways of repression. Christians were intimidated with threats; promotions at their jobs were denied; and, probably most wearing of all, they were constantly shadowed by the secret police and informers.

Since Genovieva and I were the leaders of the children's choir, we expected to be under the careful scrutiny of the law. Children were the hope of the communist party. And here we were, daring to teach the children about the very God the party insisted did not exist. No wonder they were extremely upset and determined to make life hard for us. But I really had not expected that they would come to my place of work and ask questions. This was a dangerous situation.

It is sometimes hard to explain just how dangerous it was to work with children under the communist governments. Because so many of the socialist ideas were to ignore God and to make the philosophy of the state the religion of all people, anyone who opposed the government teaching faced severe persecution. And because the work we were doing with the children in the church went directly against the ideas of our government, I knew that the police were watching our every move. It was well worth their time to shadow anyone who was teaching the young generation anything different from what was promoted among the Young Pioneers. So, I knew that the visit from the secret police to my place of work was indeed a sign of how serious they thought our work was in the church.

But as I was going about my work that afternoon, whenever the fear of persecution would rear its ugly head, I had a refuge to turn to. The memory of my Tata stopping whatever he was doing and kneeling down and crying out to God was like a vision from heaven. I could tell God all about it. Didn't He answer my prayers when I was small and determined to find out if He existed? Didn't He show me that

He knew all about me, and that He knew my size? Yes, God knew my size. He knew all that I would have to suffer for the sake of Christ, but He promised that He would never leave me nor forsake me.

All during my growing-up years, I was being prepared for just such a time as this. Our pastor, dear Brother Marcu, had constantly encouraged us that *when*, not *if*, we would be persecuted, there was One Who would stand by our side.

How much I had already been watched, I did not know. But one thing I knew, there was One Who was watching over me. Watching out for me.

As I finished up that evening and started for home, it seemed like all my senses were extremely alert. That man sitting there on the bench outside my factory—did he really just want to see where I went after work? Did I really see someone step hastily into the building as I rounded the corner to go to my apartment?

When I prayed that night, I told the Lord that I still meant it when I had told Him I would serve Him with my whole life. Regardless of what would happen, I would place my life into His hands and rest there. In spite of the disturbing events of the day, I slept peacefully.

In the days that followed, I was constantly aware of being shadowed. At times I was followed on my way home from work. We were certain that there were informers in many of our church services. At work, I had to be constantly on guard against anything that could be used to incriminate me. We were well aware of the secret police's tactics. The Christian's first offense was being a Christian. But, since we were supposed to have religious freedom under our constitution, some other charge, real or imaginary, could be used to arrest us. And I was determined that no real charge could be laid against me.

For instance, one day a lady from a department similar to mine came and asked to borrow 60 parts from my stock.

"I will return them as soon as I get my next shipment," she pleaded.

I knew that as soon as she would leave with the parts, an impromptu inventory could be declared. If I was short on any parts, I could be charged with stealing them.

"I will have to check with my boss," I told her.

"No," she protested, "I will be getting a shipment soon, and I will be in trouble if I don't have the parts for my department to work with today. Can you please let me have them?"

"I'm sorry, ma'am, but I cannot let anything go out of my department without permission from my boss. You know we are to be very strict about where all our parts go. Just the other day, the supervisor said that the problem of workers secretly taking parts home is growing. I know all of us are being watched closely. Perhaps even by the secret police." I watched her reaction closely.

She quickly looked away from me. "Ah—no. The secret police aren't in this factory."

"Then why is that man standing behind the partly-closed door every morning when we report to work? Why does he watch carefully where we put our coats and bags? And why are our personal items in our bags rearranged sometimes in the evenings?" I questioned.

"Why would I know all those things? If you are not going to let me have what I need, I'll have to do something else. I thought I could depend on you! You always say you want to help people!" she flung out bitterly as she turned and left. I was quite certain she did not need the parts and that it was a setup to frame me.

"God, I need Your wisdom. I cannot walk carefully enough on my own to keep out of the traps that are set to catch me. Help me, Lord."

One night when Genovieva came to my door, I knew immediately what she wanted. Help. Help to smuggle Bibles into a hiding place.

I hesitated. The pressures at my job seemed to be increasing. I was constantly alert to the shadows that stalked me and my activities. I thought most of the attention I was getting was because of my work with the children's choir, but I wasn't sure. Perhaps the police did know something about our work with the Bibles. And if we were caught handling contraband goods, I knew my job at the factory would be finished and I would probably be tried in the courts and jailed. So I hesitated.

I tried to reason with myself. Wasn't it more important to work with the children and teach them to sing and to learn about the Bible? Should I become involved again with Bible smuggling? Should I endanger my job, perhaps even my life?

My life? What is my life? Do I have a right to call a life that was bought with the precious blood of Jesus my own life?

"I'll come," I told Genovieva. I was willing to give my life for the sake of getting the Word of God into the hands of our people. I would continue in the work. At times it was not easy to decide to go on with this work. I was not always brave and confident that everything would work out all right. But, every time I was again involved with any of God's work, I was so blessed by His faithfulness and goodness to me that I repented of my doubts and worries about myself.

All during the 70's, there was a strong push from the communist party to project an image of strength and of nationalism. They wanted to prove to their own people and to all the world that the idealistic society was at work here and in other socialist countries. In consequence, any other people, especially Christians, were targeted for persecution and harassment.

Our children's choir became increasingly noticeable as we continued traveling to other churches to sing. When we left by train, there was always an air of excitement about us as we boarded the train and found our seats. Other passengers would watch and often some would ask questions. What group of the Young Pioneers did we represent? What? No uniforms? Who were we? Sing! In churches? How interesting!

Here was something very unusual. The choir was not a group of children legally traveling under the approval of any government official. None of us leaders were trained or licensed. And yet there were too many of us for the officials to handle.

Since we sang every Sunday evening at our church, it was easy for informers or plain clothes police to sit in and observe. Many times we could spot some different face in the audience as the program was given. At such times, I would pray that somehow the message of the songs the children were singing would penetrate some heart and the official could come to repentance and find Jesus for his life.

In spite of the constant threat of imprisonment, being in God's work was such a joy. Many times as the happy voices of the children rang out, my thoughts went to my childhood. I remembered the nights we would sing ourselves to sleep. I remembered our times of singing at church after services. Those days seemed long ago now, and yet, here we were, still teaching children about God's wonderful love. At times like this, the very heavens seemed to open and pour out blessings upon us. We were doing God's work.

15

Interrogations

The room I was waiting in was almost bare. The walls were painted an institutional gray halfway up, and the top part of the walls and the ceiling were a chalky white. One bare light bulb hung suspended from the middle of the room, and the harsh glare was reflected in little points on the shiny walls. A large, battered metal desk was facing me. The only thing on top of the desk was a round, muddy pink planter with a scraggly vine draped despondently over the sides. The vine was mostly stalk; only a few brave leaves grew at the very tip of each stem. The soil in the planter was dry and cracked.

The hard plastic chair I had been sitting on since nine that morning was definitely not designed for the human body, I decided as I shifted myself around again. I decided against standing to change positions, because I had the eerie feeling that I was being watched. Besides the door leading into the corridor, there was also a window on the wall behind the desk. The window was small and almost at the very top of the wall. It was completely dark on the other side of the glass, there was not even any reflection of the light bulb that blazed so brightly. Since the chair I was sitting on faced that window, I had the distinct impression that somewhere, a pair of eyes was staring at every move I made.

I checked my watch discreetly. If someone was watching, I was determined not to show that I was getting impatient. Perhaps if I looked calm and composed, they would get tired of waiting to see me become impatient.

And I did have much to meditate on. For instance, why I was there.

Once again, I wondered exactly how much the secret police knew about our activities. I knew they were increasingly upset as our church work with the children grew. But I still did not know how much they knew about our work with the Bibles. Just last week, I had helped Genovieva and Elena *Boghian* unload a shipment of Bibles. Elena was a Christian girl from *Suceava* whom I had met at a church service in Iaşi. She was going to college in my home town, and we had become close friends.

I remembered how Genovieva, Elena and I had worked together in order to make sure no one saw the car loaded with Bibles enter the church yard. Because Elena was slim and lithe, she had quickly climbed the tree in front of the church house so she could peer out between the leaves and watch to see if it was safe for the car to turn into the gate. I had hidden behind a bush, ready to swing wide the yard gate as soon as Elena gave me the all clear signal. Genovieva watched from the window facing the street, ready to open the church doors and help get the boxes inside as quickly as possible. This time there must not have been any secret police driving by on the first round the car made, because Elena called to me right away. Sometimes we had to wait until we were sure no one was sitting in some parked car watching the church house. If that happened, the car with the Bibles had to drive on down the road and come back later to see if everything was clear. Of course, that meant a long time for Elena to hide in the tree. But this only worked in the summertime, for in the winter there was no foliage to hide the spectacle of a grown woman in a tree!

We had found a perfect hiding place for the Bibles under the platform in the church house. We put the Bibles in the small, hollow space. But when we replaced the wooden platform, we discovered we had stacked the Bibles a little too high, and the platform rocked slightly.

When Pastor Cruceru walked across the platform to stand behind the podium to preach the last Sunday, the floor rocked slightly under his feet. I had looked at Genovieva and caught her eye. I almost had to smile now at how it seemed to have dawned on both of us almost at the same time. The pastor was literally standing on the Word of God! And during the message, whenever he made reference to standing on God's Word, we exchanged glances and smiled. His words were true!

But I was no longer sitting in church under Pastor Cruceru's encouraging words. I was sitting in the police station, wondering if we were going to have to sit here all day. I say we, because Genovieva had also been summoned to the police station. But we had not been allowed to speak to each other, and I was hastily shoved into this room and the door was locked behind me. I had almost groaned when I heard the key turn in the lock. Then I had seen the window, and felt unseen eyes watching.

When I had been waiting for over three hours, I heard footsteps approaching my room at the end of the hall. There was a slight pause, the door-knob rattled as the key was inserted, and, almost majestically, the door opened.

The officer who entered was middle-aged, his gray suit impressively decorated with stripes and his black, wavy hair carefully combed. His mouth was turned up at the corners as he turned to face me. But the dark-brown eyes that looked squarely into my face matched exactly the eyes that I had imagined had been watching me through the high window. Piercing eyes. Eyes that tried to penetrate into the secrets of minds and drag everything out into the open.

Even as he tried to smile, I felt myself instinctively prepare for interrogation. He crossed the room and sat behind the desk. The chair rolled forward silently. Without a word, he dropped a paper file onto his desk and opened it. He pulled a pen from his pocket and clicked the top. Then once more, he looked at me. He tried to appear relaxed as he leaned back. He crossed his legs and tapped his fingers on his knee.

"Well, Silvia Tărniceriu, we know all about your activities. We have been watching you and we know everything about you. We know everything about you, so there is absolutely no use that you try to hide anything from us. Anything," he repeated.

Then he smiled his oily, slick smile. "So, you may as well confess everything. You may as well tell us anything we want to know."

I couldn't help but saying, "Then there must not be anything you want to know, because you said you know everything about me."

Instantly his smile vanished. "Oh, so we have a smart one, do we? I tell you, you won't get far this way! I will ask what I will, and I want only the truth from you!" His words were said in a low, sinister voice, and his eyes narrowed into slits.

"Who were those foreigners you talked with last week?" His words shot out of his mouth like ammunition from a machine gun.

So they did know about the Bible couriers! I wondered if they had made it safely back across the border.

"I am asking you a question. Who were those people you were talking with?" the officer had abandoned his low tone. Again he shot out his words.

"Well, I really don't think I can answer you. I had never seen them before." I stalled for time, trying to find out exactly how much he knew.

"Then why did you talk to them?" he barked.

I decided against saying anything about his claim to know all about me. It would probably infuriate him even more. "They wanted to know about life in Romania," I told him honestly.

"Huh! And what did you tell them?"

"I told them about our everyday life, and church activities," I stated briefly.

"What were their names?" he asked next.

"Their names were Peter and Matthew," I said.

"What are their last names?"

"I don't know."

"You don't know! You talk with foreigners for over two hours and you don't know their last names! Where are they from?"

I hesitated then said, "I really can't tell you anything more than what I have already told you. I didn't check into their history, didn't ask how they got here, or ask them about their families."

"Then what did you talk about? Two hours is a long time

to be together."

"We sang and prayed. We talked about the Bible and shared about what we do in our churches."

"Ha, you talked about what you do in your churches. Did you tell them how you are brainwashing young children and encouraging them to rise against the government? Did you tell them that you are engaged in illegal activities and go places without permission?"

"Sir, I told them that in Romania, we are guaranteed religious freedom to worship God in the way we choose. And, yes, we did talk about the children's choir and how the young children love to learn about God and how they love to sing songs about Jesus. Yes, I did tell them that."

The officer abruptly stood up. His face became flushed and he leaned over his desk and pointed his finger at me. "You will see!" he hissed. "You think you are so smart! Well, I tell you. If you won't slip on the ice, you will find yourself slipping on the pavement!" He paused as if to let his words sink in. "We will find out about all your activities!"

All afternoon and into the evening, he questioned me. Sometimes he tried his oily, slick, imitation kindness that was very hard for me to bear, and other times he tried his shouting, threatening tactics. Through it all, I discovered a lot of how much they actually knew about my activities.

They knew when I went to work and when I usually went home, but not why I left the factory late at times. They knew I had talked with foreigners the week before. Oh, yes, they also knew that I had traveled on the trolley bus to buy a pair of shoes. That I found interesting. Someone must have trailed me halfway across the city, probably sure I was on some clandestine errand, only to find out I was going to buy a pair of shoes. But they also knew the last time I had gone home to see Tata and Mama and the family. So, I knew I was being watched and trailed.

When I was bone weary, the officer abruptly stood up and strode around the desk. He opened the door and said, "Report to our office tomorrow morning at eight o'clock. Do not go anywhere. Do not talk to anyone about what happened here today. If you do, we will find it out!"

I got up and walked out the door. It seemed almost unreal to be walking again. I walked down the corridor and when I went into the reception room, there was Genovieva.

"Genovieva!" I called out and as she turned to face me, we embraced. It was such a relief to see a friendly face again.

On the way home, of course we talked. Talked and shared our experiences, wept and prayed together. She, too, was to go back to the police station the next day. Our hearts were heavy as we thought of another day of merciless probing by the intimidating officers. We had no idea how this would end. The thought of arrest and imprisonment was very real. Ever more frequently we were hearing of sudden disappearances of prominent Christian leaders. There were reports of cruel beatings and of interrogations. And we both realized that we could easily share the same fate.

16

Pressure

"**W**hy did you go to work?" the officer screamed at me. "I told you to go nowhere, say nothing to anyone, and to come here this morning! And then, when you didn't show up, I called to your place of work, and they say, "Yes, Silvia Tărniceriu is here." And after I strictly told you to go nowhere! What do you think this is? A theater?"

I was sitting in the same chair I had sat in all day the day before. The same officer was behind the desk, but this time he was raging. His dark-brown eyes glared at me.

"Answer me. Why did you go to work, after I strictly told you to go nowhere?"

"Sir," I replied quietly. "I have a responsibility to my job. If I don't report for work, our entire department is not able to get our quota done for the day. And I know if I miss three days of work without a legal excuse, I can lose my job. It was too late last night after I left here to tell anyone to take over for me. So, I felt responsible for my job and I went to work. I had to catch up for all the time I missed yesterday. Sorry, I will not answer any more questions unless you call my supervisor and let him know where I am now and why I left early."

"You do not realize where you are!" the officer screamed. "You think you can just do what you want to. When I tell you something, you must do it! You could get years of time in jail for disobeying me. Don't you realize that?"

"I realize that I have a responsibility to my country by being at my job whenever I can," I answered. "And I will try to be there if at all possible."

This started another long tirade against me. I was told that

I was not aware of where I was, the power they had over me, the responsibility that I had to the police officers, and on and on.

I just sat there and looked at him as he raged. I felt sorry for him. He wanted to impress me with the power he had over me and how I must listen to him. And yet, he seemed powerless to do anything about it. I was reminded of the Pharaoh in ancient Egypt who tried to prevent the Israelites from leaving the land of Egypt. God had limited the Pharaoh's power over the children of Israel, and I knew that God still limited the power of these officials. I could rest in knowing that God was in control here, not this raging man.

When the officer realized that I was not going to answer any questions until he had called my place of work and informed my supervisor where I was, he tried to call.

When Mr. Nedelcu heard that an officer was calling him, he hung up.

"That crazy man!" the officer yelled. "What kind of idiot do you work for?"

"Let me talk to him, and explain why I am not at work," I quietly told him.

He hesitated a moment, then he dialed the number and handed the receiver to me. When Mr. Nedelcu answered, I briefly told him where I was. There was a short pause at the other end of the line, then he said, "Oh," and hung up.

All the while, the policeman was fuming and fussing. When the call was over, he abruptly got up, left the room, and again I heard the key turning in the lock. A prisoner again!

Is this how it would feel to be in jail? I wondered. Being locked up in this cheerless room had such a depressing effect. I had no idea how long this was going to last, or if I was going to be tried in some sham court and jailed. As far as I knew, I had not done anything against the laws of my country. I knew that handling the Bibles that were brought into the country illegally could be held against me, but I was not sure whether I could be tried for that. And I felt clear in my conscience that even if helping with the Bibles was illegal, the higher authority of God's command to spread the Gospel gave us the right to "obey God rather than men."

Yes, I was still glad that even though it meant all this interrogation, I had been willing to do the work of God. I had dedicated my entire life to serve my Jesus, and I was not regretting my decision to surrender my life to Him.

On Wednesday, and on Thursday again, Genovieva and I were summoned to the police station. Surprisingly, every morning I was still allowed to report to work, organize my department, and try to keep up with what I could until I was ordered to report to the dreaded room.

The endless questioning, the repetitious tirades against the Christians, and the long, long periods of sitting alone in the room were designed to wear me down. Late one evening, an officer opened the door and brought Genovieva into the room.

"Genovieva!" I opened my arms wide. We embraced so fervently and lovingly that the officer asked, "How long is it since you have seen each other?"

I looked at him. "We saw each other last night."

He shook his head. "And you are that glad to see each other again after having only been apart one day?"

Suddenly he seemed to have some pressing business and left us together in the room.

Genovieva moved her finger across her mouth and shook her head slightly. I knew she meant that we should not say anything that could incriminate us. There were probably listening ears somewhere to see what we would reveal as we talked about our interrogations.

So, we started to sing. Genovieva sang in her soft soprano and I sang alto. We sang a new song we had just learned. "The Lord is knocking at your door, You must open to Him."

On Friday, as I climbed the stairs to the police station once more, it was hard to force my legs into action. My entire body seemed to be rebelling against the coming ordeal. My mind kept going over and over the absolute senselessness of sitting in the same room, being asked the same questions, and being told the same things day after day. One part of me fought against the wearying ordeal. And yet, there was a part of my mind that told me that this boring repetition, this dread of the unknown, and the seeming senselessness of the entire episode, was all a part of the plan of the police. A plan of wearing us down, scaring us, making us fear the consequences if we did not listen to them and stop our Christian activities.

All day Friday, I was by myself. Not one time did any officers come to question me. After the second day, a different officer had come, and when the door unlocked I never knew who would come in to interrogate me. Even though the officers were different, their tactics were very similar—verbal abuse, screaming, or, worst of all, the fake friendliness some of them used to get information.

But one officer was different. After the usual questions about who I was, where I lived, and what activities I was engaged in, he asked me where I worked. When he found that I was employed at the electronics factory, he began asking questions about the transistor radios and tape recorders we assembled. When he found out that we also assembled ship radio transmitters, he told me about the time he spent on board the Romanian ships during his duty in the navy.

For over an hour we had visited. When another officer came to call him to report, I heard him say as they locked the door, "She is an educated person! She knows all about the assembly of transistor radios! I can talk intelligently with her!"

I knew that most of the communists thought all of us Christians were ignorant and unskilled. We were considered the scum of society, unproductive and therefore unnecessary. I guess this officer was surprised that we were normal, intelligent persons.

On this Friday evening, I was having an especially difficult time pushing off discouragement. It was Good Friday, and our church was having a communion service that night. The news of our interrogations had quickly spread through our church. Many people were praying for us, and we felt those prayers. It was really hard on me to think we would have to miss out on this meaningful worship service. I wanted so desperately to be there. All week Genovieva and I had been coming to this place. There had been no change, no variety from day to day. I had a foreboding feeling that soon we would not be allowed to leave. And we so longed to attend this communion service —perhaps the last one we could participate in for a long time.

When an officer finally marched into the room, I was ready

for him. I stood up and walked toward him before he had a chance to sit down.

"Sir," I began, "this evening is a special night at our church. We are having communion tonight and Genovieva and I do want to go. This may be our last time. I know that you are planning to do something with us girls, and I have such a longing to go back to our dear brothers and sisters and commune with them one more time. They are praying for us. Will you please let us go?" My voice quivered and I had to blink back the tears that wanted to come to my eyes. "Please, sir, let us go early tonight, so we can go to church."

The officer looked at the floor, and then back at me. "Are you crazy?" he asked. "Are you trying to convert me? And the church is praying for you? So, they know you are here? How many other people know you are here?"

"I don't know how many other people know," I told him. "But, yes, our friends from church know we are here. Our families know and when we are in trouble we ask other believers to pray for us. That is the strength of our fellowship."

Instead of speaking in his usual disgusted voice, there was a different tone in his words. "You are asking me to release you so you can go to church?" He shook his head as if he couldn't believe what he was hearing. He looked away from my face again and said nothing.

"Can you still get there on time?" he suddenly asked.

Hope surged in my heart. I couldn't speak, so I just nodded my head.

"I must be crazy," he said ruefully. "But I will take you there!" Then his voice assumed the normal brisk tone he had used earlier, "But you must be back here in the office on Monday morning!"

Our feet had wings as we joyfully went to his car out the back door. I could not believe that we were being taken to church by one of the very officers who had interrogated us!

All tiredness left us. No matter that we had been sitting all day at the police station and that we hadn't eaten anything since morning. We felt like we imagined Peter had felt when the angel had delivered him from prison. We were overcome with joy!

141

When we opened the church house door to enter, the congregation was singing the first song. Everyone could see us come in since we came in by the side door. The singing died out and with joyful exclamations of "Praise the Lord!" and "Hallelujah!" the entire congregation rose to greet us.

"Brethren and sisters!" the pastor's voice called out, "Let us kneel and thank God that he allowed our dear sisters, Genovieva and Silvia, to be with us tonight as we celebrate the death and resurrection of our Lord Jesus Christ. Our prayers have been answered!"

We all knelt. And as we lifted our voices and cried and praised God, all of us praying out loud and thanking God for His mercies to us, again the doors of heaven opened and we were in a holy place. The sweet presence of the Holy Spirit was filling the house we were in and with one accord we praised the One Who had allowed us to come. How glorious that communion service was!

----·--·-·--·--·--·--·-·--·--·-·-

That Easter weekend in 1977, an unusual event shook our entire country. Some said that it was because God was angry with the rulers of the nation. Others said it was because the police were persecuting the Christians. Even those who professed that they did not believe in God were silent at the demonstration of power and destruction that the mighty earthquake in Romania caused that early spring.

Homes and office buildings were ruined and destroyed. People were killed. Others, homeless and destitute, wandered around in a daze. On the streets, people said in fearful voices that God was judging our country for our great wickedness.

The earthquake must have also affected the officers at the police station. On Monday morning when we reported once more, we sensed a different feeling in the air as we were met and escorted to our separate rooms. We were regarded with something that was almost respect.

"Write a report about how you feel about our country," the officer said when I was seated in my usual chair. "We want a statement from you telling us that you are willing to be a law-abiding citizen of Romania."

At first I looked at him in amazement. This was almost ludicrous. Was I a schoolchild that I needed to write a report on my country?

As the officer sat at his desk, I took the paper and pencil he gave me and wrote. I wrote that I wanted to be a productive member of the society of Romania. I wrote that I wanted to promote the right things and help make our country a better place to live. Finally, I wrote that I was glad our country allowed the people religious freedom and the right to serve God.

After I handed my report to him, the officer placed it on his desk without reading it. "We will tell you when we want you again," were his amazing words!

As Genovieva and I left, we were almost giddy with joy. With a mighty shake of the earth, God had displayed to all the people of Romania Who has all power. And—we were firmly convinced—that was why we were so suddenly released. Even the seemingly hardened police officers were smitten by the reality of God's power. We rejoiced that we were recognized as His children. I still believe that is why we were released instead of put into prison. It was as though we had escaped the hungry mouth of the lions.

At least for now.

17

Failed

I awoke with a start, but the rhythmical "clack clack" of the train wheels on the track didn't sound any different from what they had the entire night we had been traveling. I had dozed off and on, waking whenever we stopped at a station. Always thankful whenever the train was in motion once more, I wondered again and again whether we had made the right decision.

I looked at Elena. Her slight body was curled up on the train seat as best she could, and she was sleeping. Her fine-boned profile was etched against the train window. I looked outside. The sky was beginning to light up in the east.

I checked our bags on the overhead shelf. We each had two bags, a large one and a small one. It seemed strange to have everything in two bags. To have left everything else behind.

We had intentionally done as little as possible for our departure. There had been no farewells, no last-minute heart-to-heart talks, no distributing of personal items. We had not even told our families what we were about to do.

It was better that way. We had learned long ago that it is very important to have as few people as possible involved in any plan. Not only so the news would not leak out, but also for the safety of those who were left behind and questioned by the police.

I looked at Elena again. I was glad she could sleep. Although she looked frail, I knew my friend had the courage and determination she needed to go with me. What a dear friend she was! Together, we had made plans to escape the country.

Yes, escape from Romania. Escape into Yugoslavia, and then eventually into the United States.

———·——·——·——·——·——·——·——·——

The events of the past four years had led us to this decision. There had been the constant harassment of being spied on by the secret police. Even after we had been dismissed from the daily interrogations at the police station, we were still trailed as we went about our lives. Hardly ever was I involved with Bible work anymore because I was a main suspect, and my journeys were constantly shadowed. Our work with the children's choir continued. But we operated under the strain of knowing that in many of our services, informers were seated among the audience. They watched our every move, taking note of who was in charge and making files of each one of the pastors and teachers.

One anxiety-ridden weekend in particular had filled us with apprehension. That was the weekend after Brother *Iosif Tzon's* booklet, *The Place of a Christian in a Socialist Society*, had been read over Radio Free Europe. This radio station was based in the West and broadcast into the socialist countries. Brother Tzon was a highly respected Christian in our circles, and he had carefully documented cases of people being fined because they were Christians, of Christian students being persecuted in school, and of the Christians' constant danger of arrest. His writings included stories of poor people who were fined severely for owning a Bible. In one case, the family had to sell their cow in order to pay the fine. Everyone knew that for a poor family to lose their cow put them on the brink of starvation.

This manifest brought recriminations to the church leaders. How the booklet had been smuggled into the West, I don't know, but as soon as it was read, it seemed like the police popped out of hiding and swarmed around the church people like a swarm of buzzing bees.

That the police had been keeping track of the religious leaders was very evident. They immediately surrounded Brother Tzon's house and marched in and arrested him. He was whisked into a car and taken to Bucharest.

I had known immediately that I was also in danger. Before Brother Tzon had sent the manuscript out, six other people had signed the work, stating that this indeed was the truth of conditions in Romania. My signature was one of those six on the manifest.

When Brother Tzon's wife wanted to go to Bucharest to see what would happen to her husband, Genovieva and I went with her. We lodged at Brother *Niculescu's* house in Bucharest. While we were there, the police came and arrested Brother Niculescu. I remember with what dignity Brother Niculescu answered the door. In spite of the rude, shouting officer who had come to arrest him, that godly brother spoke calmly and went peacefully with the enraged little man.

The three pastors who had been involved in signing this book were interrogated all day Sunday, beaten and abused, and then finally released. The small band of us Christians in Brother Niculescu's house were shocked at the treatment they had received, but the brethren rejoiced that they had been counted worthy of suffering for the cause of Christ. Even though they and we were still in danger, we had knelt and praised God for being our comfort in times of persecution. The testimony of having been able to speak for the sake of the suffering people of Romania was a real encouragement to the church.

This was only one event that had made me decide to leave the country. Another was when my dear friend Genovieva, through contacts she had made with the Bible couriers, obtained a visa and left Romania for New York. We were able to write to each other, and she had let me know that she missed me and wanted me to join her.

That was when I went to the police station and requested permission to leave the country.

"I am tired of being watched by the secret police. If you don't like what I am doing here, let me leave the country. I will go where I can serve God the way I need to," I had told them.

For several minutes the head official couldn't speak. His face got red and he shouted at me, "Serve who? You get out of here! You are mentally sick. There is no way you can leave this country alive!"

I had been literally shoved out of the office.

Furthermore, my niece, *Gabi*, had died. When her arm first pained her, she had mentioned it to her parents, my brother Mihai and his wife. It kept getting worse, so they had taken her to a doctor. The doctor diagnosed it as a form of arthritis and sent her home. But it was soon apparent that something was seriously wrong with her arm. It swelled up, and when lesions appeared they again took her to a doctor. By then it was too late to do anything, for cancer had already spread throughout her arm and was affecting the rest of her body.

To see my dear 18-year-old niece suffer was very hard on all of us. I spent hours with her after work and spent the nights and weekends with her. When she was still able to go to the park, we would take a small lunch and spend all day outside. Finally, she became too weak to leave the house, and I would sit by her bedside, attending to her needs and singing to her. In the last stages of her illness, her dressings had to be changed continually because her muscle tissue was rotting and falling away in large pieces. But her patience and her sweet disposition kept her from complaining. Her faith in Jesus was so real, and she strengthened many of her friends who came to see her. She had a constant stream of visitors — droves of her schoolmates and many others, for she was widely known.

I was with her the night she died. By that time, her arm was so huge she could no longer lie comfortably in bed. Instead, she knelt by the cot and rested her head on the bed. When I came in after work, I could tell she was very weary.

"Shall I help turn you so you can rest?" I had asked as I stroked her forehead. Her skin was hot to my touch.

At her consent, I took her arm and she slowly turned onto her back. She smiled weakly at me, and then quoted Psalm 17:15: "As for me, I will behold Thy face in righteousness: I shall be satisfied, when I awake, with Thy likeness." Those were the last words she spoke. A look of indescribable joy crossed her face, and her spirit left her young, worn-out body and went to be with the Lord.

Her pastor had used that verse as a text for the funeral. The students, the hospital staff who had come to know the sweet, soft-spoken Gabi, and our whole family gathered around the body and paid our last respects. As she lay surrounded by flowers, dressed in a simple white dress, she looked like a bride. And she was, or, I should say, *is* a part of the bride of Christ.

And so, when my brother *Costel*, now living in *Timişoara* near the border of Yugoslavia, told me how people were escaping out of Romania, I had made up my mind. I would leave. Genovieva was gone, Gabi no longer needed me, I was constantly hounded by the secret police, and I was tired of living a restricted life. I shared my plans with Elena, and she chose to accompany me.

Now here we were, on the train going from the eastern part of Romania to the southwestern part, planning to leave.

"Elena!" I called softly to my sleeping friend. "Wake up, the train is slowing down for the stop in Timişoara."

Elena stirred, sat up quickly and rubbed her eyes. For a moment, she seemed startled and she looked at me. I smiled at her and, hesitatingly, she smiled back.

"Let's pray," I said and bowed my head. All the memories of the past had vividly reminded me of the danger we faced. I needed to pray and ask God to take charge of the situation.

On Saturday night, we gathered in Costel's house — all ten of us who planned to leave the country. The plans were that we would be loaded in the back of a refrigerated truck. The truck would be sealed with an official Romanian seal, (whether real or counterfeit, I didn't know), and we would be taken across the border into Yugoslavia. We knew that once we were across the border we could ask the Yugoslavian police for political protection.

The plan sounded simple. We had been told that this had been done before with success. Our hopes were high that it would work out again. When you desperately want something, it is not difficult to believe that you will be successful.

My brother had arranged everything. As we waited in the house, I thought of the money we had scraped together to pay the driver of the truck. He was not willing to take a risk without being handsomely reimbursed. He probably also needed to reward his contacts in order for them to allow us to leave. As I looked at the group, I thought of the huge amount of money he would have if he succeeded in getting us across.

The truck was supposed to come at ten o'clock. No one spoke as we waited. We were all lost in our own thoughts. The room was lit only by the light that shone in from the hall. The air seemed oppressive. I was glad when Elena reached out and placed her hand in mine. I squeezed her hand slightly.

The clock on the wall steadily ticked on.   Ten-thirty. Eleven o'clock.   There was still no message from anyone. Twelve o'clock. We were getting restless. Costel left the house and after ten minutes passed he came back. He shook his head and sat in his chair again.

By one o'clock, we were all weary of waiting. Worrisome thoughts wanted to surface in our minds. What if? But, no, it was too dreadful to think about. Surely the driver was just delayed somehow, and he would soon come.

But by three o'clock, we knew something was wrong. A low hum of whispers circulated the room.   The air became more oppressive than before. Again, Costel left the house.

When he came back 15 minutes later, his shoulders slumped in despair. Again, he shook his head. No, he had not seen or heard anything of the truck or the driver.

Costel had no place to go to inquire about the driver. The plans had been for the truck to come to the house, and there was no one else to ask what had happened.

Most of the people were becoming noticeably upset.

"Did you give him our money?" one tall middle-aged man asked bluntly.

"Yes, I had to. He said he must have the money in order to prepare the way for the escape," Costel said miserably.

"You should have given him only part of it and the rest after we were on the truck," a sharp-faced woman told him. "You let us be swindled!"

By now, we were all convinced that the driver never intended to show up. When that realization settled in, there was a shocked silence. Then many from the group responded in anger.

Even though most of them tried to keep their voices low, the babble of voices that broke over Costel's head was anything but silent.

"You are responsible. Pay us back!"

"Maybe you are in on this!"

The people were becoming extremely upset. Two of the women were crying and moaning. Elena and I still sat on our chairs, and I realized that we were still holding hands. Elena turned a white face to me. What were we going to do? What were the rest of the people going to do? All of us had been living for this time, planning for it. I don't think anyone had even thought of this happening. Yes, we had thought of being caught, but that came with the risk of trying to escape. But not this. Not betrayal. Not being robbed of our money and left destitute here close to the border. Some of the others had probably also traveled great distances and made elaborate plans to come here. And now to have our hopes dashed!

When the accusing tones of the people turned against my brother, I spoke up. "I know that my brother did not do this to you. He was helping me, his sister, to escape. Obviously he is not responsible, because he helped my friend and me. We had best leave here before morning and people see so many of us in one house."

Costel faced the people. His mouth opened and he tried to speak. His face was haggard. Again he tried to say something, but no sound came out. He strained to talk, but nothing happened. He had lost his voice because of his extreme distress.

Another babble of voices rose. "I will see that somehow you are punished," the tall man was speaking again. "Somebody is going to pay for this! I will not stand for it." He glared at us and then left the house and closed the door with a bang.

Elena and I had to decide what to do. Really, we had no choice but to go back. We could not stay with Costel and we had no money to try again. We were trapped.

So we went back. Back into the lives we thought we were going to leave forever. Elena went back to her job in Brătuleşti—Iaşi, where she was a manager at a collective farm. And I was able to report for work at my job on Monday morning.

Everything seemed so normal, yet so unreal. Last week I had kept thinking of how I was planning to leave forever. Even in my thoughts of a failed escape, I had not thought of coming back to Iaşi to work. I had only thought of two things; escape or prison. Now here I was, back again.

I kept thinking people should be surprised to see me. Of course, they weren't surprised, because they did not know I had been planning to leave! But it was a shock for me to see everyone once more. I had thought I would never see them again. Life seemed very mixed up.

18

Try Again

It was not easy to get back into the regular routine of work. I was constantly hounded by nightmares of our attempted escape. I was more aware than ever of shadowy figures, and I often took different routes to and from work.

The tall man's threat that we would have to suffer for the aborted escape attempt was real. I began to visualize my arrest and imprisonment.

Whenever the news reached me of another Christian brother's disappearance, I reacted with fear. I became extremely jumpy. Any unexpected thing that happened, such as a jar falling onto the floor, would frighten me. I was having trouble sleeping.

One day I called Costel and talked with him. His voice was still not back to normal after the strain he had endured, and he told me he was expecting to be arrested any day. Some of the people who had wanted to escape had made contact with him again and further threatened him with exposure to the police.

I told him that I felt I had to get out of the country. I was having difficulty functioning with the threat of arrest constantly hovering over me. If he found out another way I could leave, I told him to let me know somehow. I hardly dared tell him this on the phone, but I was getting desperate. We talked in code as much as we could. We were used to saying one thing and knowing that the real meaning was something else.

_ ._ ._ ._ ._ ._ ._ ._ ._ ._ ._ ._ ._

"Silvia," my landlady called late one Saturday evening in

February. "There is a phone call for you!"

I ran downstairs and picked up the receiver.

"Silvia!" a lady's voice greeted me pleasantly. "How are you this evening? Have you had a busy day?"

I thought rapidly. This was not someone I knew. "Yes," I answered quickly. "I am doing fine, thank-you."

"Silvia, this is Mama *Leone* from *Reşiţa*. I heard that you have two tapes and I want to listen to them. Why don't you come on over on Monday and bring your tapes with you? Then we can listen to them together. Do you think you can come?"

I almost gasped. I knew what the message really meant. "I think I can come," I answered. Then I repeated, "Yes, we will be able to come."

"O.K. I will have to find a rose for you for a present. Do you like red ones?"

"Yes, Mama Leone, a red one will be fine," I laughed a little.

"All right. Good-bye. I will see you on Monday, then."

I replaced the receiver and went back upstairs. I sank onto my bed as the real message of the telephone message sank in.

I was to go. Arrangements had been made for another attempt to escape the country. And I had to be in Reşiţa in less than 48 hours! Reşiţa was south of Timişoara, the city we had tried to escape from the other time! I had never heard of Mama Leone, but I understood the code language.

I had to contact Elena. We had agreed to try it together if ever the opportunity came again. She would have to come down from Suceava on Sunday in order to leave with me on the train Sunday night.

But as the reality of everything sank in, I sat on my bed to think. Was I really ready to face trying to escape again? I remembered too vividly the terrible disappointment of the previous attempt to escape, seven months earlier in August, 1980. Could I go through another try and perhaps have that also turn into defeat?

Then I thought of my present life. Being shadowed constantly. The ever-abiding fear of exposure for trying to leave the country, and the sure-to-follow arrest, interrogations and imprisonment. I thought of how, even at four-thirty in the morning when I wanted to leave for work, I would check through my darkened window to see if someone was spying on me. I thought of the wild elevator rides, going from floor to floor in order to go out another exit from the building so I would not be followed.

I would try again, I decided. I was too weary of this kind of life. Most certainly I would be arrested if I stayed, and perhaps I would be arrested if I tried to escape. But our escape just might succeed, and I could leave all this behind.

As I prepared to leave, I carefully chose each item I would take. I knew this time that we were going to try to escape in a different way than what we had before, because this time there was no money involved. Both Elena and I had barely been able to get the money together to pay for our supposed ride in the truck.

Sunday morning at church, I again went through the agony of a silent separation. Would this really be the last time in church? I could hardly join in the singing, but the message of the songs sank deeply into my heart. I thirstily drank in every word of dear Brother *Morcan's* sermon as he spoke lovingly of being true to our Lord, Jesus Christ. He encouraged us to remain faithful, regardless of the circumstances we found ourselves in. I knew he was trying to prepare us for any persecution any of us might face.

That evening as we had the four o'clock rehearsal for the children's choir, I fought with my emotions. Those dear little faces wanted to swim in front of my eyes. I forced myself to keep my emotions under control and direct their singing.

Again, there were no farewells after church that night. Brother and Sister Morcan's little daughter, *Andrea*, seemed unusually attached to me that evening. She called me Mama *Lila*, and when it was time for me to go home, she begged to accompany me. I stooped down and buried my face in her curly hair and this time I could not keep from crying. I gave her a final hug, put her in her father's arms, and went quickly out of the church yard. My heart seemed to be breaking.

I gave the keys for my stockroom at the factory to a friend and asked him to deliver them to my supervisor the next morning. I wrote a note and told the supervisor that I would be missing for three days. Something unexpected had come up. I guess in the back of my mind, I thought if this escape didn't work out either, perhaps I could be back at work by the next Thursday.

—··—··—··—··—··—··—··—

"There she is," Elena told me as we stepped off the train in Reşiţa.

"Silvia!" Mama Leone, wearing a red rose pinned to her coat, greeted me. "And who is this?" she wondered, extending a friendly hand to Elena.

"My dear friend, Elena, who is traveling with me," I told her. We met Mama Leone's husband and went with them to their house.

We were told that plans were for us to escape across the river with a reliable guide. Yes, he had done this many times before, so he knew the way, and this time, he himself was planning to escape with his family.   But there was one problem. The river was unusually high because there had been a warm spell, and it was swollen with melted snow and ice from the mountains.

However, we were to go that night by car to *Oraviţa* and meet the rest of the group. Our guide would tell us what he was planning next.

So, we went into the first car. Every time we neared a police checkpoint, we were filled with apprehension. And we prayed. It seemed during that trip through the night that my every breath was accompanied with a prayer. I was constantly talking with God, telling Him everything and asking to be led by Him.

Three times we changed cars, because all the area policemen knew the few drivers from their locale. It would not do to have a car from Reşiţa driving to Oraviţa late at night.

When we finally reached Oraviţa early on Monday morning, we were exhausted. We were told which house to go in and there we met our guide and his family.

"The moon is too bright to try anything tonight," the elderly guide told us. "Plus, the river is so high, we cannot

156

wade through. We must somehow get a boat."

"How long will that take?" I asked. "Will it be safe to stay here while you get a boat?"

"It will be safe, if you stay hidden. The problem is where to get a boat. No one is allowed to have a boat here in this village because we are too close to the border. I think someone must go to Timişoara and get a boat there."

All day Monday we stayed inside. We did not go near any of the windows and we did not talk. The winter daylight faded early, and it was after dark before our guide returned with the good news that he had been able to get a boat. I did not know how he could bring a boat successfully through all the police checkpoints, but somehow, he did.

There were eight of us who were planning to leave: the guide and his wife, who were in their 50s, their teen-age son, another son and his wife, one man from Bucharest, and Elena and I. You might think that we became well acquainted with each other as we waited all day Monday, but we didn't. Again, it was better that we did not get to know each other, for if we should get caught, the less we knew about each other, the better. And we were under such tension that no one really wanted to visit.

When we had bundled ourselves up to brave the cold winter weather of February, we left the house silently and headed for the river. We walked through the dark village and came to the brink of the water.

I looked at the river and my heart sank. The river was so big, it almost looked like a lake stretching out into the darkness. The dark water swirled in the dim light and occasionally a chunk of ice went drifting past. And when I saw the boat, my heart sank even more. It was a flimsy-looking thing, small, and did not look at all like it could carry anyone across the river.

"You two boys go first," the guide directed calmly. "I will tie a rope to the boat, and after you are across, we can pull the boat back and then two more can go."

His sons were barely on their way, when we heard muffled exclamations followed by loud splashing.

"The boat was hit by ice," the mother exclaimed sharply.

157

The father quickly removed his coat and waded into the icy water. "I know *Petru* can't swim," he said, and struck out for the capsized boat.

How they were able to get the boat right-side-up again, get in, and get to the other side, I will never know. But I know to us who were waiting it seemed like a long, long time.

When our guide finally reappeared, he took us across two at a time. My memory blurs as I think of the agony we went through in waiting to cross; in crossing the treacherous, swollen river in a tiny boat barely riding high enough to keep the water from coming inside, watching for ice chunks that could crash into us; and in waiting on the other side hoping that everyone would make it safely across.

It was windy that night, and cold. The unexpected thaw had ended and the ground was frozen on the top again. Underneath, the soil was wet and swampy. I do not know how our guide could keep from freezing because he was soaking wet from rescuing the boys. Perhaps sometime he got other clothes from his wife's bag. But I know that most of our clothes were far from dry.

"Follow me," the father ordered in low tones, and led the way through the tall marsh grass after he had hidden the boat in the reeds. Single-file, we followed.

Our boots sank down through the frozen layer of ice that covered the marsh. Every step was difficult, for the mud under the ice seemed like glue. We plodded on and on through the night. I made sure that Elena was always in front of me, for I did not want her to be left behind somewhere. The guide and his family were in front of us and behind us was the man from Bucharest.

Right, left, right, left. Lift your foot, pull it free from the mud, lift your other foot, pull it free from the mud.

Several times we had to stop and backtrack because the marsh became too muddy for the guide to lead us on. Other times we would come to open expanses of water and we had to turn back again and again.

Were we really headed into Yugoslavia? How did we know we were not going back into Romania again? I knew the river rounded a bend where we had crossed and my mind kept playing tricks on me. It seemed we were heading back the way we had come. Would we suddenly find ourselves standing back on the bank of the river, looking into Romania again?

It became more windy. Suddenly from behind us, the man said, "Stop! I lost my shoe!"

We stopped and he hunted around in the mud for his shoe. "Where are your boots?" I silently wondered. Who would wear shoes to escape across the river, especially shoes that you could lose?

"We must go on," the guide called back to us in a low tone. "We cannot wait."

I pitied the shoeless man, and he kept lagging further and further behind. "Perhaps I could carry him," I muttered to Elena. He looked so skinny and he had such a hard time trying to keep up with the rapid pace. I say rapid, because in spite of the treacherous footing, we were walking as fast as the group could go. We had to in order to keep from freezing. The old woman kept right after her husband, and I marveled at how Elena kept up.

My mind was numb and all I could do was concentrate on taking another step forward. When Elena stopped in front of me, I bumped into her.

I looked ahead. The border!

A wide stretch of raked sand was right in front of the guide. "You must follow me very carefully," he instructed us. "There are wires stretched across this sand and those wires are attached to land mines. We can get across if we step between the wires. You must keep your eyes on the sand and follow me very cautiously. See that white pillar out ahead? When we reach that pillar, we are in Yugoslavia."

No time to stare now. We cautiously followed our guide. "Stop!" he said sharply.

"See the wire? Line up here beside me. Make sure you can see the wire."

I stared intently in the dim light. I could see the innocent looking wire stretched out several inches above the sand. Innocent, yet there was something grim about the wire. Attached to land mines, he had said. Explosives that could blow us to pieces. Innocent? Hardly.

"One, two, three, STEP!" our guide called out.

We stepped across. "Stop!"

Again we strained to see if there was another wire in front of us. Another step. And one more step. Inching slowly forward, barely daring to move. I am sure we all held our breath as long as we could.

Freezing cold wind blowing steadily across the isolated border. Eight people in a row, hearts pounding, pulses racing, concentrating on finding the next wire that could kill or cripple. But now there was no time for us to think about those things. Concentrate. Find the next wire. Be ready to step if the guide counts and calls.

I don't know how long we walked. It seemed like the trip across the river and the march through the swamp had faded into the past. Time stood still. Looking for another wire. Another count, another step.

"Look!" our guide said after we had stepped again. We straightened our backs and right there, within several meters of us, was the white post!

I experienced a sudden surge of emotion as I realized that we were now in Yugoslavia. Freedom! I was no longer in Romania! We had successfully escaped! I wanted to shout! I was aware of a prickling of my scalp as I relaxed.

Now where was the village to which we were going? As far as I could see, and that was not very far because it was still quite dark, all I could see was more marsh grass. Somehow, I had expected that it would look different on this side of the border. The ground was still muddy underneath the ice. It was just as hard to walk as it had been before. And, yet, there was something different. I knew it was just inside of me, but I felt free. Somehow, freedom felt different from anything I had ever experienced before.

Whoosh! There was a loud crashing in the reeds just to my right. All of us froze. Because of the state of mind I was in, that horrible noise scared me so badly that, as we waited in complete silence, I could feel my eardrums pulsate.

I had no idea what kind of wild animals roamed the marshes of Yugoslavia, and I envisioned some terrible monster coming out of the reeds and attacking us. My mind raced at the thought of having escaped the perils of drowning in the river and being blown apart by the explosives. Were we now going to be devoured by some ravenous beast? I quickly made a choice. If that animal came out, I would go to meet it. I would offer myself as food and then maybe the others could escape. I was not married, I had no one dependent on me, and I carried a lot more meat than Elena.

Now, I wonder if those thoughts did not come from near hysteria, but as we crouched there in the dark marsh, I calmly awaited my fate. When the creature, whatever it was, finally lumbered away from us, our heartbeats returned to as normal as was possible under the circumstances, and we continued.

Finally, we crested the top of a low hill. And there in front of us was a village.

I was close to 30 years old, but I had never been out of my country. I had seen many pictures of foreign scenes, but to actually see a Yugoslavian village was a momentous occasion. I eagerly looked at the houses. I examined the fences. The houses had chimneys just like ours. Woodpiles rose in orderly ranks in the backyards. Even the windows had curtains! I don't really know what I expected, but as exhausted as I was, I know I was amazed. Trees grew with their roots in the ground, dogs ran and barked as Romanian dogs do, and everywhere I looked, things looked similar to what I was used to seeing in Romania. I thought they shouldn't. Because we were now free! We had escaped!

Our guide tapped on the window of a house, and the door opened a few minutes later. Words can't describe how good it felt to huddle beside the stove, dry our wet clothes and sip the hot tea we were offered.

But one thought kept coming back to me. We must move on! We must not stay near the border! The black threat of the Romanian police was only a few kilometers behind us! I wanted to get as far away as possible! As soon as possible!

There were differences of opinion. Some thought we should stay together. I wanted to split up. A big group was too easy to spot. I decided that Elena and I would go to the train station and go to Belgrade. From there we would go to *Triest* on the border, cross over into Italy, and then travel on to

America. I was sure that it was better to go separately.

But "No, no!" our hosts insisted. There was no danger. We should stay there, warm up and report our escape to the police. The police would take our information and then we could ask for safety as refugees. That was how they handled people who escaped from Romania. The Yugoslavians knew how the Romanians suffered and their police did not send Romanians back.

The word "police" was enough to make me want to run out of the house. "Elena, let's go!" I whispered to her. "We have to get out of here!"

Elena looked up at me, and for the first time I noticed how exhausted she was. "I can't," she answered weakly. "I have to rest."

I struggled between the two choices. All my reasoning told me to get as far away from the border as possible. I panicked at the very thought of being turned over to the police. Not after all we had gone through. Yes, they said their police were sympathetic, but visions of my interrogations at the police station rose before my eyes, and I knew I didn't want anything to do with any police, whether they were Yugoslavian or not.

I even thought fleetingly of joining the man from Bucharest, who declared he was not going to stay. He slipped out the door and left. I wanted to cry out and tell him to take me with him.

Then I looked at Elena again. She sat on the chair with her eyes closed. She looked extremely weary.

I could not leave. We were in this together. Whatever happened, I would not leave her. I knew she would do the same thing for me. We were sisters in Christ and we would stay together as long as we could.

I sat down and waited to see what would happen next.

19

Turned Back

All of us were silent as we bounced along in the police van. The Yugoslavian police had come and interviewed each one of us at the village house. We had given our names, birth dates, addresses, and other information. They, too, assured us that they would only detain us for 21 days, and then we could apply to move on as political refugees.

For some reason, I could not get rid of a sinking feeling of doom as I unwillingly entered the police van. All the assurances we were given by the Yugoslavians did not erase my feelings that this was not the way to freedom.

Freedom? To be taken back to the Yugoslavian border town in a police van? And once we got there, we were escorted under guard into a large comfortable room where we were told we needed to stay. Our personal belongings were recorded and taken away from us. Our watches, our purses, our bags, even our belts, were taken away.

"Why do we need to be detained here in this prison?" I asked the Yugoslavian officer who was busily writing down a list of all our possessions in a file.

"Lady, you have crossed our border illegally, and we cannot just let you go on your way. When we have detained you, and checked with the Romanian authorities to make sure you are not escaped criminals or some other dangerous people, we will allow you to leave." He bent over his papers and continued writing.

I was glad he was not looking at me. My face must have turned white under my brown skin. Check with the Romanian authorities! Would my reports go all the way back to

Bucharest and to Iaşi? I was sure I was considered a dangerous person! Oh, why had I agreed to report to the police?

The guide's wife, their daughter, Elena and I shared the one room together. We were well provided for. A toilet and plenty of warm water with which to wash ourselves. Fresh bread still warm from the ovens every morning. Jam, butter, and hot coffee! A good warm meal every day, always potatoes and sometimes some other vegetables. And meat! We could hardly make ourselves believe we were in prison! Such wonderful food in prison! Why, even at home we didn't have such good food!

However, the locked door, the barred window, and the fact that we were not allowed out of the room were constant reminders that we were indeed in prison. Even the privileges, such as providing us with yarn and letting us crochet, were not enough to erase the thought that, as nice as we had it here, we were still not free. Still at the mercy of the authorities.

On the fourth day of our stay, this was reinforced.

I was escorted by a Yugoslavian guard into a room down the hall. There was an officer sitting behind a desk.

"Sit down. I have questions for you."

I froze. This man was not from Yugoslavia! He was from Romania! He had a perfect Romanian accent! I could hardly breathe!

"What is your name?" the familiar bark of the police broke the silence. "What is your address?"

I answered mechanically. I knew that he did not need to ask. He was not writing anything down, but was looking at his papers. My file.

"How did you escape the country?" He clipped every word short.

"What is this?" I asked. "Why are you asking me all these questions? I am not in Romania, I am in Yugoslavia. What right do you have to interrogate me?"

"Shut up! I ask the questions," he flung at me. "How did you escape?" he persisted.

My mind was whirling. Where was I? Had I not passed the white post that marked the border? Had we not been treated with kindness and been given meat every day? Had the Yugoslavian police not told us that we would be released and allowed to register as refugees?

"I asked how you escaped across the border!" the officer screamed at me. "What train did you take from Iași? How did you get here? Who brought you here?"

I calmed down. I must not let fear overtake me. I had enough experience with the intimidating tactics the police used to know I must not cower.

"We are grown people. Don't you think we can walk by ourselves? Why do you think someone had to bring us here?"

"So, you are one who likes to talk, huh? You are one of the smart ones. Listen, Silvia Tărniceriu, you think you have escaped us by coming into Yugoslavia! I tell you, you have not escaped." He lowered his head and glared at me. Then he spoke slowly and distinctly, stopping between every word. "We—will—get—you—yet!"

Then came the hours of grueling questions. How did we get to Bucharest from Iași? Who helped us at the station in Resița? How much money did we pay to be smuggled across? Whom did we pay? On and on, trying to pry information out of me.

I answered as briefly as I could. I was determined not to incriminate people. And now it was again very good that I knew as little as possible about the people who had helped us. Most of the time, I could answer, "I don't know" when I was asked to supply names. I could not tell him the family names of Leone, the guide and his family, or the man from Bucharest. I did not know why the others were escaping from Romania. I could not tell the officer to what village we were taken, or whose house we had stayed in while we waited. There really was very little information that he could get from me about our flight across the river.

This seemed to infuriate him. "There will come a day when you will be glad to tell us!" he hissed. "We will show you yet that we will not be beaten! We have ways of helping you remember!"

The next day, I was called in again. The same officer, the same questions, the same snarling voice that hammered on and on against what I had done.

"You are guilty of embezzlement," the officer charged me. "You have taken state property from your job and sold it to collect money to escape. You will be tried and convicted."

The charges he brought against me washed over me. It seemed like nothing worse could happen.

———·——·——·——·——·——·——·——·———

Back in our room, the guide's daughter, *Anica*, became angry. She blamed me for bringing all this trouble upon our group. Her mother tried to quiet her, but to no avail.

"If it weren't for you, we would be released like the other people who escaped," Anica fumed. "More than 60 other women have already been moved through this women's compound while we've been here, and yet our group has to stay here because of you. What did you do that they are keeping us? Why didn't you tell us you are a wanted person before you escaped along with us? Do you realize what suffering you have brought on our entire group?"

"We must not blame Silvia," the old woman said patiently. "We do not know why God allowed this to happen. My husband has helped many people escape before, and this is the first time this has happened."

At first, I had thought our guide and his entire family were Christians, but now it seemed evident that his daughter was not. When her mother and Elena and I prayed, Anica did not join us. In fact, she tried to have as little to do with Elena and me as possible.

The rest of our 21-day stay in Yugoslavia was a constant barrage of questions and interrogations by the Romanian officials. The Yugoslavians did not seem to bother about us except to feed us. The excellent meals continued, but after awhile it was difficult to really enjoy the food. Our hearts still yearned to be released, to experience freedom.

We were given no promises, no certainties. Since we were in Yugoslavia, every once in a while I could build up my hopes that perhaps, somehow, we would still be released.

Exactly 21 days after we had been in Yugoslavia, we were told to prepare to leave. Not a word of where we were going, what was going to happen, nothing. Just, prepare to leave.

Our bags and belongings were brought back to us and we waited.

Then the door was unlocked, and we were escorted under armed guard down the hall. There, at the end of the hall, was an open door. What I saw there seemed to be a premonition for worse things to come.

A black van had been backed up to the door, and both back doors of the van had been opened. When I first saw the van, I had a wild thought of fleeing out the door, dashing past the van and to freedom. Then I saw that flight was impossible. The small space on both sides of the van was blocked by wire gates. We were prisoners in the truest sense. Helpless. Just like cows being loaded to go to the slaughter house, I thought to myself as we were herded into the van. The back doors were slammed shut and locked, and the van drove off.

The four men who had escaped with us were in the van, too. All eight of us were together again. The man from Bucharest who had left the house in the village had been picked up by the police, too. He had not escaped.

"Where are we going?" was everyone's question.

No one knew for certain. I definitely had no idea which direction we were traveling. The van had no windows. The front part where the driver sat was completely blocked off.

"Does anyone have anything in their bags that would incriminate us?" It was our guide who asked the question. "If you have any Yugoslavian money with you, get it out. If we are going back to Romania, it will be better to not have any foreign money on us."

We stuffed our *dinars*, the Yugoslavian money, into cracks in the van. And then the import of the old man's words hit me. "Going back to Romania," he had said. He must know. He must have been able to sense which direction we were headed.

I bowed my head and prayed. What was going to happen to us?

Our ride lasted only about an hour and 30 minutes. The van slowed down and we heard voices outside. Then we moved forward again. We stopped, the van backed up several meters, and we stopped again. The motor stopped. All was quiet inside.

Outside, there were voices. Words. Sentences. In the Romanian language.

All at once, the back doors of our van were swung open. We looked out into an open courtyard that was milling with soldiers. Dressed in uniforms. The uniforms of Romania.

As if to remove all doubt, a signboard over the gate we had driven through declared, in large letters, "The Socialist Republic of Romania"!

The last vestige of hope died within my heart. We were right back in Romania! We were helpless prisoners in the grip of the very people we had tried to flee! All our efforts of crossing the swollen river, going through the bewildering swamp, and finally crossing the treacherous border, had been in vain!

"Why, God?" I cried in silent anguish. "Oh, why? Why did You not take us away when we crossed the icy river, or allow us to be blown to pieces by the land mines? Why did You allow us to get into Yugoslavia, where we began to breathe the air of freedom, only to bring us back into Romania? Where are You, God? What have we done to deserve this?"

"Get out!" The military bark of a commanding officer yelled at us. We scrambled out from the back of the van.

"Where are you from?" he asked us. His voice was cold and detached. "Who helped you escape?"

No one spoke from our group. We stood still and waited.

"I asked, who helped you escape?" he yelled. His face was turning red.

"We are grown people," I answered. "We are able to walk by ourselves and escaped by ourselves."

"Oh, so you are the leader, the one who can talk. You are the funny one." He looked at me for a long time.

"Maybe a shadow came and helped you cross the border. I tell you, if you cannot remember who helped you cross the border, we can make you remember!" Again the threats, the efforts at intimidating us.

We were herded into an open courtyard.

"Face the wall!"

I looked for Elena. She was next to me, and she looked ill. Her face was white.

168

"Elena!" I whispered.

"No talking!" The guard yelled at me. "I said face the wall. No whispering, no turning!"

For a long time we stood there. The cold March wind whipped around our legs. Outside the courtyard, we could hear the noise of the army camp. Soldiers drilling, the chanting of voices, marching footsteps. But inside the courtyard it was quiet, except for the footsteps of the guard going back and forth.

Some official had evidently given an order, for a number of young soldiers entered the courtyard. "Turn around!" they shouted at us.

It was clear that they knew the identity of each of us prisoners.

"You traitor," they hissed at the son-in-law. "We will show you what we do with people like you who leave the country!" One soldier kicked him so hard that the man was propelled several steps away.

And then the torture began. From one to the other of the soldiers, the man was kicked. His grunts of pain were met by yells from the soldiers. They used him like a football. Back and forth from one army boot to the other.

I wanted to hide my face in my hands, but I did not dare to move. The old woman gave one low moan, and the guard raised a threatening hand, glared at her for a minute, then turned back to watch the spectacle.

My breath was coming in short gasps. I thought I could not stand to watch the awful scene.

Once the young man fell, and a circle of soldiers surrounded him and kicked him viciously until he struggled back onto his feet.

The other men from our group were visibly trembling. The young son was shaking and crying.

With a final push, the soldiers sent the son-in-law back to the wall. He leaned against the wall, sobbing and moaning.

Then they turned to the old man. "You are the one who helped the rest escape! You have helped people before! Take this!"

I could not bear to watch. I closed my eyes. But I could not shut my ears. And the sound of an open palm smacking against the old man's face cracked like a pistol shot. My eyes flew open.

The soldiers were not kicking the old man. They were hitting him. Slap after slap stung his cheeks. His head swung from side to side from the vicious blows.

Curses and yells filled the air. Then the soldiers began beating the teen-age son and the man from Bucharest. The men were beaten and kicked. Fists rained on their heads, and all the while, vile language poured out of the soldiers' mouths.

That scene is etched in my memory. The courtyard of vicious soldiers attacking the helpless men. The four of us women, trembling, standing in a row, forced to watch. The animal-like yelling, the hate-distorted faces, the sounds of thuds and kicks against the victims. I still tremble to think of that awful event.

And then that part was over. We were again forced to stand in a row, facing the wall. The men were groaning in pain, and the old woman was sobbing. Several times, I heard a very quiet moan from Elena. I wanted to put my arms around my dear friend and comfort her, but I did not dare to move.

The day dragged on. I had no idea what time it was. It seemed like we had already been in this courtyard for hours. And still we were forced to stand. Facing the wall. Not allowed to move. Facing the wall. Not allowed to move. Facing the—

My mind was reeling. I tried to pray. It seemed I could not think. No words would come. All I could manage to say over and over again was, "Oh, dear God. Oh, dear God."

I needed to use the rest room. Did I dare ask? Would that make the guard angry? I was sure that the other women needed to go, too.

A calm came over me. I would ask. Not just for my sake, but for the others, too.

"Sir," I called out. "We need to use the women's room."

The marching footsteps stopped.

I waited to see what would happen.

"Only one at a time," the guard yelled.

He called for another soldier and we were escorted to the

women's room one at a time and then back again.

For some reason, this gave me back some of my courage. That small act of kindness seemed to be a bright ray of hope in this place.

It was evening. I did not know how long we were going to have to stand in this place and I was determined not to ask. It was as if I knew that we were being tested to see how long we could endure the waiting. And I knew that it was worse for the men, beaten and bruised, trying to stand.

But I was hungry. We had not eaten all day. Should I ask for food?

I heard the exchange of words as the guards changed duty. The new sentry began to walk back and forth. The light was fading from the sky, but huge, yellow floodlights lit our courtyard.

"Prisoners, turn around!" It was a new voice.

The officer who stood surveying our group looked almost human, I decided. He was dressed in the usual uniform, but there was something different about him. He did not have that haughty look so many of them had.

"Sir," I addressed him. "We have not had anything to eat all day. I have some money and I wondered if we could buy something to eat."

A long silence. As he looked at me, I looked right back. I did not lower my eyes, and I could not tell what he was thinking. "Please God, have mercy on us! Move his heart!"

"Go get them something to eat," he told the guard.

And we were given bread. And meat! It was good.

We were put into an unheated room for the night. The wind whistled in through the broken windows. A guard was watching all the time. There was no time to relax.

"God, I thank You. In this awful place, You have shown me that You know who I am. Just as You revealed Yourself to me so long ago when I was a child by sending me clothes that were just my size, so You now revealed Yourself to me by allowing us to have had this food. I don't know why we must be in this awful place, but I know that You know where I am. I know it was You Who sent that officer to us tonight and it was You Who gave him a soft heart. Thank-you, God."

20

Crazy Girl

"**W**hy are all the places that have to do with the police or the military so drab?" I wondered to myself. Again, we were standing in line. Again, we were waiting to be questioned. I knew the questions that would come. What is your name, your age, your address, what are your parents' names, where did you work, how did you escape, who helped you, where did you think you were going? The questions were asked over and over again.

We had not stayed long at the first place. That was a training camp for soldiers. Did they train them there how to lose human decency and how to hate and how to beat people? I wondered. Training camp. Training to wound and to kill.

A second camp. And I was pondering to myself the reason for this drab, colorless, institutional atmosphere that appeared everywhere we went.

"Perhaps it is because the lives of these men, these police, have no meaning," I mused. "If we have no direction for our living, we become insensitive to beauty, to attractive surroundings. Surely it would not have cost more to paint these walls a pleasing color of blue or green, rose or yellow, than it did to concoct this muddy gray that is splashed all over the wall. It creates such an atmosphere of depression. And the officers work in here day after day.

"I thank God that my parents taught me to appreciate beautiful things. Even though Mama was busy with her work, she would always let us put a bouquet of wildflowers on the table. And even though we were poor, she still liked to see that the clothes we wore were attractively made and neatly mended.

"I believe God wants us to love beauty. He made a beautiful world. The hill behind our house when I was a child held so much beauty. The deep, dark woods; the fragile wild flowers; the musical thrush; and the delicate ferns."

I was brought back to reality with a jolt by a harsh voice yelling, "Stand at attention! You will be searched!"

"Stand at attention!" I thought wryly, in spite of the situation. What did he think we were doing for the last hour or so? We had been forced to stand at attention until our legs felt like sharp needles were being pricked into our skin. That is why I had welcomed the flood of memories.

The officer started at the other end of the line. I had entered the room first, and so I was farthest from the door. Now, I would be last to be searched.

It was always humiliating to be searched. There was no respect of privacy when we were searched. The officers would try to make sure that there was nothing hidden anywhere. First, they would search the personal belongings. Then, they would start to search the person.

Personal belongings! There was something about that phrase that niggled at my memory. My bag. What was in my bag?

My address list! I felt my knees begin to shake. I still had my address list in my bag! "Oh, Lord!" I prayed. "I must get rid of that address list! They must not be able to see who I was going to contact after we escaped! I don't want to get my American friends in trouble!"

The officer was still searching at the other end of the line. I eased my arm down my side slowly. I bent over slightly, but I kept my head up, gazing straight ahead. I bent my legs.

There! My hand was touching the bag. I had to stoop lower in order to reach inside. I bent my knees even more. The strain on my leg muscles was hard to maintain. But I had to keep my back straight in order to be as inconspicuous as possible. I wondered if Elena was thinking about what was going on, but she kept standing at attention, not looking at me.

My hand was inside the bag. I felt around. No, that was my Bible. Not that, either; that was the rest of the garlic I had carried with me when we fled across the river.

There! I felt the familiar cover of the notebook. I pinched the small book between my two fingers and slowly raised myself. My legs were shaking from the strain of holding my body in such a difficult position and from the desperation that I felt.

As soon as I was upright, I went to the back of the book. I lowered my eyes enough to see where the page was. As soon as I found the address of my contact in America, I stopped. David Troyer, Millersburg, Ohio. On the same sheet were other addresses I needed to get rid of. I ripped the paper out.

At first, I did not know what to do with it. I could not just crumple it up and hold it. I did not want it to be anywhere on me when I was searched. I knew the officers searched everywhere.

I tore the paper into smaller bits. The officer was moving up the line. He had started with the women, now.

I pretended to stifle a yawn, and stuffed the torn paper into my mouth. I slowly ground the paper between my teeth. The paper was tough. It was hard to chew. It wanted to lump together into an unmanageable lump. I tried to separate it into small pieces, but it just wanted to stick together. It tasted terrible!

I chewed some more. Believe me, it was more difficult than it sounds. I agonized with that little wad of paper until the officer came to Elena, who was standing right beside me. Then, with an extreme effort, I swallowed the disgusting mass. I was afraid I would choke. Ugh, I wanted water to wash the lump of paper out of my throat! It stuck there and I thought I had to cough. But I tried not to change expression. I forced myself to look straight ahead. I forced myself to ignore the wad of paper in my throat. At least now there was nothing that I did not want them to see.

"Show me your ID," the officer held out his hand.

"What is your—" his voice died away in surprise as he studied the card I had given him. He looked for a long minute at my picture. Then he looked squarely in my face.

"Everyone else out!" he yelled suddenly. "Get moving! Out into the front hall!"

"You stay in!" he commanded, pointing to me.

Once more I prayed. "Lord, did he see me eat the paper? Please, what will he do with me? Protect me from all evil!" Fear knocked at my heart. What was I going to suffer in the hands of this man?

The officer shooed Elena out the door. She looked beseechingly at me, but she knew she had to leave with the others. We all knew it was dangerous for an official to detain one of the women. He locked the door and turned to face me.

The officer took my ID card and sat at the desk. He motioned me to a chair and looked at my card again. Then he shook his head.

"You crazy girl! I can't believe it! The Crazy Girl is here and I meet her again." He looked at me. "Don't you know who I am?"

He thought I was crazy? I was wondering if he wasn't crazy. What did he mean, did I know him? I studied his face.

"Don't you remember me? Don't I look familiar to you?"

There was something about him that tugged at my memory. "Crazy Girl." That was what they called me in Iaşi. That was what my teachers and classmates called me when I was going to school.

But I did not know this man. He definitely was not one of the police who used to interrogate me in Iaşi. How was I to know who he was? His voice sounded somewhat familiar. Somewhere I had heard him before.

"Do you know me now?" He took his hat off. His hair was black and curly. It did make him look very different. And more familiar.

"Silvia! We went to school together! I remember you. We called you the Crazy Girl! You were the Christian!"

Memories of school flooded me. Yes, now I recognized him!

"Remember Mr. *Alexandru*? Remember how he would make us all go outside, regardless of the weather, for what he called the Getting-Rid-of-Lazy-Brains exercise?"

As we sat and talked of our school days, I kept shaking my head in disbelief. Here, in this forsaken place, I had met someone who recognized me! Would he have recognized one of the other hundreds of girls he went to school with? But he did remember me, the Crazy Girl! I said a silent prayer of thanks to God for having been remembered. This was one more sign that God knew exactly where I was. Just as He had known that I was a girl and had known the correct size of my shoes, He again showed me that He was with me and knew all about me. This meeting was bringing a sense of reality into my life.

"What are you doing way down here? You are all the way across the country from Iași. Oh, I just remembered something. When is your birthday?" He checked my card. "Yes," he said excitedly. "I thought so. We are twins! My birthday is on September 29, 1951, too. I didn't want anyone to know when we went to school. I didn't want to be a twin to the Crazy Girl!" he laughed. "But I remembered. Seven years we were in the same class! And now I meet you down here! Isn't that something? As soon as I read 'Silvia Tărniceriu' and saw your picture, I knew who you were!"

Then he sobered. "Silvia, you don't know how lucky you are that I recognized you! I was given orders to 'do away' with the dangerous runaway who tried to escape. I know what that order means and so do you. I am one of the commanding officers here, but I got those orders from the commander at the camp you just left. He felt that it is not worth our time to mess with you!"

The death sentence! I had been given the death sentence by the officer of a soldier's training camp! I realized how little human life meant to many of these people. How little my life meant.

I stared numbly at him. I couldn't speak.

"What shall I do?" he asked. "I was supposed to search all of you and then we were given orders to beat you. 'Don't bring her back,' he said. But I can't do that. What shall I do?"

I again felt calm in my soul. "The angel of the Lord encampeth round about them that fear Him, and delivereth them." I could sense that God was directing my life, even in this horrible place, by sending this man from my school days to be a commanding officer here. I did not know what he would do with me, but I could tell he did not want me harmed.

"I must send you on," he decided. "You cannot stay here.

If I send you to another camp, you will not be on our records.

"I realize that someone is planning to get rid of you. Do you know that for every prisoner who is returned to us from Yugoslavia, our government must give a train car load of grain in return? Our diplomatic relationship with Yugoslavia is not overly friendly. So, only the people our government officials really want back are paid for with grain. Someone must want you back in Romania for a special reason. Perhaps to make an example of you to warn others what happens when Christians try to escape!"

My mind instantly flew to the manifest I had signed. When Brother Tzon's booklet had been read over Radio Free Europe, it had brought national attention. My signature had been in that book. And that made me worth a train car load of grain!

"I must talk with my colleague. Which one is your friend?"

I described Elena and he called her in. Then he brought his colleague in.

He briefly explained the situation.

The other man looked at us and shook his head. "You crazy people!" he said. "All this trouble because you serve your God."

As all eight of us jolted from that camp to the next one, I felt that we had escaped the lion's mouth. I told the bewildered Elena about my meeting with my school classmate, and we marveled together at how God was in control over this situation. I told her we had narrowly escaped a beating, but I did not tell her about the threat of being beaten to death. She did not need to know that. But I told the Lord all about it.

21

The Shield

"Where did you get this? Why do you have this book in your bag?" Another officer. Another camp. My memory almost fails me at how often we were moved and how many times we were searched, questioned and yelled at by different officers. Sometimes the officers don't even have faces any more, they are just memories.

I looked to see what he had. My Bible! Even in that desperate situation, my heart leaped for joy when I saw my Bible!

Tata had given me that Bible. I had carried it to church for years and it was never far from my side. I had marked verses in it; there were notes carefully penned in the margins; and probably the most valued addition was what Tata had written inside the front cover. "This book of the law shall not depart out of thy mouth; but thou shalt meditate therein day and night, that thou mayest observe to do according to all that is written therein: for then thou shalt make thy way prosperous, and then thou shalt have good success" Joshua 1:8.

Tata had written that in my Bible to encourage me to read and meditate on God's ways. The handwriting was crooked because an accident had crippled his right hand, but that had not kept him from writing to me, his daughter.

"Why do you need this book? We have a bible you should read. You need to read the writings of Karl Marx and the other great party leaders. You do not need this Bible. Where did you get it?" He turned the pages carelessly.

I did not want to tell him that Tata gave it. I was afraid he would use my sentimentality to harass me further. "I have had it for a long time," I answered.

"Oh, so nobody gave it to you? You just happened to have it?" He spoke in an affected, mocking tone.

"Well, here is what we do with trash. We just take it from the prisoners so they cannot read the worthless thing anymore." He tossed the Bible and my handwritten songbook on his desk. "I have heard that things happen to people who destroy a Bible. Well, we will see!" He laughed a cruel, mocking laugh.

Destroy my Bible! When I was still in Iaşi and lived under the daily fear of arrest, I had thought I could make it quite well in prison if I were allowed to take my Bible and my guitar with me. I felt as long as I could read God's Word and sing, I would be able to face anything.

"Back to the wall!" the officer shouted. He had already searched me and all my belongings.

I was so weary as I joined the others at the wall. The relentless grilling by the officers was doing what they planned it would. I was worn out.

"God, I'm sorry. I just can't thank You right now. To have my Bible taken away from me is too much. You know how much I depend on Your Word. I have verses memorized, but I still need my Bible! You know how much that Book means to me! Even if I could get another Bible later, this one has all my notes written in it. And Tata's verse to me! Oh, Lord, please! How can I bear to give it up?"

On and on I prayed. I think sometimes I complained rather than prayed, but I was talking to God. I simply cried out my deep, innermost feelings to Him and told Him everything.

For several hours we stood, facing the wall. If we tried to relieve our tired leg muscles, the guards yelled at us. It was torture to be forced to stand, doing nothing. I could not see how the guide's wife could endure it. I was having a terrible time. My legs tingled, then burned, then itched. I wanted to rub one leg against the other to relieve the itch, but I did not dare. I never knew if the guards were looking at me just then or not.

Sometimes, when I thought I could not bear the itch in my

legs any longer, I would slowly ease my feet together and try to lift one foot enough to rub against my leg. To concentrate on doing one small thing like that could take a long time, and even though the itching did not stop, it gave me something to do.

The day stretched on. We never knew how long we would be forced to stand, we never knew what they were going to do with us next, and we never knew what plans, if any, were being made. Any questions we had were never answered. We were not given any satisfaction as to how long this time of being shuttled from place to place would be. Somehow we had found out that we were going to be tried in court and sentenced. But, we did not know when.

I heard a door open. I heard the voice of the officer who had taken my Bible. "Take the prisoners and lock them up for the night! You, come with me!"

We turned to leave. "Hey! You, the one who had the book. Come with me!"

I looked at the officer. He was looking straight at me and pointing. "Come in here," he commanded, motioning to the room behind him.

My thoughts racing, I followed him reluctantly.

I noticed the cot in the corner. A stove was radiating heat in another corner. A desk and several chairs were at one end of the room. But there was no comfort in my heart. I had a sinking feeling. I was afraid. I had heard and read of horrors that occurred in places like this. I silently cried out to God.

The officer went around me and closed the door. Then he locked it.

"Sit down," he invited. His voice was somehow different from before. I did not know if I dared trust his new voice.

He must have sensed my feelings, for he said, "You don't need to be afraid. I will not touch you."

He sat at his desk and began feeling in a drawer while he talked. "I don't know what happened," he began. He found my Bible and handed it to me. I clutched it tightly and held it against my breast.

"I started to read in that book when I came in here after I took your books. Ever since then I have been reading it. Page after page. Book after book. Why," he glanced at the clock on the wall, "I must have been reading it for three hours!

"Why did you underline some sentences? There are a lot of underlined words in the back part of the book."

"I underlined those verses because they mean something to me," I answered. "If something speaks to me while I read or while someone is preaching, I underline it."

"I could not burn this book. I was just going to look at it a little bit, then throw it into the fire." He made a motion toward the stove. "But there was something about it. I couldn't stop reading it. My grandmother took me to one of your churches when I was 5 years old. And when I read your book, that memory came back. I remember some of the things that happened then.

"I have a question. What is it that keeps you from hating us? We have tried to get rid of you Christians. We have persecuted you, imprisoned you and told the people that you Christians are dangerous. And yet you don't hate us? Why?"

I looked at him and smiled. "If you continue to read the Bible, you will find out. You will get to know the Author, and once you get to know Him, you will find out what keeps us from hating anyone."

"With my signature, I can put you into prison. But I have seen it before. I cannot take your faith out of you. Why? What makes you willing to suffer for your faith?" His questions seemed to tumble from his mouth.

"It is all here," I said, indicating my Bible. "All the answers to the questions that you have."

"Then I will ask you something. I have the power to confiscate your Bible and keep it. I will not do that. But I will ask you to give it to me so I can read and study it some more. This is the first time I have ever seen a Bible. Will you give it to me?"

My Bible! The Bible Tata had given to me! How could I bear to give it up? I clutched it tightly to me for a second.

Wait! Whose Bible was it? No, it was not my Bible, it was God's Bible. And I knew this man needed it more right now than I did.

I got up and placed the Bible in his outstretched hand. He

placed it gently on his desk. It seemed as though he knew the struggle I went through to give it to him.

"I know it is not easy for you to give me your Bible. I saw what your father wrote inside the front cover. That is one reason that makes me want to read it some more. I must find out what makes this book so precious to you."

Then he seemed to pull his thoughts together. He rubbed his hands together slowly.

"I want to prepare you for tomorrow. They have plans to beat you before you go to court. They will make sure no marks can be seen that you were beaten, but they want to scare you so you will say what they want you to say.

"I will ask to be in charge of your beating. When you see me, do not give any indication that you know me. No sign. Nothing.

"When you come into the room where I am, I want you to scream. I want them to think that I am beating you. But I will not touch you. Something keeps me from doing any harm to you." He glanced at the Bible.

"To any questions they ask, say the truth. They already know all about your escape. They found your tracks by the river and they know how you escaped. You will be given prison terms and you will do forced labor.

"That is all I can tell you. Now, you may go, but remember what I told you about tomorrow." He paused a minute and looked at the Bible again. He glanced around the room. "I have to find a good place to hide the Bible. I could be ruined if anyone finds out I kept it instead of burning it. But something keeps me from destroying this book."

He gave a rueful chuckle. "I have heard that something happens if someone destroys a Bible. But I tell you, something happens even if the Bible isn't destroyed. I don't understand myself! I have never been this strangely moved before!"

I understood! The Word of God does wonderful and strange things to people. Even to what appeared to be a hardened communist military officer!

Again, I had been spared. I felt unworthy. My mind went back to my prayer that afternoon. I remembered my pleading with God to allow me to keep my Bible. I had thought that I could not live without it. And now I had given it away!

I realized the precious gift that a Bible is. How I longed to be able to read the words printed in the holy pages. But I suddenly realized that, even more necessary than having the actual printed Word, was having the Word written in "the fleshly tables of the heart." I thanked God for the hours of Bible memorization I had had in my childhood. And I thanked Him for the years of preaching and teaching that I had been able to have.

I had given my precious Bible away. But the Word was still in my heart! No one could take that away. Or so I thought.

22

Tears

All eight of us prisoners were gathered in the cultural hall. We had been herded through the streets of the town from the police compound that morning. The people from town looked curiously at us at first. Somehow, word must have spread that we were the ones who had escaped across the river into Yugoslavia. A murmur went through the watching crowd. Announcements had evidently been made about the people who had been so disloyal to the country and had tried to escape. When I looked at the faces of the townspeople, I saw pity and understanding written on their faces. They knew too well about our hardships in Romania. The long lines to get bread. The high utility bills for the apartments. The deteriorating work conditions. And they lived close enough to Yugoslavia to know that conditions in the West were better. So, there were no accusations hurled at us, but rather the people were sympathetic and understanding of our plight.

The sentencing in the cultural hall was brief. The presiding officer read off our prison sentences in a bored voice. The guide who had organized the flight was sentenced to five years. Mama Leone's husband, whom the police had somehow found out about and linked to us, was sentenced for three years. The rest of us—the guide's wife and his family, the man from Bucharest, and Elena and I—were each sentenced to two years in prison.

Two years! I believe that it was the maximum sentence they could impose on us. Even prostitutes were only sentenced to six months. We were considered four times more dangerous than prostitutes! I felt devastated.

Back to the police compound we were sent, chained together like a gang of slaves. My mind was heavy and I did not even try to speak to anyone. A dark cloud seemed to cover me.

As we stood outside the gate, waiting for the guard to open up, I felt something wet on my cheek. I glanced up briefly. A combination of icy rain and snow had started to fall.

Once we were inside and the gate was locked behind us, they unfastened the chain. Then one by one, we were taken inside and questioned. The same questions. The same tiresome procedure that we had gone through so many times.

I groaned. My spirit was so heavy. If only I had gone on when we had reached the Yugoslavian village. If only Elena had not been so tired. We might have been able to reach Triest and then go on into America.

I began to cry. Not once since we had been taken into police custody had I cried. I had not even cried when the reality of being brought back into Romania had hit me. But now, the tears started to fall.

I cried for myself. I cried for my family who might not even know where I was. I cried for our desperate situation. Visions of the cruelty that the men had endured when they were beaten came to me. And I cried for them. Yes, I even cried for my Bible. Memories of all the things that had happened to me were crowding into my mind.

I began sobbing loudly, taking huge gasps for air. I did not care where I was or who heard me. All I was aware of was an enormous weight that lay on my heart.

Through my agony, I heard Elena say, "She is going to die! I have never seen Silvia cry like this!" She turned to me, "Silvia! Please don't cry! Oh, what shall I do if you die!"

I tried to talk to her. At first I could not speak because of my tears. "I—will—not—die!"

"Oh, please do not cry," Elena was crying herself. "I don't know what will happen to me if you die!"

"I—promise—I—will not die!" I sobbed. "Just let me cry!"

Finally it was my turn to answer the endless questions. I

restrained myself the best I could and answered everything they asked of me. No longer did I have any quick answers to their obvious questions. I was no longer the brave girl or the girl who liked to talk. I was broken in spirit and I had nothing to say.

In my misery I was but dimly aware that the guide's wife and I were taken downstairs until we came to a cell. My mind refused to grasp what was happening.

But I became acutely aware of where I was by the time we were thrust into the cell and I heard the key turning in the huge iron door. I looked around me through my tear swollen eyes. What I saw brought a fresh flood of tears. A cell so small I could easily touch both walls by stretching out my arms. Five easy steps covered its length. When I stumbled weakly and grabbed at the wall for support, I quickly jerked my hand away from the wall. The concrete walls were damp and slimy. Since we were underground, everything was damp and the air was heavy and moldy. The metal cots flanking both walls were covered with skinny mattresses, and when I sank down on one of them, the straw inside did not even rustle. Everything had hardened together into a lump.

I had thought I was done crying, but the condition of the cell brought a fresh flood of tears. When I saw the filthy floor under my feet, I lifted my shoes away from the floor. I felt so wretched. I had not had a bath for over a week, my hair felt so stringy and I knew I looked awful. Nothing was clean. I had my fur coat and another set of clothes with me, but everything I had was dirty.

Again I sobbed. It seemed there was nothing I could do to help it. All the feelings and emotions I had tried to control just broke loose. I sat on the cot, drew my legs up, and cried. Hot, searing tears coursed down my cheeks. I had never cried like that before.

Then, like the voice of an angel, I heard the guide's wife saying, "Don't cry, honey. You will make yourself ill." She gently rubbed her hand over my back.

Her compassion soaked through to me. My crying was no longer bitter tears that scorched through my heart, but tears of defeat. I no longer felt like I was being torn apart by my wretchedness.

I don't know just when I began to pray, but I found myself talking to God. "I don't know how to praise You in this cell, God. I really don't know why You allowed me to come to this place. I would much rather have drowned in the river or been killed when we were going across the sand strip than to have to endure this awful place. God, where are You? Is it possible that You know where I am? I know You said You will never leave us nor forsake us, but right now, God, I don't feel that You are here. If You hear me, please watch over me!"

I don't remember how I could sleep that night, for the damp, moldy smell that came from my mattress and the stench that came from the toilet down the hall added to my anguish. A dim light bulb cast an eerie glow through the opening above the door.

The days that followed were like a continuous nightmare. Early in the morning we were offered a chunk of moldy bread and a cup of colorless liquid that was supposed to be tea. I refused the bread, and one small sip of the tea was enough to make me sick. Later in the day, the small hatch was opened in the door, and a plate of something that was supposed to be soup was thrust in.

I could not figure out what the greasy mixture was supposed to be. If I had thought the tea was colorless, I had been mistaken. This stuff was much worse. There were some nameless chunks floating around on the bottom. I gagged and returned it out the hole. My cell mate returned hers, too.

After the third day, I began to get desperately hungry. I did not know that a person could get this hungry and live. I knew people could go without food for a long time, but even in my imagination I had never realized how hungry I could get. But for over a week, I could not eat that terrible food.

I thought constantly of food. I remembered the delicious mămăliga Mama made for us. I thought about the bread we used to eat. I remembered the wild cherries we had picked on the hill behind our house when I was a child. I wished I could reach some of the leaves on the trees and chew on them. I wished I could somehow reach some grass and chew on the grass. I even wished for paper. I remembered the page I had eaten from my address book. But now even that was gone.

Everything except my clothes had been taken away from me. My watch was gone. I had no idea what time it was. It was difficult to even know how many days were passing. And it seemed like I really didn't care. Everything was just one long nightmare. I had read a number of books about what people endured when they had been put into prison. But this was no book. This was real. I was the person in prison now!

In that dark time, I grabbed at any ray of hope that I could. When I remembered the paper I had eaten, I began to think about Genovieva.

I began to wonder if somehow my family had found out where I was and if they had let Genovieva know I was in prison. I could picture Genovieva telling her American friends about my plight. I visualized David Troyer coming to our rescue. Perhaps the Romanian officials would be in awe of him and allow this brave man to take us to America. Surely David would be tall and muscular, and the officers would bow to him and allow him to do what he wanted to do.

We had been told that we would be able to choose an attorney and ask to be represented at our court trial. Perhaps there was hope to be able to get out of here!

Something in the back of my mind told me that I was building air castles, but I was desperate. I had to think of something to relieve myself of the sordid conditions I was in.

And in that damp cell, another problem arose. My sinuses became infected. The damp, musty air aggravated my nose. I was constantly sniffing.

Every morning and every evening we were escorted, one by one, to the toilet room. Here was a faucet where a pathetic trickle of cold water would sometimes come. There was nothing like soap to wash with. It was far too cold to undress in order to wash. One time I begged the guard for money to write home and ask them to send me some soap and a toothbrush. Some kindhearted soul actually gave us some soap. I wrote a letter asking for a few things, but I did not know whether the letter was mailed. We were told nothing. It did no good to ask information about anything.

Meanwhile, my sinus infection became worse. My face became swollen and my nose was constantly plugged. I still was not eating and I was getting weak.

One day when the same revolting mixture was offered to us I asked the guard, "Are you planning to starve us? When will we get food?"

There was no answer and I bent over to look out the hole. I saw the guard's helper, a trusted prisoner, making motions for me to be quiet. He was shaking his head vigorously behind the guard's back and putting his finger to his lips. Later, as the guard was pushing his noisy cart down the hall away from us, the helper came to our door.

"Do not complain!" he whispered. "If you complain, they will put you in solitary confinement. It is much worse there! The food that you get now is what is scraped together when they wash the dishes at the army camp. In the solitary confinement you will get nothing!"

I did not know how that could be possible, but I was not going to try to find out! I resolved to never complain again. I would try to be brave until the day I died.

My sinus problem grew worse. Finally, I was so sick that the guard took me to see the doctor. In my misery, there was little that I remember about my surroundings. The doctor prescribed antibiotics. "Take these pills every six hours," he instructed.

After my visit with the doctor, I was locked up in a different room. To my joy, Elena was among the seven or eight women in that room. We were overjoyed to be back together again. But I was so sick I could hardly do anything. Plus, I was afraid that I would not be given my pills at the proper time. I knew I needed the pills to relieve my sinus problems.

That evening, when the guard came to hand us the daily ration of what was considered food, I asked him for my pills. I had been escorted to the toilet and just before I was locked into the cell, I mentioned the pills.

"What do you think this is? A hospital?" He smacked the

side of my face with his open palm.

I reeled back from his blow and fell against the wall. Slowly, I lifted my hand to my face. I staggered and almost fell.

When I regained my balance, I looked straight into his eyes.

At first, he glared right back at me. His cruel eyes seemed to bore into my face. But as I continued to gaze calmly back at him, I could see him change. He seemed to realize that I was a person. He shifted his glance to the floor, and then back to my face.

"I'll get your pills," he said suddenly. His voice was almost apologetic. And he waited until I tottered into the cell before he closed the door.

I collapsed onto the cot. And when the guard returned with the pills and some water, I sat up. I thanked him, but he hurried away.

It took over a week for my sinus problem to clear up. Finally, I could breathe easily again.

However, there still was nothing we could call food. Daily, the same swill was offered to us. Finally, one day, I was so desperate for something that when the bowl was thrust in the hole, I pinched my nose shut, tipped the bowl and swallowed the entire contents. Pushing the bowl away from me, I tried to ignore the protesting rumblings of my stomach. I forced myself not to throw up. Elena still declared she could not swallow any of it.

One day, we met with a horrible sight. The door opened and a woman with blonde hair was pushed into our already crowded cell. We were shocked when we saw her face. As she sat on a bed and moaned, we could hardly keep our eyes away from her. She had huge bruises on her cheeks, and her lip was cut and bleeding. One of her ear lobes was torn and blood had dried on her neck. She put her hand to her mouth and spit blood out between broken teeth. Sobbing and moaning, she rocked her body back and forth.

Later we found out she had tried to escape from prison, but was caught and returned. She had been severely beaten by the police. Suddenly it came to me what we had been spared. If my former schoolmate had not recognized me, we would have been subjected to the same fate. Now, the miseries I was experiencing did not seem so heavy after all.

"Silvia Tărniceriu, come out! There is a package for you!" The older police officer at the door almost looked kind as he called me one day. Perhaps it was the words he said that made him appear kind, but whatever it was, I was so pleased that someone had sent something for me!

I followed him down the hall. "Your father was here this morning and left this package for you!"

My Tata! Here! And I did not see him!

"Why was I not told he was here? I have the right to see him. Prisoners are allowed to see their families!" My words tumbled out in my excitement. I so badly wanted to see someone from my family! They knew where I was! I could have wept.

"He left you this bag," the officer pushed it toward me. "I was not here when your father was here. Someone must have decided he may not see you."

"I was told that I could have an attorney to represent me. I want a retrial!" I was desperate to do something about our situation.

"You will have a trial," the officer told me. "But, lady, you must not expect anything to happen. Our system does not change very often."

I looked into his face. He did have feelings. I saw compassion as he looked at me. It was so good to be shown some consideration. His elderly face reminded me a little of my Tata.

My Tata! He had come all the way from Iaşi to see me and bring me this package! How I loved him! It was extremely disappointing not to be able to see him, but being able to handle the things that his hands had touched was comforting.

Soap! A toothbrush! Some personal items and bread! And some biscuits! That was the most wonderful package I had ever received! I went back to the room with the other women, and I shared the bread. We savored that bread with every bite.

We took small nibbles and rolled the crumbs around in our mouths. Even though it was not fresh, it tasted wonderful to us!

However, I was not allowed to take all the food with me back to the cell. And later, when I asked for the rest of the contents of my package, there was only a pitiful amount of food left. When I asked what had happened to my food, the guard shrugged his shoulders disdainfully and marched me back to my cell. I could have cried, and not only because I missed that special extra food. But the thought of my loved ones having packed it especially for me, made it all the more difficult to think of some guards sorting through my things and stealing whatever they wanted.

———————————————

One day we were treated to an unexpected kindness! Maybe the soldiers got tired of bean soup and refused to eat it, because our cell was treated to a big pot of bean soup. Along with an onion! We could hardly believe it! Soup with enough beans in it to be called soup! And a tasty onion! Whatever had happened that we should be treated so royally?

Cutting up the onion, we stirred it into the soup. We tried eating slowly to savor every bite, but we were too hungry. We eagerly wolfed down the first real food we had had in weeks. I wanted to make the delightful treat last as long as possible, but all too soon the pot was empty.

When the guard came back to collect the empty utensils, I handed them to him out the hatch. And then I saw who had given us this wonderful treat. It was the same guard who had hit me on my face when I had asked for my pills! I thanked him for the delicious soup and he jerked his head at me and quickly left. I am convinced he gave us the soup to try to make up for what he had done to me earlier. Somehow, our situation seemed just a bit less horrible. There were some guards who did have feelings!

That night, I suddenly awoke. I grabbed for my stomach. I was horribly sick! The bean soup had been too much for my starved stomach! I needed to go to the toilet room as quickly as possible. My moans awoke some of the others and I told them I was sick. No one knew what to do.

As I moaned on my cot, several of the women started banging on the door of the cell. No one wanted me to stay in this room if I needed to use the toilet.

When the guard came to see what the disturbance was about, they told him to get me out of their room. They said I was sick and would soon foul up the entire room.

"I don't have the key!" He growled at us. Then he turned around and left.

"I just can't wait," I whimpered a few minutes later.

"He can get the key," the others decided. They began screaming and banging on the door again.

For a long time, nothing happened. My stomach cramped and I thought I was going to explode! My forehead was hot and sweating. I knew that soon there was nothing I could do to control myself. I thought I would pass out.

When the noise that the women were making continued, the guard appeared again. I guess he saw how serious the situation was, for this time he did get the key and escorted me to the toilet room.

I still don't know how I kept from fainting. I went through horrible agonies as my insides boiled and churned. I gasped for breath. Dimly, I could hear the guard shouting at me. But I could not answer. I could do nothing. My entire body was too helpless.

I don't know how long it was before I could drag myself out of the room. When I was taken back to the room, I had to lean against the wall all the way. I could barely walk. Even though we were not allowed to lie down during the day, and it was now morning, I collapsed on my cot. I was totally drained of energy. The good bean soup had been too much for my weakened condition.

23

Not My Size

I could hardly believe it! I had seen Tata! We had been taken to the courtroom, and, even before we had entered, we had been strictly warned not to turn our heads and look at anyone in the visitors' benches. And as we were being officially charged and sentenced to what we already knew, I hardly paid attention. There had not been a single chance to ask for an attorney to represent us. We had not been allowed to see any one of our families or friends. But out of the corner of my eye, I had seen Tata!

What is it that makes you aware of someone you know in a room filled with other people? Whatever it is, I sensed that someone was there. I knew better than to turn my head, but I slowly swivelled my eyes as far to the right as I could. I could not see very clearly at all, but that one form looked familiar. I dared turn my head very slightly for a better look. It was! Tata was there! Right there in the same room I was in!

I wanted to jump up and run to him. I wanted to be a little girl again and feel his loving arms securely wrapped around me! I wanted him to take me away from all this horror, this nightmare of cruelty and prisons. Tata was there!

But I did not dare. I had already learned too many of the harsh rules of being a prisoner. While I could hardly keep my body under control, my mind was warning me. I did not dare do anything now. I was not allowed to. I breathed long and deeply.

As we were being led out of the courtroom, I wanted to check again. Had it just been my imagination? No, there he was! Tata, and beside him was Victor!

I was weeping silent tears as we were forced to move on. Tata and Victor were there! Tata! My father who loved me and cared for me like no one else ever did. Victor! My brother who was so much more than a brother. My friend. My spiritual advisor and mentor! My whole being reached out for them.

Suddenly I heard my name. "Silvia!"

We were outside, going from the courtroom back to the truck that had transported us here. The truck was inside the fenced area where we were being loaded.

"Silvia!" the call came again. The voice was not nearby. It was shouting.

This time, I turned to look in the direction of the call.

"Eyes forward!" shrieked the guards who were trying to rapidly herd us onto the truck.

But we had to go in the direction of the voice in order to board.

"Silvia!" again the voice rang out, closer this time. "'The Lord is my Shepherd'!" Each word was yelled clearly. "'I shall not want'!"

It was Tata! I could not help it. I turned my head and looked. There, etched against the sky, was Tata, hanging over the top of the wall. He was calling out to me and encouraging me. And instantly, I knew how he could reach the top of the high wall. We had often done it at home in Iași if we wanted to see over a wall. Victor had knelt on the ground, and Tata had scrambled on top of Victor's back to see if he could catch a glimpse of me.

"'He maketh me to lie down in green pastures'!" Everybody could clearly hear the wonderful words of comfort. "'He restoreth my soul! Yea, though I walk through the valley of the shadow of death, I will fear no evil! Thy rod and Thy staff, they comfort me'!"

We were in the truck now. The driver started the truck and we lurched forward. I could not hear Tata's voice anymore, but I continued the Psalm in my own mind. "Thou preparest a table before me in the presence of mine enemies . . . my cup runneth over. Surely goodness and mercy shall follow me all the days of my life: and I will dwell in the house of the Lord for ever!"

My heart sang as we rolled down the highway. I had seen Tata and Victor! They knew where I was!

Several days later, since our files were closed and because we had been given our sentences we were transported to a prison.

Our belongings had been returned to us. As I rummaged through my bag, I found a small jar of coffee and sugar that had miraculously escaped being confiscated. I unscrewed the lid, dipped my finger in the mixture and tasted it. It tasted wonderful!

I shared some with Elena. Then I began passing the jar around to the other prisoners on the bus.

An armed guard patrolled the aisle. He first walked the entire length of the bus to the back, then turned around and walked to the front. At least 30 prisoners were being transported.

I used my small hand mirror to see when the guard turned around at the back of the bus. Whenever it was safe, I would distribute the coffee.

Maybe it was the effects of the caffeine on my system that made me pretend not to see that the guard had caught on to what was happening. I caught his eye in my mirror when he was marching to the front of the bus, and quickly jerked the mirror away as if I did not want him to know what we were doing. He kept his orderly march to the front of the bus.

On the way back, I got a little bolder. This time when he came close, I motioned with my eyes, asking him if he wanted some.

It almost seemed like a glimmer of a smile crossed his face. He shook his head slightly, motioned in warning toward the armed guard at the back of the bus, and kept on walking.

We continued our cautious licking of the mixture, always pretending to keep the whole episode a tight secret. I think the marching guard was amused at our little game.

— · — · — · — · — · — · — · — · — · —

"I understand there are Christians among this new group of tramps!" a woman's screaming voice greeted us as soon as we got off the bus and were marched inside the prison.

"Come on! Which ones are the Christians?"

I did not check to see if anyone else raised their hand or not. I raised my right arm as high as I could reach. This was one area I was not going to compromise in.

"You crazy people! I will show you what happens to Christians! Look here!" she raised her fist. "I promise you will forget your God in two years! You will find out that there is no God and He does not know anything about you!" Her grating voice went on and on.

I began quoting scriptures to myself from memory. "Who shall separate us from the love of Christ? Shall tribulation, or distress, or persecution, or famine, or nakedness, or peril, or sword? . . . . Nay, in all these things we are more than conquerors through Him that loved us." These verses from Romans 8 were very fitting for my situation. Regardless of what this woman was screeching, I was determined that two years would not separate me from God.

"God, You know my size. You know just where I am. Thank-you that I can have that security. Whatever they do with me on the outside, they cannot take away what You have done for me on the inside."

"Get in there! What are you waiting on?" The women guards allowed us no decency, screaming and cursing at us for being hesitant to go into the place where we were to undress. There was absolutely no modesty allowed us as we undressed.

Somewhere we had gotten the impression that we were going to have a shower. But as soon as we had removed our clothes, we had to stand in line. In front of the line I could hear other women guards giving orders. "Take this. Move on!" More screaming orders.

When my clothes were taken away and I joined the line of other women, I ceased to be a person to the guards. I was just one of about 200 women in the prison. Only one of this big group of women. Silent women. For we were not allowed to talk or motion to each other. In fact, at this stage, no one really seemed to want to make any contact with each other. We were all embarrassed at our lack of privacy and we all felt the shame and humiliation of being exposed. We had no place to hide.

I thought about when Jesus was crucified. They removed his clothes, too. The shame He bore, the exposure, the lack of decency—all of this He did for my sake. Tears came to my eyes as I thought of what He went through to redeem the world from its sin. To redeem me from my sin.

"Jesus, I can bear this. I know You suffered much more for me than I have ever suffered for You. Oh, how I thank You for knowing what humiliation and shame I am going through. How I praise You for becoming a man and being tempted in all ways just like we are tempted, so that You can help us. I know that You understand what I am going through. Thank-you!"

We got our only warm shower the first day in this prison. But the comfort was short-lived. Just as the good feeling of having had a shower was warming me, it was all spoiled by what happened next.

I was leaving to get my prisoner uniform when suddenly gasoline was dumped on my head. I supposed it was to make sure we did not get lice. That awful, rank smell of the gas stayed with me a long time and took away all the pleasure of the warm shower.

The outfitting woman barely glanced at me when my time finally came for prison clothes. I could see the blouse she shoved at me was too small, but I gratefully put it on. The white and gray striped woolen skirt was a better fit, but it had large holes in it.

"Excuse me, madam, this skirt has big holes in it." I showed the skirt to the woman. "It needs mending."

"'Holes in it'! 'Needs mending'!" she mocked. "What do you think this is, a clothing store? You are in prison!" She motioned me away with her hand.

Boots. Big, rough, prison boots. I slipped my feet into the boots, and they were several sizes too large.

I tried again. "These boots are not my size. I will get blisters if I wear these boots, especially without socks."

"Not your size! Get out of here! You will have plenty to think about in here and you will forget if your clothes are your size! Here is your number. Make sure you wear it all the time if you know what is good for you. This is no motel!"

Number 224. I lost my name. I lost my identity. I was now

merely a number.

All of us women prisoners were now dressed in the same uniform. Gray and white stripes. It did not matter what shape or size anyone was, we were now blended into a blob of humanity. Nobody cared about what size we were. We were forced into a mold so that we would no longer think for ourselves. We were no longer people with names. We were just numbers. I was number 224.

I lost something that day: stripped of my clothes, stripped of my identity, stripped of my name and assigned a number like some animal. Something inside of me seemed to shrivel up and die. To be totally ignored as an individual and to have no respect shown to me was extremely hard. It was not that I felt I was important or needed to be recognized by everyone. It was that no one cared. I became a blank. Only a number.

Room number 13. I was not in the least superstitious, I thought, but I noticed that number when we were entering our assigned sleeping room. It seemed like another attack from Satan. "An evil omen!" he seemed to be whispering. I prayed for protection and trusted that God would care for us.

The room Elena and I were shoved into was large enough to hold 15 women, but we saw almost 30. The cots were barely wide enough for one person, and now two people were to share each small strip of straw-filled mattress.

For some reason, the thought crossed my mind that this must be what hell looks like. The women who were crowded into that room had such looks of anger and hate and despair written on their faces that I flinched. Here, away from the restraining hands of the guards, they seemed to be like demons. Suspicion, resentment, and belligerence furrowed their foreheads, and their eyes flashed fire at us. We were two too many for this room, and we felt their resentment.

At one end of the room was a tiny cubicle that contained a toilet. Inside this cubicle and spilling out of it were women, smoking. This was the only place they were allowed to smoke and so many of them were addicted to cigarettes that they tried to crowd into that one corner. The stench and smoke of the cigarettes, the foul language they used to address each other, the crowded room—this must be a little like hell must be. I shivered in horror as the shock of having to spend two years in here sank in.

There is no getting used to prison life. How can you get used to a fluorescent bulb without a cover, burning all night just a few inches from your head where you are lying on the top bunk trying to sleep, spoon fashion, beside another woman, even if she is your friend? How can you get used to picking up stones in bitterly cold weather every day and wondering if you will ever get warm again? How can you get used to being screamed at, cursed at, and yelled at all day long? How can you get used to prison food that never is enough, never is good, never is satisfying?

In the mornings, a tremendously loud, jangling bell startled us from our sleep. We needed to leap out of bed, try to quickly use the toilet and be ready to stand at attention when the second alarm went off. It did not matter that the bell rang every morning. That loud, jangling noise always made me leap up in terror.

The work in the fields went on day after day. Spring was still slow in coming and the rains drenched us as we worked. The mud sucked at our boots, blistered feet were shown no mercy, and we worked until we were exhausted.

I lost track of time. Every day was just the same. Spring out of bed. Gulp down some tasteless food. Board the truck with 150 other women and go work the land. Return in the evening to the crowded, smoke-laden room, so exhausted, so hungry, so tired, that every move was an effort. The next day, do it all over again.

Many nights I was so weary that I could not sleep. I would pray and try to quote scripture by memory. I longed for my Bible. And when I did fall asleep, I would wake in fitful starts, thinking the rising bell had gone off.

Every little kindness was a ray of sunshine in our dark world. One time Elena and I were working in the field and the man who was our work director picked us out to work in the greenhouse. When we entered the warmth of the greenhouse, he turned and spoke to us.

"You are new here. I want you to work in here and transplant these seedlings. You girls are different. I don't think you belong here." He was whispering because there were other guards outside, and no one was supposed to have any conversation with the prisoners.

In the days that followed, he showed us small favors. Once we were told to work in a room where we had to sort apples. He quietly told us we were allowed to eat whatever we wanted. "I know why you are here and what your charges are," he said in a low tone. He looked at us with a searching look and shook his head. I could read compassion in his eyes.

"Lord, You have shown me that You do know where I am. Thank-You for the kindness shown us here in this awful prison by this man. You know just when we need encouragement! Even if the prison officers are not interested in my size, I know You know my size. You know where I am!"

24

Broken

I could feel the heat building up outside. The rhythmical sway of the train was enough to make me sleepy, but there was no room to sleep. This was the first day of our transfer from one prison to the next. Suddenly, without warning, we had been told to get what few things we had, and get on the truck. We had been taken to the train station, and, thank God, Elena and I were still together.

We prisoners had an entire train car. One half was for the women, and in the other half, the men were chained together. I wondered if the passengers in the other train cars knew that they were on a train with prisoners. I tried to remember what it had been like to be free and to be able to travel.

The windows had been covered with sheets of tin. There were eight of us together in one compartment. Eight, in a place constructed to hold four. That meant some of the people always had to stand.

I wiped my forehead with my hand, sweating so much that my clothes were already wet. I looked at Elena. Her hair clung damply to her skin and she looked white. I pressed my face against the tin sheet. It felt cool at first, but then I felt that the tin was actually hot. The sun was probably shining directly on it.

The day wore on. The train constantly slowed down, stopped, and started again. We could hear the whistle blow for road crossings. We took turns sitting down, trying in vain to find a place of comfort. As the heat increased, we longed for some air, some cool breeze to relieve us of the stifling heat. The door to our small compartment was locked and when I put my hand to the crack under the door, I could not feel the slightest cool air come in. In fact, it felt like it was hotter in the aisle than in our room.

A dim light burned overhead. We went on mile after mile. In that heat, we felt like we were dehydrating. The small amount of water that we had had that morning was not nearly enough to last through the day. Yet the train went on. Every time the train stopped, I listened in vain for some footsteps bringing us something to drink. But nothing happened.

There was only a little relief late that day when the sun finally went down. And by the time the door was opened and a portion of dry, moldy bread spread with lard was thrust in the door, none of us were interested in eating. All we wanted was water. Our eyes greedily watched as the aluminum cups were filled. When I heard the sound of water trickling into the cup, I felt a shiver go through me.

I wanted to make the cup of water last as long as possible, but I was too thirsty. I tipped it and felt the wonderful liquid go down my throat. It was ecstasy!

The next day, again we sweltered. Some of the women removed their clothes and sat in exhaustion as the heat again took its toll. I tried to press my burning face against anything that might feel cool. I thought I was going to faint. My mind became numb. All I could think of was water. I fantasized about water. I wanted to think of something else, but always my mind went back to water. Oh, to have some water.

My tongue felt swollen. When I licked my lips, I was startled at how dry and cracked they were. Adding to our misery, the air was so putrid with the odor of our unwashed bodies that I thought I couldn't bear it.

"Please, Lord, let me die quickly. I have longed for death before, but this time, I just pray for a quick death. I don't know how much longer I can stay sane in this awful heat. I have never known such a terrible thirst. Won't You just come and take me home?"

Another night. Once more the temporary relief of having water. A cup of water. The value of water was beyond anything I had ever owned.

It was on the third day, when I wondered how much

longer we could endure this torture, that I was shaken out of my stupor.

"Oh-h-h!" the long-drawn-out cry came piercing through the door. "No, don't do it again! I am so sorry that I asked for water! No! Oh, no! I shouldn't have asked for water!" The plea was suddenly cut off.

I started in horror! The voice was that of a young boy. And I could hear a guard cursing and swearing. The sound of a club whacking against the boy's body made me flinch.

Again the anguished cry. "Please! No! No! I don't want water! Please don't!" There was a gasp, then all was silent.

Did they kill him? My hair prickled on my scalp and I felt a numbing sensation all over. I had been thinking of calling for mercy and asking for someone to bring us water. Oh, I did not dare now. That horrible scream reverberated in my mind. What had they done to the poor boy?

The nightmare ended. Somehow, we managed to survive, and when we stumbled off the train and into the next prison compound, it seemed I couldn't get enough fresh air. And when we were shoved into a room, I cautiously drank only a little water at a time.

So here we were at another prison. Another horror story.

This was a special prison for women only. During the daytime, the prisoners were forced to labor at sewing machines, making uniforms for the police. I had never thought I would miss the other prison, but once more I found myself cringing as we were screamed at, sworn at, and rudely introduced to a new schedule.

They separated Elena and me. The parting was extremely hard. I depended upon Elena's friendship so much and I knew she depended on me. But by that time, we dared not protest. We were the new prisoners. We were the ones who received no mercy.

I was put into a room of 60 women. Everyone seemed to have only one interest—survival. There was no friendly feeling at all between anyone. Very seldom does anyone make friends in prison. It costs too much. Most of the prisoners don't want to become involved in other prisoners' lives. Only occasionally did I find out why someone was in prison. There was hardly any speech, only short, terse words from one to the other. For the most part, each one of us went about in a world of our own.

At times I felt I should try to talk to some of the women around me, but most of the time I was too wrapped up in my own misery to try. The faces of several women awoke feelings of compassion in me, but since I seldom saw the same women, the feelings died.

———————————————————————

"I don't want to hear any noise from a single one of you! Get your food down and shut up!" I could hear by the voice that the woman guard was young, but her face was twisted with hatred. We were in the dining room, 500 of us, and as much as we tried, it seemed like we made a good deal of noise. But it was an eerie noise. Only the scrape of a stool or bench on the floor. The noise of eating. The occasional clatter of some spoon or utensil being dropped, then the sudden silence following the clatter.

"I said, 'No noise!'" I looked up to see the young guard advance upon an older woman sitting across the table from me. The woman had turned to her neighbor and asked for salt.

Wham! The guard viciously shoved the old lady's head on the table. The sound of her head slamming against the table was terrible.

I felt a hot tide of blood rising up within me. I was so angry. The vicious cruelty of that guard made me seethe.

The guard must have felt my eyes staring at her. She glared back at me for a minute. She didn't say a word, but we locked eyes. Finally, she spit on the floor and walked away.

I felt drained at the emotion that had surged through me. But I was so upset with how she had treated the defenseless old woman. I didn't want to be angry, but I was. These people had no mercy.

This prison held horrors that I had not experienced in the other one. One of these horrors was the isolation room that we walked past to get to the dining room. One day as we lined up to go in to eat, I heard moans of deep distress. "Mercy! Someone have mercy!"

My blood chilled. The moans came clearly through the bars. I moved closer. Again the moans and cries of someone in deep distress.

I put my mouth close to the bars. "Be strong," I whispered. "Don't give up!"

A sharp dig in my back made me straighten up. The prisoner behind me frowned at me and motioned at me to move with the line.

I moved. It was the lady who was said to be in prison because she had killed her husband and then ground him up in her meat grinder. She had a wild look in her eyes, and everyone left as large a space around her as possible. She had a nervous twitch in her shoulders and she constantly grimaced.

It was the remembrance of scenes like this that made me draw ever more into myself. I was constantly in fear of being punished or put into the isolation cell.

One desperate night, I was lying in bed, trying to pray. Something was happening to me. I felt so strange. I tried to concentrate, to think of what to say, of what to pray. Nothing came to my mind.

I wanted to quote Scripture verses. I could not think of any. Not a one. All the hundreds of verses I had committed to memory during my childhood were gone. I could not think of a single phrase from the Bible.

I felt so weird. So empty. I wanted to think of a song. There was none there. I hunted in desperation for some phrase that would trigger a tune, or some tune that would bring words to my mind. But there was nothing there. Not a shred of a song. Not a single Bible verse.

A darkness came over me. My memory was going. As hard as I tried, I could think of nothing. And to haunt me, my mind kept echoing the words of that woman in the other prison. "You will forget God! You will forget God!"

I fought against this horrible darkness. There was war in my mind. I cried out to God, "Lord! You must keep me! I don't know what is happening to my mind! I am scared! I remember almost nothing!"

I worked in a daze the next days. Mechanically, I sat at the sewing machine and sewed the uniforms. I worked with Maria, a deaf mute, as a team. I had won her friendship earlier, and we worked side by side.

While at work, I decided on a course. I would go on a hunger strike. For I was convinced that I was losing my mind. I could barely remember who I was and where I was from. I could think clearly and knew exactly what was happening right then, but the past was slipping away . . .

I suspected that I was being drugged. And I determined I would not eat anything. I would starve myself rather than go insane.

By this time Elena was with me in the room I shared with the other women. I had dared ask the guard in charge to allow Elena to come into our room because she was so scared of sleeping in the room where a large bunch of gypsies had been raising all kinds of riots. But even having Elena with me was not any help this time. I was losing my mind.

During this time, Maria was moved away from my sewing area, and a woman named *Lenuţa* took her vacancy. This constant changing was all part of a plan to keep our minds in turmoil and to prevent us from getting to know anyone. I had been so used to Maria, and even used some sugar that I had received in a package from home to win her friendship. But now all that was gone.

Lenuţa was one of the prostitutes who was serving time in prison. Haughty, cold, and seemingly indifferent, she banged into the chair and started sewing.

My job was to sew the first pieces of the uniform together and her job was to finish the uniform. The constant monotony of the sewing was so boring that I had made a point of seeing how carefully I could sew each seam. It gave me a goal to be able to sew straight without having anything wrong when the inspector inspected our work.

With Maria as my partner, we had worked out a system where we were well able to get our quota done for the day. But now with Lenuţa, it was different.

"Look here!" The man who inspected our clothes was standing behind us. "This uniform is awful! You will not do this kind of work!" He glared at us.

"It is not me," Lenuța whimpered. "I do the work right. I can't help what she does."

I did not open my mouth. I knew that the seams I did were all right. I had not had any trouble since Maria had shown me how. The seams Lenuța did were crooked and the uniform did not lie flat.

"Shut up! I didn't ask who did it! I want only perfect uniforms coming out of this division!"

Lenuța scowled at me and went back to work.

"God, I don't know what to do. You know it is not my work that is at fault. Show me what to do!"

What neither of us knew was that the inspector had already taken things into his hands. Each piece of fabric was stamped with a number, and when the next stack of uniforms was delivered from our division, he traced the faulty seams back to Lenuța.

He severely scolded her, and when he left I could tell that Lenuța was desperate. I told her quietly that I would show her how to sew the seams the right way. At first she rebuffed my offer, but when it became obvious that she had to have help, she allowed me to help her.

—·—·—·—·—·—·—·—·—·—·—·—

For four months, I wrestled with trying to get my memory back. I still prayed, but I could not remember any scrap of song or any Bible verses. I became like a robot. Because I had no will left, I had not gone on with my hunger strike.

When a package arrived from my sister Rodica, at first I did not know who had sent the package. Rodica. Oh, yes, I had a sister, Rodica. I stared at the package on the table. It had been opened.

"Where is the rest of my stuff?" I asked the officer.

"It was too heavy. You may not receive more than one kilogram in one package."

I knew what had happened. He had opened the package and taken out what he wanted and gave the rest to me. They did that. I had heard the story of one prisoner who had seen that his package had been opened. He became so enraged that he had leaped on the police and choked him. He was willing to face the death penalty for getting even with the one who had stolen things from his package.

There was bread in the package. Some sugar. And some meat. I looked longingly at the meat, but it was spoiled and I did not dare eat it.

When I was back in our room, I threw the meat into the trash can. Several of the women saw it and said they would fry it on one of the irons they used to press the uniforms. Maybe that would make it fit to eat.

When they fried it, the odor of fried meat filled their workroom. The inspector rushed in and demanded to know what was going on. No one wanted to take the blame and then someone said that number 224 had gotten a package. But because I was not even in their workroom, and told the inspector that I had thrown the meat out, I was not held responsible. There were times when justice did prevail.

One evening, a woman named *Veronica* came back into our room. She had already been gone for days and I had almost forgotten about her. But when she staggered into the room, I could scarcely believe what I saw. She was a wreck. Her eyes stared straight ahead and she moaned and cried. She babbled about the horrors of the isolation cell. She raved madly and rocked herself back and forth on the cot. I stared in horror!

"Number 224! And number 226! Follow me!"

I jumped up wildly! It was the same guard who had banged the old woman's head on the table. Had she seen me whisper to someone in the isolation room that one day when I was in the supper line? Was that where I was going?

It did not comfort me that Elena was the other one called. I was terrified!

The guard stopped in front of the isolation cell and unlocked the door.

My heart beat with great huge thumps! What was happening now?

"You two go in and clean the room! Everything!" She pushed us inside and left.

We took one look at the room, and Elena burst into tears. We could not believe what we saw.

Human waste was all over the floor. The smell was so

horrible that it burned our eyes. The cots were not covered with any mattresses, but only a network of thin wire. They were locked up against the wall for the day so that no one could sit down. That would have been too much of a luxury. There was absolutely no light in the room, only the light that shone in from openings around the door.

I had no idea where to begin. We stood in silent shock. This was the isolation room! And Veronica had been in here ten days! No wonder there was the cry for mercy!

"Why aren't you cleaning?" the shrill cry of the guard assaulted our ears. "I told you to clean and you stand there. Get to work!" She shoved us forward, further into the room.

"We need a broom, or—or something," I stammered.

"A stream of vile words was flung at us. We were not going to use a broom. We had hands, didn't we? We were to clean the floor and fill the buckets that she had brought. We stared in horror as the realization struck us. We had to use our hands!

"God, how can I? When I said I would give You my everything, my whole body, my hands and my feet, did You mean this? Oh, I don't know how it is possible!"

There was no water. There was no shovel or anything with which to scoop. So we used our hands. There simply was no other choice.

We gathered the waste together and filled the buckets. We did all the cleaning with our hands.

When we were finished, it was time for supper. We walked with our hands held away from our bodies. We did not look at our hands. Once we were in the washroom, we rushed to the sinks. We had no soap; no hot water with which to wash. We washed and washed but we could not get our hands clean. It did not matter that they looked clean. We knew better. Our hands were not clean. Those hands were not our hands.

It was time to go in for supper. We went in, but we could not eat. I still kept my hands from touching any part of me. I could not bear to look at them. I felt so unclean, so polluted.

That night as I lay on my cot, I could not sleep. I tried to pray. I just had those terrible visions of that room, that awful job that we had been forced to do.

"Give me some scriptures, God. I need some Word from You!" It was a cry of desperation.

"Love your enemies!" Suddenly a verse came to me!

"Lord, I don't want a commandment! I want some promise from You that I know You care for me! I went through something awful! Please comfort me!"

"Love your enemies!"

For such a long time, no Bible verses had come to me. And now, suddenly, this verse came back. I tried to think of other verses, but I couldn't. "Love your enemies!" It was as if I could hear that verse being spoken. "Love your enemies!"

I tried to think of other verses. I could picture my Bible. I knew how the pages looked. I knew on which side of the page some of the promises were. But I could not think of a single verse to comfort me. Only one, "Love your enemies!"

I was so tired and so miserable. Finally I gave up . "O.K. God. I will do that. I will tell the guard who made us clean that room 'Good morning' tomorrow. I choose to love her!"

The next morning after the alarm had shrieked us awake, the same guard came to inspect us. I gathered up courage and said, "Good morning!"

She looked at me in astonishment. Then she cursed me. "What are you trying to do? What made you say that to me?"

"It was God," I told her.

"You keep your God to yourself," she yelled at me.

That day during work, I felt different. Something was different. I felt a lightness that I had not felt for days.

I was bending over my sewing machine. "Silvia!" I was startled to hear someone call my name. No one called me Silvia. I was number 224!

Again the call, "Silvia!" I looked up and stopped sewing.

I could see no one. There was only a calm hush. Lenuţa was still busy sewing. No one else was paying any attention.

"Silvia! 'The Lord is my shepherd! I shall not want! He maketh . . .'"

It was Tata! I had a clear vision of Tata clinging to the top of the courtyard wall while we were being taken to the bus. "'He restoreth my soul.' Silvia, do you hear me?" Tata's voice was so real it seemed like Lenuța would hear it too.

I remembered I had nodded my head slightly to let Tata know I heard him. "The Lord will be your shepherd, Silvia!"

"'Though I walk through the valley of the shadow of death, I will fear no evil: for Thou art with me; Thy rod and Thy staff they comfort me!'"

My memory was back! I clasped my hands together! I could clearly remember everything!

I was free! Oh, I cannot tell in words the freedom that came over my soul. I was no longer in prison! My spirit was free in Christ!

"God, I praise You. I adore You. You are all I want. I love You. I thank You for being with me in this place. I thank You for letting me be in this place! God, my life is Yours! Oh, Lord, thank-you for breaking me! I thank You for bringing me to the end of myself. I was no longer anything to anybody. I was just a number. But now You have set me free! You called me! I am Yours, wherever I go! Thank-you, Jesus!"

I could not stop praising God, and I could not stop quoting verses. Songs came back. I laughed and cried. I had to keep on working, but I could not keep from singing.

"There's no other friend like Jesus," I sang. I could not keep silent. A well of joy was flowing from me.

And in that room of women working, of sewing machines humming, I was amazed to hear other voices joining me. Hesitantly at first, and then stronger. There were other people in here who knew hymns! I was so surprised!

We sang other songs. I whistled. The joy was sweeping over me in waves!

All at once, the door swung open. The director stood there, his brows bunching together. "What is going on in here? Is this a church? You are not allowed to have a church here!"

Even though our voices quieted, I was still singing inside.

That evening back in our room, I could not keep silent. I began telling Elena what had happened. Others listened to what I was saying. There were interested faces as I related how God had given me my memory back. And as I began quoting Bible verses, they listened quietly.

Anica, the daughter of the guide and his wife, was in our

room. She had resented me from the beginning, and now it seemed that what was happening pricked her conscience.

She huddled in a group of some of the other women. I felt that they were ready to break up our meeting.

Nothing had happened yet, however, when the door opened and a guard hauled Anica out into the corridor. We could hear her yells and screams of pain as she was beaten again and again.

I had nothing but compassion for her. And when she came back into the room, she cowered in her cot. I was convinced that God did not want the spiritual work stopped that was begun in our room that night. I continued quoting scriptures and sharing the words of songs.

Evening was so different. I had a purpose to live for. No longer did I have that dark cloud hovering above me. Now, everything was free and light. It made a difference how I viewed the other prisoners. I tried to let them know that I cared about their lives. It made a difference how I looked at the guards. I no longer resented them, but rather pitied them. Christ had set me free!

It was so wonderful to be free! I was so thankful to God for allowing me to go through all those horrible experiences so I could completely come to the end of myself and break my will before God! The price had not been too much to pay for the wonderful freedom that flooded my soul. Regardless of what would happen in the future, I had the assurance that God truly was with me! I knew again that He knows my size!

25

Hopes Dashed

I woke up early the next morning. Even before the dreaded alarm bell had shrieked its harsh tones over the entire prison, I was awake. I lay there, not moving, for fear I would disturb Elena.

"In all Thy ways acknowledge Him, and He shall direct Thy paths."

"I am the Way, the Truth, and the Life."

"I am the Good Shepherd, the Shepherd gives His life for the sheep."

I could scarcely believe it. The Bible verses that came flooding into my mind were so wonderful. How had this happened?

I reflected on the one verse that had come to me. "Love your enemies." When I had been willing to do what God had wanted me to do, He had restored my memory. God had heard my cry! This lesson has stayed with me. If I want God to answer my prayers, I have to be obedient to whatever He reveals to me.

"Dear Lord, I am willing to do whatever You want me to do. Thank-you for making it possible for me to have my memory back again. Help me to know how to keep on trusting You even when things seem to be going out of control. I care not anymore what You have in store for me, I will trust in You."

I decided that every morning, I would quote all the memory verses that I could, reciting them to myself alphabetically. And when I came to the letter L, I would always remember, "Love your enemies!"

The days in prison were still long, the food was still bad, the working conditions did not change, and there were times when the unknown future stared me in the face. But one thing sustained me through it all. God was by my side. He had called me by name. I was in the protection of His hands.

I carefully scraped my spoon against the bottom of the bowl. Even though prison food was not tasty, I was no longer very picky when it came to what I ate. I was glad to eat what was provided. There was no extra weight on my large frame. How I wished I had been able to eat the carrots and onions before they had been cooked to a pulp in the watered-down soup I had just finished. I almost forgot what fresh vegetables tasted like.

Elena and I had been working in the prison kitchen garden for several days. I had longed to eat the carrots and onions that we weeded, but we were strictly forbidden to eat anything. The guard would see us and report us. Neither of us forgot the isolation cell and its terrors.

It was now August, 1981, and whenever we were sent to work in the garden, I was reminded again of how slowly our time in prison went. The days inside, working at the sewing machine, seemed unending. And when I was again sent outside, I was always surprised how little time had passed. We had been in prison for six months, but it seemed like years.

However, my newly restored joy was still with me. No one had been able to take it away. I often wondered if something had been added to my food to make me lose my memory, but whatever had happened in the past, it never happened again. Wonderful promises of God's love and care flooded my mind every time I called upon the Lord.

Our supper was over. I was waiting until the signal came for us to leave the dining room and go back to our rooms.

"Attention!" the voice of the prison director broke in upon my thoughts. "I have an announcement for you!"

This was unusual. Something out of the ordinary surely must have happened, for announcements were almost unheard of. Normally, we were just shouted at while we were working.

"Our Great Leader, *Ceauşescu*, is granting amnesty for many of the prisoners. Tomorrow morning someone will come to your sleeping rooms and read the names of the people who will be released. You need to be thankful to our kind and generous ruler for this consideration."

In spite of the rules against noise and talking, a murmur of voices rose after the words had sunk into our minds. Sure, at times we had dared to dream about being released early, for we all knew that the prisons all over Romania were crowded almost beyond capacity, and that Ceauşescu often eased the problem by releasing hundreds of prisoners in August. But I had not dared hope that it would really happen here.

Back in our sleeping room, we were unusually quiet. At first, no one seemed to know what to say. I am sure that everyone had one thought. "Will my name be called tomorrow, or will I have to stay and serve my sentence?"

I knew there were prisoners there who had already served 15 years. To these old-timers, it seemed that hope for their freedom had almost disappeared. But as for us, we couldn't help but hope.

I was not in bed yet when I heard someone crying. It was *Sofica*, a woman who slept on the bottom bunk of my bed. She was huddled in a heap, trying to stifle her tears.

I went to her. "Sofica, what is wrong?"

"I am so afraid I will not be released. I do not know what will happen if I do get released and I don't know where my husband or children are. I can't think what will happen to them if I don't find them. I just feel so awful!"

"Sofica, remember I have often told you that God is in control of our lives? Can you just trust God to take care of your family? I know it is hard to wait and wonder if our names will be called for release tomorrow, but it is wonderful to trust in God and let Him give us His rest. Will you try?"

Sofica swallowed and nodded. I patted her shoulder and left. I knew Sofica's story. She and her husband had tried to break up a fight, and in the following melee, everyone had been arrested and put into prison. Since she was in prison, she had not received one word about her husband or her children.

It seemed so unjust to see her languish in prison because she had tried to stop the fight.

Naturally, Elena and I had many questions that night. What would we do if one of us was released and the other wasn't? I told Elena that if she were released, and I wasn't, she was to go to my home and tell my family about my condition. Even though I had seen Dănuţ during a brief visit, I was not able to have much conversation with him. He had told me that Tata was very ill, and my one chief concern was that Tata would no longer be alive when I was released from prison.

Later, when Rodica had sent a package and Dănuţ and I had had several more minutes of precious conversation, he had told me just how sick our Tata was. He had finally been diagnosed with leukemia.

And now, when I even dared to think that I might be released in the morning, one thought kept coming to me. I would be able to see Tata again! I don't think any of us really slept that night. At one moment, I was convinced there was no hope that my name would be called. I remembered all the harsh and sneering remarks made to us by the guards. I thought of the words of the one who had asked who among us were Christians. "I will make you forget all about your God!" No, it did not seem possible that I could be released.

But hope seems to grab at anything. The announcement had been made that Ceauşescu was pardoning prisoners. If it was true, someone had to be pardoned. And it could just possibly be me.

I tried not to think about it. Freedom? Would I really be free? What would my life consist of? I would have the stigma of having been in prison. Could I get a job? What would happen if I went back to Iaşi? What would happen if I did not go back to Iaşi?

I tossed and turned. Elena was as restless as I was. I knew her mind was traveling in the same way mine was. It did no good to talk about it. It was something that we had to fight through on our own.

On our own? I was not on my own. "I will never leave thee, nor forsake thee!" God knew all about what I was facing.

"God, I will bring this to You. I will allow You to be in

218

control of what happens tomorrow. I cannot know, but I know You do know. You knew my size when I was a little girl, and I know You answered me when I lost my memory. I will trust You now."

—·—·—·—·—·—·—·—·—·—·—·—

Sometimes I have had certain feelings about what is going to happen. But that morning as the director came to our room and began reading the names of the women who were to be released, I had no idea, no feeling whatever whether my name would be called or not.

Often I have wished that my last name did not begin with a T. Even in school I had to go through the agony of waiting until the teacher came to my name to see if I had passed or not. And this time it was the same way.

I cannot tell you how tense the room of 60 waiting, expectant women was that morning. And how can I describe the feelings as the names were called out? The involuntary exclamation of those whose names were called. The gladness that sprang into the dull eyes as the realization dawned on them that they were going to be released. The spring in their steps as they went out the door!

Or how can I tell about the dashed hopes of the ones who were passed over—when realization came that the director was past the place where their name would have been? The slumped shoulders. The looks of despair. The wretched cries and banging of heads against the bars in frustration!

I was reminded of the Judgment Day. The director was like the angel reading the names in the book of life. The joy of the released. The despair of the lost.

But yet, how different. Here, man seemed to be in control. Here, man seemed to have the earthly destiny in his hand to release or not to release.

But in the judgment, all will be just. And God is in control. We do not need to fear, for we Christians have been washed by the blood of Christ. We have been redeemed by His sacrifice. Our pardon has been signed by His grace through faith in Him. So, I waited, knowing that even though man seemed to be in control, it was God Who knew all things.

Even when Elena's name was called out, I was still forcing myself not to hope too much. Better not to expect, for then the disappointment would not be so great.

"*Stănescu, Ileana!*"

"*Stoicescu*, Maria!"

The director was coming closer to the T's. My heart began beating rapidly. I couldn't keep myself from hoping. I gripped my hands together.

"*Tănase, Tereza!*"

"*Tărniceriu, Silvia!*"

I listened to my name being called. At first I wondered if I had heard correctly! He had called my name! Never had my name sounded so good. I could claim it as my very own. Now I was no longer just a number!

Then I was in the outer room with the other released women. We were crying and laughing and hunting for dresses or skirts and blouses among our possessions that had been returned to us. I hastily shoved my arms into one of Elena's too-small blouse sleeves. It didn't fit, because even after having been in prison for six months, I was still larger than slim Elena. But it didn't matter. We were going to leave! Any civilian clothes were wonderful. It didn't really matter if they fit. Size was of no importance right then. We had been freed! Our names had been called!

And our bags had been returned, with our personal belongings in them!

When Elena and I walked together out the first gate and into the courtyard, we could scarcely contain our excitement. The big iron gates that were always closed and locked unless we were under armed guard, were standing wide open. Just a few more steps and we would be outside those gates!

But we were still inside when we heard a shout. "Stop!"

My heart sank! Surely that command was not for us.

"Stop! You four women! You cannot go free!"

It was the director, screaming from behind us. He sent a guard to bring us back. Another guard stood at attention, ready to slam the gates shut.

"There has been a mistake! You cannot go free! You must return and go back to work!"

In our shock, we could not do anything. We had no questions, we had nothing to say.

We went back to our room. All that day, we went through our work as if we did not have feelings. I sewed my usual quota of uniforms. I went to the dining hall for supper.

I felt the looks of the other prisoners and of the guards as we performed our duties. Yes, Elena had cried at first, and I imagine everyone thought we would become hysterical after going through the tension of not knowing if we would be released, then being released only to be called back again.

But in my mind, I could only whisper, "Lord, whatever You want. Perhaps I have not learned yet what You want me to learn. Maybe it will take the full two years of going through Your school before I have learned what You want me to learn. Thy will by done."

Each of us prisoners was assigned a certain time to be on watch whenever our cell was occupied. I am not sure for what reason, except perhaps to add to the constant strain of being under surveillance. That night, I had to be on watch from midnight until two-thirty. Elena stayed up with me, and when we realized that we still had our bags, we began looking at Elena's pictures.

I guess we were quite emotional after having gone through the stress of the day, because we started laughing at some of the pictures. Memories of times past came sweeping over us. We had to stifle our giggles and as we struggled to laugh silently, I am sure some people would have thought we had gone crazy. We laughed until tears streamed down our cheeks. It seemed we needed an outlet for our emotions.

The hope that had sprung up in hearts was soon dead again. Two days later, when the director called our names again, we were absolutely not expecting to be freed.

"No, you will not do this to us again," I thought to myself as the director took us to the room to change clothes again. "I will not believe that we have been released unless we are outside the prison and the gates have been locked behind us. I will not go through the horrible process again of being yanked back at the last minute."

Wordlessly, Elena and I again dressed in street clothes. We

walked toward the first gate. It was open. We passed through and walked toward the second gate. It, too, was open.

At every step, I expected to hear the director's voice screaming, "Stop!" Every nerve in my body was ready for the command. We walked closer to the gate.

We were at the gate. Now we were passing through.

No yell. No command. Nothing.

My breath was coming in short gasps. My heart was pounding.

The guard behind us shut the gates. I heard the rattling of the chain as he locked the gates.

I looked at Elena. She stared back. But we kept on walking. What if this was a trick? They could still send the guards after us, just like Pharaoh had sent his army after the escaping Israelites when they were crossing the Red Sea! My skin prickled.

Then I heard something. My name!

"Silvia! Elena!"

I looked down the road leading to the prison. Someone was running toward us. Two people! As the figures came closer, I recognized a pastor from Bucharest, *Daniel Brânzei*, and his wife, *Dana*!

We collapsed into their arms, all of us weeping and praising God. It seemed impossible! How had they known that we would be released that day?

"We've been waiting for you three days already!" Brother Daniel explained. "We saw in the newspaper that Ceauşescu was granting prisoners amnesty. When you did not come out, we went to the Minister of Internal Affairs and demanded to know why you were not released.

"At first they did not listen to our questions, but I said I would not leave until I had an answer from him that they would release you. Finally, they gave the word that you would be released."

Of course, we had not known what was happening outside prison. But it was evident that someone had not wanted us to be released. That thought was like a troubling cloud in my mind.

But I pushed the thought away. We were free! I could see

for miles without a wall or a fence or a guard keeping me in a certain place. The road ahead of us stretched into the distance. The earth around us seemed immense.

We went back to Brother Daniel's house in Bucharest. There we could take a bath. There we could sit in comfort. It didn't seem real.

Mica, Daniel's mother, prepared the best of Romanian food for us. It was a feast! But the vast supply of food was too much. Our stomachs had shrunken and all we could do was nibble at the delicious meal.

"Silvia," Dana said gently. "Are you all right? You seem different. I don't just mean that you look thin and unhealthy, but your mannerisms are different. You don't talk, or something, like you used to."

I smiled at her. I knew everyone remembered me as the talkative one. I used to be able to talk for hours. And now, I had almost nothing to say.

"Yes, Silvia, you do seem different. I guess you went through some things there in prison, didn't you? We will pray that God will bless you with His strength."

I wanted to tell them that I was different. I wanted them to know what had happened to me in prison. But for some reason, I just couldn't talk. I guess I was still in a daze.

I walked around in Daniel's house. I touched the soft upholstery of the couch. I drank in the beauty of simple things like a picture on a wall, or a vase of flowers. I reached out and felt the curtains at the window.

"Tomorrow we will take you home to Iaşi on the train," Brother Daniel planned. "We will have to leave early to get to the train station on time."

That night when I went to bed, I could not sleep. I was alone in the bed. The bed was soft. It had clean sheets and a pillow. I had been able to take a bath. And in my stomach, there was good food. Even though Brother Daniel's home was modest by any standards, I felt like I was in a palace.

I don't remember what I prayed that evening, or even if my prayers were words or not. But I do remember the praise and thankfulness that welled up inside me as I communed with God.

26

Home Again

I felt something touch me lightly on my shoulder. Instantly I sprang out of bed and stood at attention.

"Silvia!" Dana said in astonishment. "Whatever is the matter?"

I gazed at her for a moment. Then I relaxed. I was no longer in prison.

The habits that I had learned in six months behind bars were not easy to overcome. The first morning we were released, I was still in a daze. I wandered around in Daniel's house, trying to get ready to leave by train. I didn't have any personal things to prepare. I had no clothes to wear except what I was wearing from Elena's bag when I left the prison. I did not know what to do with all my freedom. There were no loud clanging bells directing me when I should line up. No one told me what to do.

One thought kept coming to me. How would the people at Iaşi respond to our return? Would the church be embarrassed about us because we had tried to escape but were caught? Would my family be glad to see me after I had spent time in jail as a criminal?

We left the apartment and boarded the train to go back to Iaşi. Brother Daniel insisted on accompanying us. I was so glad, for even though we had been released from prison, I was still apprehensive about our safety. Why had we been called back after our names had been on the list for release? Why did Brother Daniel have to go to the Minister of Internal Affairs and demand our release? Who was trying to keep us in prison?

The ride on the train was not comfortable. Too many memories of being transported by train from one prison to the next kept coming back. Even though we had comfortable seats and could open the windows, the thought of that hot, airless room and the screams of the boy kept wanting to come back.

Brother Daniel tried to be friendly. "When did you last hear from your family? I called them last evening and told them that you are released and what time we will arrive in Iaşi. Even though your Tata is ill, I am sure your coming home will be a great cheer to him."

I managed to smile at him. But I could not bring myself to talk. Something inside me held me back. As happy as I was to be out of prison, there was also something scary about being released. In prison, my life had been planned, forced. Now, I did not know what I was supposed to do. I did not know what I could do.

We were nearing the outskirts of Iaşi. I could see the familiar landmarks along the railroad tracks. A part of me wanted to hurry the train onward, and another part of me wanted to slow the wheels.

Clickety-clack. Clickety-clack. I could hear the train slowing.

I gazed out the window. The station was just ahead.

When the train stopped, our car was directly in front of the station. And I couldn't believe my eyes!

The station was filled with people! People I knew! People holding bouquets of flowers and searching the train windows for us! There were the sisters and brothers from church! There were the children from the children's choir! My family was there! And—my throat choked up—there was Tata!

The chorus of welcomes, the warm embraces, the tears of joy, and the gifts of flowers that were pressed on us were overwhelming! This crowd of people to welcome us home was more than I had ever expected.

Dear Mama and Tata! When I felt my Mama's strong arms around me, I laid my head on her shoulder and wept. It was wonderful to relax against her capable bosom.

At first I hardly knew Tata. He was dreadfully thin and pale. I could see what his sickness had done to him. But in spite of it all, when he lifted his frail arms and I went to him, I was like a bird returning to its nest. My beloved Tata was here to welcome me!

A couple from England, Les and Mair Peters, was there. They had been aware of my imprisonment and had managed to come to Romania to welcome me home. And when they came to our house, they gave us boxes of clothes. Clothes that fit me. Clothes that were just my size. I marveled once more at the providence of God. He knew my size!

In spite of all the joy of being reunited with my family and my friends, there was still the black cloud that loomed in the background. Even at the train station while I was busy greeting everyone, I was conscious of silent figures at the edge of the crowd. Men in dark suits, wearing dark glasses. And I knew I was being watched. The police knew just where I was. I was considered an enemy to my country. I was to be watched. To be shadowed and observed.

When I went back to the factory to seek employment again at my former job, I was greeted with cries of amazement from the workers.

"Silvia!" I heard from every side. "We did not know you are back! You really threw the whole factory in a tizzy when you left. Your department was behind for weeks until someone else could take over your job."

I hardly knew what to say. I had expected to be shunned, but now I was almost given a heroine's welcome. "How did you dare to try to escape? Tell us, did the police really catch you on the other side of the river? We heard that while you were walking away from the river, the Romanian police surrounded you and brought you back. But where were you from the time you left until they said they caught you?"

I knew immediately what had happened. The police had released distorted news about our escape and capture. I pictured the image they had tried to portray. A group of us fugitives, lifting our skirts daintily, tiptoeing around water puddles, and the mighty Romanian police boldly apprehending us. They wanted the people to believe that our pitiful plans for escape were no match for the vigilant efforts of the police.

My former supervisor, Mr. Nedelcu, had many questions for me, too. "You crazy girl!" he said almost fondly and grinned at me. He shook his head. "What have you done to me?"

He crossed the room and closed the door. "After you were gone for several days, the police swarmed all over this department. They sealed your warehouse and we had to shut down our department. They went over the inventory and it was good that you were so orderly because otherwise it would have taken much longer. They checked and rechecked your figures and pried and asked questions and questions. They tried to find out if there had been any workers who had helped you prepare for your flight.

"I was very upset. We could not work. They declared that you had stolen components from our factory and sold them. They wanted to insist that somewhere there was a mistake and we must be short on supplies somehow.

"And when I told them it was quite the opposite—that we had a surplus of components because we had so little waste—they wouldn't believe me until I showed them where our surplus was. Then they got mad and tried to intimidate me and told me that I was going to have to pay for helping you. Then I got mad and told them to leave the factory and let me go on with our work. I tell you, it was quite hectic!"

But when I tried to apply for a job, he was sympathetic, but helpless. "I can't give you a job. We are full and there is no position available. If I would hire you, I would be in deep trouble. The police know where you are. They would know that you came back here to work. I'm sorry, I cannot help you."

When I turned to leave, he held out his hand. "When I realized that you had left, I knew you were trying to leave the country. I prayed for you!"

I thanked him and left. How remarkable! He had prayed for me! Prayed! I didn't even think he believed in God! And he had wanted me to get out of the country!

Everywhere I went to look for work, it was the same. My identification papers were still at the prison, and without those papers, I could not even be considered. I was qualified for a number of positions I applied for, but every time, I was told, "No, we have no place for you."

Again, I was summoned to the police station, and there I was sternly told that I was considered a parasite to the country if I did not work. When I tried to explain to them that I could not work if I did not have my identification papers, I was shrugged away. "Go work in a construction crew!" was the reply I got.

One day, shortly after we had come back to Iaşi, Elena and I had just left for the day when two men came to our house and asked for me. When my mother told me about it that evening, I knew that we must not stay at home. I did not want my parents to be harassed constantly and go through the anguish of not knowing what is happening to me.

For a year and a half, we were constantly on the move. We lived with friends, we lived with relatives, we stayed in vacant apartments. And always, we were being watched.

— . — . — . — . — . — . — . — . — . — . — . —

In spite of the many times I had gone up the familiar steps to the police headquarters before, my heart still pounded faster than normal. I opened the dark green door and went inside.

I approached the front desk. A look of recognition crossed the official's face.

"Sir," I said directly, "I have come to ask for a passport to leave the country. You will not allow me to work here and get a job for which I am trained. If you do not want me here, I want to apply for a passport and go where I can be useful."

A slow tide of red rose over the official's face. "You stupid woman. You can get a job! All you have to do is sign a paper saying you will be loyal to our government, and you can get a job!"

We had gone through this before. "I will not sign a paper stating that I am loyal to the communist government of Romania. I will not become a part of a corrupt system. You say that there is freedom of religion here in Romania. Yet you discriminate against the Christians and try to force us to sign papers saying that we are loyal only to the communist party. And the tenets of the communist party declare that we shall

229

give our total allegiance to the Party. My heart belongs to God, and I cannot serve another god." I spoke calmly, for I had learned to fear the police. I no longer had quick, bold answers like I used to have.

But my testimony infuriated him. He jumped up from his desk and literally shoved me out of his office. "Get out of here, you crazy woman! You will never leave this country!"

But I prayed about it constantly. One bright spot during this time was my continued contacts with Genovieva and her friends. Soon after we had been released, Christian Aid for Romania had urged all their supporters to pray for us and write or call the Romanian embassy in Washington, D.C. for our release from the country. Later, I learned that the embassy had to unplug their telephones because the calls from the Christians jammed the lines.

We were also grateful that God miraculously allowed CAFR to send food parcels to poor Christians throughout Romania. Many large Christian families like my own were suffering from lack of food as the country's economic system kept deteriorating. This outpouring of food from Christians in the West was such an encouragement.

Constantly skulking and hiding, we somehow managed to survive. Tata, weak and ill from his sickness, managed to give us a loaf of bread every day. I knew that his meager pension was barely enough for himself and Mama, but he insisted on helping us. *Tudorică*, Genovieva's brother, was a student in medical college, but he, too, managed to share for our needs.

One day we were handed envelopes. One had my name on it, and the other one had Elena's name on it. When we opened them, there was a month's salary in each one. I had just helped another poor person with the last of my money, and now God had given it back tenfold. We had no idea who had sent the money. God had provided for us.

Another time, *Lidia*, a godly woman with 11 children, gave us some flour, oil, and sugar. The entire Christian community shared with each other. We tried to help out in return, but we could not get jobs, so it was very difficult.

At that time, we were staying with Tanti *Florica*, Victor's mother-in-law. Finally she told us tearfully, "You must find another place to live. The police are coming almost every day and questioning me about you. It is not safe for you to stay here."

We went to our pastor, Brother Iosif Morcan. He listened to our plight, then offered us several rooms in the back of his house. The rooms were used as storage rooms, but we scrubbed the walls, cleaned the floors and moved in. The bare necessities, a mattress on the floor and several odd pieces of furniture, were all we needed.

Many days we spent inside. If we left, we tried to leave early in the morning or late at night. We were literally in hiding.

After much praying, I returned to the police station. I would try again to get a passport to leave the country.

Elena went with me. And this time, I was handed the application! I still don't know why I was given the forms. Probably the officer thought he would get rid of me.

"Elena cannot apply here. She is from Suceava. She must apply there. And you must get all these signatures before we will process your application."

I looked at the yellow form. Signatures. From my place of work. From the city government. From a doctor.

We left the office. The task seemed hopeless. How could I get all these signatures when I had no place of work? Signatures were not given to anyone in any case unless he was employed there. Each worker had to have a business stamp from his employer in order to obtain the proper signature. Nevertheless, we began our task. Elena went back to Suceava to apply there, and I started trying to obtain the signatures I needed. I realized full well that the officer who had given me the form did not expect me to bring it back completed.

I talked to Tata about my plan. Sick, lying in bed most of the time, he looked lovingly at me. "Go," he said softly. "You have no life here. God bless you." He patted my hand.

I took gifts along. Gifts from the food parcels from America. I went to the doctor's office. Somehow, I gained entrance. Telling him what I needed, I asked what he wanted for pay. I told him I could give him some American coffee if he wanted some.

He looked at the coffee I offered. "Give me your form."

He signed and stamped my application.

Then I went to the city government office. I stood in line. I talked with different officials. Some were indifferent, some were rude. But I persevered. I waited. And I prayed.

Sometimes my task seemed hopeless. But many times the gifts I took along from the food parcels helped to open doors and gain admittance to the right people.

Slowly, I gained the precious signatures I needed. Every time I got one more signature, one more stamp, my hopes rose. But I also repeatedly told myself that this venture, too, could be doomed to failure. I prayed constantly and committed this to God. I was going to trust that He would provide the open doors that I needed.

It took me over a month to get the needed signatures. It was now a year since I had been released from prison. I still look at each signature as a miracle from God. And when I laid the completed form on the officer's desk, it looked like he thought a miracle had occurred, too. He stared for a long minute at the application. He scrutinized the stamps and the signatures.

"We will have to send your file to Bucharest. They will have to decide. It is not up to us." He took my application and dismissed me.

Elena, too, had miraculously gotten her signatures and submitted her application. Now there was nothing to do but to wait. And pray. How we prayed. We pled with God to hear us. And, yet, in all our pleading, we still prayed, "Not my will be done, but Thine."

—·—·—·—·—·—·—·—·—·—

Months later, I was still waiting for an answer to my application requesting permission to leave the country. I was 31 years old and wanted to be able to go on with my life. I had been going to the police office every morning. I no longer tried to hide from them. I was weary of all the cat and mouse games, of going out and not knowing who was watching me and not being able to get a job. So, I decided to check every day if my passport had come.

Every day they said the same thing. No answer from Bucharest. But I was determined to see if I could find out what was happening. So one day, after the usual denial of not hearing anything from the office in Bucharest, I asked. "Mr. Mureşan, what is happening to my request? I want to know. I have the right to know if my application has been processed."

"Huh, now you are coming to us. What do you want us to do? We cannot give you the answer. The answer must come from Bucharest."

"Mr. Mureşan, you say you know everything about me. Then why don't you know about my passport? You say you know everything when you want to scare us. And now you say you know nothing. You know you can do something about my passport. I will come every morning until I receive an answer."

He was silent for a moment. Then he looked straight into my eyes. "You do have the necessary signatures from our office to leave. But we have not received any notice from Bucharest, so we do not know whether they will release you or not."

"When did you send my report to the Bucharest office?" I was not going to give up now.

"I don't know, several months ago."

"Then we will go to Bucharest and find out where my file is. I have the right as a citizen of Romania to know what is happening with my request."

He glanced away and merely shrugged his shoulders.

—·—·—·—·—·—·—·—·—·—·—

Then, we got some very good news! David and Erma Troyer were coming to Romania to visit us! I know it was God's timing, for we were getting very weary in our struggle to live as strangers in our own country. We were not allowed to leave, and neither were we allowed to live a normal life. It was now July, 1982, and we had been out of prison nearly a year.

When David and Erma arrived at Genovieva's parents' home, I was very eager to meet them. And when I first saw David, I had to smile at myself for my earlier attempt to envision him. This was not the strong, muscular man I had thought could elbow his way into prison and release me. This black-haired, kind-faced man was of medium height, and his mild manner did not suggest anything of a knight to help people in distress. His wife, Erma, I could tell, seemed more nervous than he about being in a communist country.

They brought boxes of food and clothing. Genovieva had sent gifts to her family and friends. Tudorică and Costică, Genovieva's brothers, were there, and their English was good enough that we could converse. David and Erma arrived in the evening, and we soon saw that our guests were very tired. It was already past midnight, so we decided they could sleep at the house instead of going to the hotel where they were registered.

_._._._._._._._._._._._._._._._

I struggled to my feet from where I had been sleeping in the front room. What was that noise?

Bam! Bam! Loud, repeated knocks sounded on the front door. Someone opened the door and instantly two policemen were in the room.

"You have broken the law! You have allowed foreigners to be in your house overnight! That is not allowed! Where are they?" The police shouted the questions.

"They are in bed. They are our guests," we replied.

"They must report to the police station immediately!" The commanding officer started for the door.

"Wait! I will go. You are strangers to them. I will call them."

I darted into the room where David and Erma slept. "David!" I whispered.

Erma jumped and was instantly awake. "What's wrong?" she asked anxiously.

"David," I called again, and then saw he was awake. "Police here! They want you!"

I could tell that David understood what I was saying. But for a minute, he seemed lost in thought.

"David," I said again. "Hurry! Police want you!"

But David did not seem to be in a hurry. He slowly got up

and smoothed his hair. Then he followed me into the front room.

"Where is your wife?" the question was barked out in commanding tones.

Someone interpreted for him and David replied that she was still in bed.

"Bring her. You both must come to the police station. It is not allowed that foreigners stay in a house for the night. You must sleep only in the hotel."

"She is tired." David protested. "Can she not stay here? I will come with you."

This was interpreted, but the answer came back. "No! She must come, too."

They ordered Genovieva's mother to accompany them. After the group had left, the rest of us paced the floor.

We were so humiliated. That our country should treat our guests in this rude and insulting manner was horrible. We had not been able to give them anything to eat. And what would the police do with the Troyers?

All day long we waited. Several times small groups went to the police station to see if we could get any information, but to no avail. Finally, to our relief, we saw them coming. It was already evening.

They told us that the officials had been almost kind to them. The officials had explained that it was illegal for foreigners to stay in homes overnight, so they would need to fine them. Genovieva's mother would be fined as well. The officials did welcome the Troyers to our country, but told them they must not stay in homes for the night. Of course, this all happened after they had sat at the police station most of the day, waiting.

After our excitement died down, David told us that he and Erma would accompany us to the Bucharest office to see if they could help us get our exit visas. I believe that David began to see how desperate our situation had become.

—·—·—·—·—·—·—·—·—·—·—·—

David, Erma, Elena and I traveled the weary miles to Bucharest by train. We had to stand in line for a long time with the other people who were filing for the right to leave the country. Since the rest of the world was becoming more and more aware of the Christians' situation in Romania, there was a continued outcry against the persecution that we faced.

I did not know at that time that the requests for Elena's and my exit passports were continuing to flood the Romanian embassy. I did not know that entire churches were praying and fasting, contacting their state senators and putting pressure on the leaders of America to do something about our plight. I just knew about our frustrations at getting an answer to our request to leave.

"You are a parasite in our country!" the officer screamed at me when I was finally allowed to state why I was at the Bucharest office. "Six months in prison was not long enough for you to learn anything? Then you will learn some more. You have no reason to leave. You were born in this country and you will die in this country! Get out of here!"

Then I introduced David to the officer. "This is my sponsor from America. He wants to see my file. We have waited a year for an answer and we have not heard anything. He wants to know why nothing is being done."

At first, the official barely looked at us. Then he spat out his words. "No foreigner needs to come and tell us how to run our country."

"Excuse me, he is not trying to run your country. He just wants to know why our laws have allowed my request to go unanswered."

"Give me your documents." The officer addressed David.

David looked in his briefcase and found his passport. He handed it to the officer.

"There is no visa in this passport. You are not legally here in Romania."

Then he realized that David was not understanding his rapid Romanian. So he spoke to me. "He has no visa. He is here illegally. There is no way he can do anything for you. How did he come?"

I turned to David. "Need you visa," I stammered, my broken English aggravated in my haste to make him understand. "Where is visa?"

David understood. He began shuffling through his papers in his briefcase. He was not in a hurry. It did not seem like he thought there was any major problem. I marveled at his calm behavior. I thought he must not know how to deal with Romanian officials.

When he found his visa and handed it over the counter, the officer studied it.

Then David spoke. "I need to report to my senator about Silvia's case," he said clearly and slowly.

The officer listened. Then he left the room.

We waited. The clock ticked on. Would there be any answer today?

Then the officer came back. He had a file with him. "You are lucky. You have the approval to leave the country."

Just a few words. Words that could change my entire life. But I knew that something could still come up to prevent me. I was not given my passport immediately. No, the official said, they could not get my passport now. Another office did that. I would have to wait.

"Excuse me, my friend Elena Boghian is here, too, and we want to know the answer to her request."

They had not allowed Elena to go into the office with me, and she was waiting outside.

"You go out," I was instructed. "She can come in."

While I was waiting, I remembered the time we thought we were released from prison, and then the gates had closed us in again. Was this answer for real or was it just another trick? I could not trust any of the officers. However, my heart beat with joy. I had been granted my request!

I did not need to ask what the answer to Elena's request was. One look at her face when she came out gave me the answer. Her request was denied.

Elena's father died when she was young, and her mother, unable to care for all her children, had placed Elena in an orphanage. There, the state government raised her. The officer said they had put too much money into raising and educating Elena to allow her to leave the country. She owed the country $18,700 for her education.

We were stunned. How was this possible? There was no

joy at my news anymore. How could I leave Elena behind? My dearest friend who had suffered all the agonies with me throughout the last years? All my elation at my news turned to sorrow at the mere thought of parting and leaving Elena behind.

After the Troyers had left, we traveled back to Iași. I tried to comfort Elena, but there was nothing I could say that sounded comforting, even to me. I was going to leave, but Elena could not. How was this possible? What was I going to do? Should I stay for her sake?

27

Good-Bye

In the following days, I struggled with my emotions. Should I leave and allow Elena to stay behind? Is this what God wanted me to do?

Again I poured out my heart to the Lord. And I received the assurance that if God opened the doors for me to leave, I should go. It really would not help matters any if I stayed. Perhaps I could do more for Elena's release from America.

Time moved on, and I tried to live as normal a life as possible.

"Si-lent night, Ho-ly night. All is calm, all is bright . . ." The children's treble voices sang the beautiful Christmas hymn softly. Seventy upturned faces intently followed each beat as I directed the practice session.

This was something I loved. I had joined Tudorică in the work with the children of the church, even though I knew I was doing something dangerous. But I was determined to do something that would give my life some purpose. And I found fulfillment in working with the children. Even though I had the word from the Bucharest office that I was going to be able to leave, I still kept on with helping at church with the children's choir. I had to do something to pass the time.

"Good night! God bless you!" I helped some of the smallest ones into their winter coats. I knew many of them were shivering with cold beneath their thin coats or threadbare jackets. Yet they continued to come for chorus practice, and since we were getting ready for the Christmas program, I was glad so many had come.

"I have no idea what we should give them for Christmas gifts," I told Elena. "We don't even have enough money to buy an orange for all of them. I feel so terrible about not giving them something to brighten the day for them."

Christmas in Romania was something that only the Christians observed. The government had no use for a day celebrating the birth of Christ. For many of the children, this day became special after they started coming to church. Their love for the Bible and for the story of Jesus intensified when they grasped the importance of the birth of the Son of God.

That night, another shipment of Bibles arrived. Since I had applied to leave the country, I was more apprehensive than ever about helping with the distribution of Bibles. If I helped, I would not only endanger myself, but also the others who were involved. So usually, I did not even know when a shipment arrived.

But now, it seemed that God was answering my prayers in an unusual way. For here I was, looking into a box that I had thought was filled with Bibles. But this box had something different. Something else had been shipped along with the Bibles.

Children's books! Beautiful children's books filled with stories about children. Children who knew about God and obeyed the Bible! I looked closer. My dear friend, Genovieva, had written this book!

How was this possible? Never in all of Romania had a book been published for children with Christian stories! And now, this shipment of books had arrived just before Christmas! Just when I was praying for gifts for the children!

The excitement of having something to give the children was almost forgotten as I began to turn the pages and read the stories. I recognized the children Genovieva was writing about! These children were the ones we had worked with during the years Genovieva was still in Romania! These children were still in the church!

My eyes filled with tears. This was a miracle! A miracle from God. Beautifully colored illustrations and good, solid, Bible teaching. I hugged the book to myself and thanked the

Lord.

The books were a sensation! I passed them out right after the Christmas service was over. Every child who received a book looked at it with shining eyes. They wanted to read it right away. They had never seen such a book before. They lovingly turned the pages, read snatches of the stories, and gently ran their fingers over the beautiful illustrations. They could tell that such a book was expensive, for even the cover was beautifully illustrated. And it was a present for them! What a special Christmas!

"Don't take these books to school!" I cautioned them. "They are not printed in Romania, and it could cause trouble if your teachers would see them. They are just for you!"

I knew that these books could cause a storm if they were to catch the attention of the authorities. Not only weren't they printed in Romania and therefore did not have the sanction of the communist party, they even taught about God and how He answers prayer! The very thing from which the party was trying to wean the people!

But I have to think of what the leper did in Mark after Jesus healed him. Even though Jesus had told him to "tell no man," the healed leper could not contain himself. The leper began to "publish it much, and to blaze abroad the matter." The children could not contain themselves. Somehow, the books did get into school.

"Silvia! I must speak with you! I want one of those children's books that you gave to the children in your church! My *Larisa* is begging and begging for one. I will pay you for it!"

"Why—why," I stuttered. "What—what book?"

"Silvia, you know what book. When Larisa saw her friend *Natalia* in school who is in your children's choir, Natalia had this book. And Larisa wants one. Her friend said she got it from you."

My heart sank. The books were in school! And worse, it was no secret from whom the books had come! I was in trouble!

However, the message in *Zion I, For Unto Us A Child Is Born* was doing a marvelous work. When dear Edica and Carmen, who had not ceased coming to church in spite of their parents' harshness and criticism, had received their Christmas present, they cherished it and read it whenever they could. But they did not dare read the book openly. So they devised a plan. Whenever they could not safely read their book at home, they hid it behind some other books on the bookshelf. They considered this a safe hiding place, for their parents hardly ever touched the books on the shelf.

But how interesting are the ways of God. Edica and Carmen's mother decided to clean the house. And when she removed the books to dust them, she discovered the book her daughters had hidden.

All alone in the house, she began to turn the pages and read the stories. She was fascinated by the pictures, and even more by the true stories of children in Romania who trusted in God. At first, she was skeptical about the testimonies she read. Did God really answer prayers? But something made her keep reading.

When she was finished reading the book, she thoughtfully replaced it in its hiding place and finished the dusting. Her mind was not at rest. The stories she had read were real. The people were real. And the answered prayers must be real, too.

The next day, and the next, she got the book out and read the stories again. She began to take notice of her daughters' lives.

The things she had read about in the book were mirrored in the lives of the girls. Even in their childhood, she sensed that the faith her girls had was not just a trust in some idea of man.

We had no idea what was happening until Edica breathlessly announced one evening during revival meetings, "Mother is coming to church tonight!"

All of us prayed for Edica's mother before the service. When she came rather hesitantly in the door, the usher, not knowing who she was but wanting to welcome the visitor, showed her to the front bench.

For the first time, she heard the children sing. She watched and listened to her daughters as they sang about Jesus. She saw the joy on their faces.

When the pastor preached, she heard the wonderful story of Christ. After the message, when the pastor asked if anyone wanted to respond to Christ, she raised her hand.

"I want the God of my children in my life," she spoke clearly and yet with feeling. "For several years I have watched what was happening in their lives. I did not understand why they wanted to come to church and what they were attracted to. But what they have, I want."

Then she turned to her daughters. "I am not worthy to be your mother. I have tried to keep you from coming to church, but now I see you have what I need."

Our hearts were filled with praise. God had used the faith of two young girls to speak to their mother. And He had used the children's Bible story book to make her want to come to church and learn more about Christ. The church house was filled with rejoicing!

— · — · — · — · — · — · — · — · — · — · — ·

At last, I received my passport. As usual, I was frustrated about the condition of my passport. I was sent to the office in Iași to be stripped of my Romanian citizenship. I had to give up my Green Book, the identification that every Romanian received at birth. This book was needed to do anything in the country. No one was allowed to travel anywhere, get any job or perform any service without this important book. Now, I had to give it up. I was no longer considered a Romanian. I was a person without a country. No, I was a person without an earthly country. I truly was a stranger and a pilgrim. But I still had a heavenly country.

The passport I received did not have an exit visa. My questions were answered with the usual shrug. Every week I had to return to the office for a stamp that allowed me to be in the country. The stamps were filling up the pages in my passport.

The long days of March went by. No visa. April arrived. Still no visa.

"The Americans don't want you. We gave you the right to leave. Now they don't want you." This was how the officers taunted me when I went to check if my visa had come.

During this time, the city of Iași decided to demolish all the houses that were in my parents' village to make way for new apartment buildings. So, my aged parents were to be moved into an apartment and my childhood home was going to be dozed over.

I pitched in to help with the move. We had decided to take the firewood to the church since the apartment would be heated with natural gas. And when we cleaned out the attic, I found some Bibles that had been hidden there years before.

I decided I would hide the bag in the firewood and take the Bibles to the church house. I carried the bag of Bibles outside.

I was so used to checking to see if I was being followed or not that I immediately saw a dark figure under a tree down the street. I was instantly aware of what I was carrying. But I decided it was too late to try to hide anything. "Someone must have come to see us move!" I said loudly.

The figure moved out from under the tree. "Silvia Tărniceriu!"

My scalp prickled. It was Mr. Mureșan from the police office. I tensed. What was I going to do? The bag became incredibly heavy. I leaned it against the wagon.

"Mr. Mureșan! What are you doing there?" I called. I tried to speak in a natural voice, as if to see the head police officer in my street in the evening was a normal thing. "Come in. Meet my parents. I am sorry we can't give you tea, but our things are packed for they have to move." I chattered on and tried to distract him from what I was carrying.

He met my parents and sensed their fear. "Don't be afraid. I need to talk with Silvia tomorrow at the office. Someone from the Bucharest office has come. No, I can't stay. I must go back."

I made a bold move. "May I ride along with you to my sister's house? I don't want to go with the tractor and wagon and you will go right past my sister's place."

He looked at me in surprise. "Where—where does your sister live?" he stammered.

"Mr. Mureșan! You don't need to ask. You know where my sister lives. You have been in her street many times." I was so tired of playing their game of pretending they did not know everything about me. I was not going to let him pretend anymore.

To my surprise, and probably to his, he consented. "Drop me off at the National Theater," I said. "I will walk the back way from there."

I thanked him for the ride. "See you at eight o'clock tomorrow morning," he said and then drove slowly away.

I walked toward Margareta's house. As I cut through the alley by the orthodox church, I was hidden from the street. I raced along the alley and turned down the path that led to the front door of Margareta's house. As I ran, I jerked my sweater off and stuffed it in my handbag. Then, instead of going inside, I went out the yard gate and sped down the street. I paused briefly, then crossed the street and walked swiftly to church.

When I heard a car coming from the direction that Mr. Mureşan could be coming to check up on me, I hid behind a bush until the car passed. It was not his car, so I continued.

When I arrived, I helped unload the wood and took the sack of Bibles inside. Then we went back to Margareta's house.

I tried hard to go to sleep that night. Why had I helped hide the Bibles? I wondered if Mr. Mureşan just pretended he did not know what was in the bag. Why was I spoiling my opportunity to leave the country by again being involved with something illegal? What would I say the next day in the office?

I talked to God. And I was reminded that God gave Moses words to speak when he appeared before Pharaoh. He would give me words to say.

"You will be called in a few days to sign your passport." I could scarcely believe the words from the officer from Bucharest. He said nothing about the night's activity. I walked home in a daze.

But I was not called. Days passed. Another week. Still nothing.

The pages in my passport were being filled up. "You must give us your passport to put new pages in if the visa does not come."

This news filled me with dread. Must I also give up my passport? Even though I was considered an alien in my country, the passport I had at least acknowledged my existence. True, I had to pay a month's salary for every month I stayed in Romania with this passport, but I did have some identification. Without my passport, I would have absolutely nothing.

But before my passport was completely full, my visa arrived! I had the ticket and all my papers were in order. Now I could leave!

———————————————————

It was April 20, 1983, and all at once things were happening rapidly. Before, it seemed the days had crept by on heavy feet. But with a bewildering quickness, the time came that I had longed for—the day of my departure. Sometimes I was not sure if this was real or not. My hopes had been dashed so often before. Now, I was resigned to anything that might yet happen to keep me from leaving.

And when I was at the train station and all my family and friends came to tell me good-bye, I thought for a wild moment that I would give it all up and stay with my loved ones. There was nothing in my future that seemed secure. My early obsession to leave the country and escape to America had died away. I still wanted to leave, but when the actual time came to tear myself away from my family and my friends, I could scarcely go.

It had been terribly hard to say good-bye to Elena. She had given me a wild hug and then locked herself into the bathroom. I tried to say comforting words to her, but all I said seemed to fall on deaf ears.

I saved my last farewell for my parents. I hugged my mother close. I was leaving Mama. A Mama I had learned to love and respect beyond what I had ever thought possible. I looked lingeringly into her face. She smiled at me through her tears and I was able to smile back. Our special bond was still there, even though I was leaving.

I shall skip over most of my farewell with my Tata. Even now, years later, I cannot think of parting with my earthly father. He had taught me about God, both by his example and by his teaching. Oh, I thought I could not leave him, for I was sure I would never see him again on this earth. His disease-ridden body, covered with open sores, did not keep him from coming to the station. I had begged him not to come, but as his feeble hand stroked my hair in a parting blessing, I was glad he had been able to come. I could barely tear myself away from his arms.

I looked out through the train window, hardly able to see through my tears. I waved as long as I could see the station. Several of the children from church ran alongside the train until we gathered speed and traveled toward Bucharest.

So many times I had dreamed of this moment. Why was I not more elated and joyous? What had happened that this time was in some ways nothing special?

I had been through the school of suffering. I had lost my self-assurance and God had shown me how desperately I needed Him. I was willing now to accept whatever my loving Father had for my life.

The arrival in Bucharest, the waiting in line for my ticket to be stamped and approved, the waiting period at the gate—it all seemed unreal. I constantly thought something might still turn up. I could still be turned back.

But finally, the time for boarding came. I said good-bye to the pastor and to Victor who had accompanied me. Taking my guitar and my small traveling case with my Bible and my personal things in it, I went down the stairs. I was leaving.

"Silvia!" A call came to me from across the runway. It sounded like Tata!

"Silvia! 'The Lord watch between me and thee. The Lord make His face to shine upon you'!"

It WAS Tata! I could not believe it. He had somehow followed me all the way to Bucharest to say good-bye one more time. One more time on this side of eternity!

I could not speak; I just waved my hand. The last thing I could see through my tears was my Tata's familiar hand, waving back and forth, back and forth. I thought the sobs would burst from my throat, so I hurried up the steps and boarded the airplane.

The jet engines roared and we started down the runway. The plane shuddered and trembled and we left the ground.

We roared into the blue sky.

I had left Romania. I was headed for America. I would have a stopover in Italy, then fly directly to the United States.

I was no longer a citizen of Romania. I had left my country, my friends, the church and my family behind. And I was frightened. The unknown seemed too large for me. I felt like a tiny speck in a vast ocean of sky. I had no idea how far it was to Rome. I had no idea how big the Atlantic Ocean is. In America, everything would be different. Different people. Different customs. A different language. Life would be totally different.

———————————————————

I had no way of knowing then that Elena would be released within a year after I left. I had no way of knowing that God would move the leaders of Romania to change their laws, not requiring anyone to pay for leaving Romania, just after the money had been raised to "buy" Elena out of the country. I did not know then that Elena would also come to America and that we would be able to go through many of our adjustments in a new country together. I did not know those things then.

And I had no way of knowing that I would be able to help my fellow countrymen in their dire needs more in America than I ever could have helped them in Romania. I did not know that the communist government would collapse, that the entire structure of the country would change, and that I would be able to travel back and forth to Romania to help my people. I did not even know that one day, I would be able to live once more in Romania among my friends.

All of these things, I had no way of knowing. I never dreamed that I would be asked to share my testimony with thousands of people. And that a mighty moving of hearts would cause sharing, giving people to pour out food, clothing and money not only to the people of Romania, but also to other needy people around the world.

———————————————————

But I had learned. I had learned where to go when nothing was the same anymore. High above the earth, flying toward an unknown future, I began talking to God. "Lord, You see this scared daughter of Yours. You know how much I need You. You have kindly helped me see my own helplessness. You have proved to me that You know everything. So I will put my life once more into Your hands. I will give everything, including my past, my present, and my future, to You. Do with me what You want. I love You, my Savior, my Helper, and my Friend. You know everything. You know my size!"

THE END

Epilogue

After arriving in Ohio, Silvia immediately began working at the Christian Aid for Romania (the name was later changed to Christian Aid Ministries) office. Her first task was writing thank-you notes to CAM supporters. Her initiation period in America was brief, because she felt a consuming desire to plunge into the work of helping her suffering countrymen.

To gather prayer support and to inform the Christians in America about the terrible poverty and plight of the Romanian Christians, Silvia traveled with Genovieva to speaking engagements all over the U.S. and Canada. With her warm, cheerful personality, she won friends everywhere she went. Her story, *God knows my size!* was told in hundreds of churches and schools. To hear Silvia tell her own story and watch her animation and expressions, along with her Romanian accent, is something never to be forgotten.

Between her speaking engagements, Silvia worked at the CAM office, maintaining and updating the list of names and addresses of food parcel recipients in Romania.

After the demise of the communist government in late 1989 and Ceausescu's execution on Christmas Day, Silvia did what she had never dreamed she could do. She went back to Romania. But she was not able to go in time to reunite with her beloved Tata, for he had already left this world for his heavenly home. However, Silvia was able to meet with her Mama and the rest of the family. And she marveled at the newfound freedoms in her homeland. Now she could travel unhindered from church to church and the Christians were no longer forbidden to have services.

Returning from Romania, Silvia continued working in the Ohio office. Her knowledge of the Romanian customs and culture was a valuable aid to CAM. After several extended visits to her home country, Silvia returned to Romania, in 1993, in order to better help the poverty-stricken Christians.

Today, in 1999, Silvia has her own office in a CAM building in the town of Suceava. She works as a translator and is a link between the Americans and Romanians. She also works with the distribution branch; teaches at the orphanage; assists on the farm; and gives language and orientation classes to new workers at CAM's base in Romania.

Although Silvia has her U.S. citizenship papers, and can travel freely between the United States and Romania, she is most at home among her own people. Long are her days, and fulfilling her life. In spite of her many duties with CAM, her large heart has time for all her friends and she is always ready to make new acquaintances. But most of all, the faith she received in her young years is still the guiding beacon in her life. The God Who revealed Himself to her in such a wonderful way is still teaching her that He, indeed, knows "her size."